# INFORMATION THEORY MODELS OF INSTABILITIES IN CRITICAL SYSTEMS

# World Scientific Series in Information Studies
(ISSN: 1793-7876)

**Series Editor:** Mark Burgin *(University of California, Los Angeles, USA)*

World Scientific Series in Information Studies — **Vol. 7**

# INFORMATION THEORY MODELS OF INSTABILITIES IN CRITICAL SYSTEMS

## Rodrick Wallace

The New York State Psychiatric Institute at Columbia University, USA

**World Scientific**

NEW JERSEY · LONDON · SINGAPORE · BEIJING · SHANGHAI · HONG KONG · TAIPEI · CHENNAI · TOKYO

*Published by*

World Scientific Publishing Co. Pte. Ltd.
5 Toh Tuck Link, Singapore 596224
*USA office:* 27 Warren Street, Suite 401-402, Hackensack, NJ 07601
*UK office:* 57 Shelton Street, Covent Garden, London WC2H 9HE

**Library of Congress Cataloging-in-Publication Data**
Names: Wallace, Rodrick, author.
Title: Information theory models of instabilities in critical systems /
    by Rodrick Wallace (Columbia University, USA).
Description: [Hackensack?] New Jersey : World Scientific, [2016] |
    Series: World scientific series in information studies ; volume 7 |
    Includes bibliographical references and index.
Identifiers: LCCN 2016024941 | ISBN 9789813147287 (hardcover : alk. paper)
Subjects: LCSH: Artificial intelligence. | Chaotic behavior in systems--Mathematical models. |
    Systems engineering. | Information theory in research. | Conscious automata.
Classification: LCC TA347.A78 W35 2016 | DDC 003/.54--dc23
LC record available at https://lccn.loc.gov/2016024941

**British Library Cataloguing-in-Publication Data**
A catalogue record for this book is available from the British Library.

Printed in Singapore

# Preface

Real-time information processing structures perform critical duties in natural systems ranging across gene expression, cellular metabolism and repair, the immune response, neural process, small-group 'cockpit' actions, and, for humans and other colonial living things, the operation of elaborate 'institutions' of various forms, dynamics, and purposes. Draconian evolutionary selection has determined the form, function, and stabilizing mechanisms of such structures over the billion years of our interacting biological, social, and, more recently, cultural histories. In spite of this, natural real-time cognitive systems fail. We age, become ill, and die, and our socioeconomic institutions collapse, in large measure consequent on the failure of critical regulatory processes (Wallace 2015a, b).

Now, we are entering a new evolutionary dynamic – sometimes called 'anthropocene' – dominated by artificial cognitive structures at varying scales and levels of organization. Evolutionary selection pressures are poised to act on the 7 billion humans enmeshed within those structures. The purpose of this book is to develop a set of information-theoretic statistical tools for analyzing the instabilities of real-time cognitive systems at those varying scales and levels of organization, with special focus on high level machine function.

In particular, technological momentum, driven by relentless economic interests, will see massively parallel computers widely deployed to control a great swath of critical real-time phenomena ranging across transportation, power, financial, and communication networks, individual vehicles, chemical production facilities, refineries, nuclear reactors, and the like. It is increasingly understood that stabilizing cognitive systems and devices is as inherently intractable as programming them – something we do not really know how to do well. This book formalizes that understanding for cognitive process in general, using tools adapted from recently developed biological perspectives on cognition. It is, in addition, something of a *Caveat Emptor* for those confronted by golden-tongued computer salesmen and their academic and government collaborators, a close parallel to investment firms selling mathematically complex financial instruments based on aggregations of subprime mortgages.

The book's foundation is a set of published materials, listed below, that explores the inevitability of serious dysfunctions in cognitive systems including highly parallel machines as they become ever larger and are tasked with ever more demanding real-time duties. The arguments apply similarly to 'cockpit' human-human and human-machine distributed cognition.

In spite of longstanding evolutionary selection pressures, at any moment in Western societies some two to three percent of the population is afflicted with mental disorders that interfere with the ability to carry out socially expected duties. Indeed, most people, over their lifetimes, will suffer one or more periods of similar inability. There is, however, little or no understanding that massively parallel machines or cockpit structures controlling essential real-time services must inevitably experience significant rates of analogous dysfunction, particularly during periods of peak demand. Failure need not be 'graceful degradation under pressure', but is more likely to be a highly punctuated collapse, for fundamental reasons related to the inevitability of phase transitions in information systems. This is not a failure mode to welcome in critical systems.

Something of this has emerged, albeit heuristically, in the artificial intelligence literature. Atkinson (2015), for example, writes

> Psychopathology is the study of mental illness, mental distress, and abnormal or maladaptive behavior. It is the study of *fault modes* of the human mind. As yet, we have no equivalent area of study for intelligent autonomous machines. ...[T]he technology of intelligent, autonomous systems gives rise to novel fault modes that are not seen in other types of automation... As a consequence, autonomous systems may provide new vectors for cyber-attack that could lead to subversion, degraded behavior or outright system failure... [T]here are fault modes for autonomous systems that remain unexplored and their implications unknown. ...[I]t is possible that some psychopathologies of machine intelligence could be *induced* in

a new form of cyber-attack, thereby creating new risks with potentially very serious consequences... Despite the rush to implement multi-agent systems for important and critical applications in health, finance, transportation, defense and other domains, we simply do not yet have an understanding of fault modes that are likely to occur due to emergent behavior.

Here, we provide formal address to some of these matters.

Chapter 1 reviews and extends some fundamental results from information and control theories.

Chapter 2, written in collaboration with the biologist R.G. Wallace, broadly reviews recent studies on high level animal cognition and their implications for machine design.

Chapter 3 explores human mental disorders from the perspective of those studies. These supply an introduction to the formal methodology and provide a basis for examining similarities and differences arising from the more rapid machine timescales.

Chapter 4 examines in extended detail how stabilizing large networks of cognitive devices is as difficult as programming them, applying quasi-symmetry methods that greatly expand the formalism.

Chapter 5 shows that highly parallel real-time machines are inherently coevolutionary, since elements of a dynamic structural hierarchy always interact, an effect that will asymptotically dominate system behavior at great scale.

Chapter 6 presents a model for programming highly parallel devices in which an 'epigenetic farmer' directs machine behavior by increasing the probability of a desired developmental pathway, leading to a computed answer that may range from some simple fixed point to, in a coevolutionary machine, a particular highly structured dynamic behavior. The approach leads toward further understanding of the failure patterns that must afflict these machines.

Chapter 7 expands consideration of the similarities of the failure modes of real-time, massively parallel cognitive machines, analogous man-machine distributed cognition systems, and the broad spectrum of developmental disorders afflicting organisms that have had the relentless benefit of eons of evolutionary pruning. The results are not encouraging.

Chapter 8 examines a case history, the catastrophic failure of computerized operations research methods in management of the New York City fire department.

Chapter 9 applies the theory developed in earlier sections of the book to canonical instabilities likely to afflict forthcoming systems of autonomous vehicles on intelligent roads. Such systems, it appears, will experience massive failures resembling large-scale regional power blackouts.

Chapter 10, in a sense, completes the circle, applying parts of the theory to biologically ubiquitous molecular-scale fuzzy logic gates that are increasingly attractive for machine design.

The final chapter summarizes the overall message: *Caveat Emptor.*

The book is largely written at an advanced undergraduate mathematical level, with special topics introduced as needed and in a Mathematical Appendix. The material should be accessible to the broad technical audience concerned with computer design and security. Indeed, considering the ease with which developmental disorders can be induced in living things by toxic exposures or stressful experiences during critical periods, those taxed with matters of homeland security would do well to take note of these arguments.

**Sources**

Wallace, D., R. Wallace, 1998, *A Plague on Your Houses*, Verso, New York.

Wallace, D., R. Wallace, 2011, Consequences of massive housing destruction: the New York City fire epidemic, *Building Research and Information*, 39:395-411.

Wallace, R.G., R. Wallace, 2009, Evolutionary radiation and the spectrum of consciousness, *Consciousness and Cognition*, 18:160-167.

Wallace, R., 1993, Recurrent collapse of the fire service in New York City: the failure of a paramilitary system as a phase change, *Environment and Planning A*, 25:233-244.

Wallace, R., 2005, *Consciousness: A Mathematical Treatment of the Global Neuronal Workspace Model*, Springer, New York.

Wallace, R., 2005, A global workspace perspective on mental disorders, *Theoretical Biology and Medical Modeling*, 2:49 (online).

Wallace, R., 2006, Pitfalls in biological computing: canonical and idiosyncratic dysfunctions of conscious machines, *Mind and Matter*, 4:91-113.

Wallace, R., 2008, Toward formal models of biologically inspired, highly parallel machine cognition, *International Journal of Parallel, Emergent and Distributed Systems*, 23:367-408.

Wallace, R., M. Fullilove, 2008, *Collective Consciousness and its Discontents*, Springer, New York.

Wallace, R., 2009, Programming coevolutionary machines: The emerging conundrum, *International Journal of Parallel, Emergent and Distributed Systems*, 24:443-453.

Wallace, R., 2010, Tunable epigenetic catalysis: programming real-time cognitive machines, *International Journal of Parallel, Emergent and Distributed Systems*, 25:209-222.

Wallace, R., 2012, Consciousness, crosstalk, and the mereological fallacy: an evolutionary perspective, *Physics of Life Reviews*, 9:426-453.

Wallace, R., 2014, A formal approach to the molecular fuzzy lock-and-key, *International Journal of Unconventional Computing*, 10:93-110.

Wallace, R., 2014, Embodied cognition, embodied regulation, and the Data Rate Theorem, *Biologically Inspired Cognitive Architectures*, 8:70-81.

Wallace, R., 2015a, *An Ecosystem Approach to Economic Stabilization: Escaping the neoliberal wilderness*, Routledge, New York.

Wallace, R., 2015b, *An Information Approach to Mitochondrial Dysfunction: Extending Swerdlow's Hypothesis*, World Scientific, Singapore.

Wallace, R., 2016, Subtle noise structures as control signals in high-order biocognition, *Physics Letters A*, 380:726-729.

Wallace, R., 2016, Canonical failure modes of real-time control systems: insights from cognitive theory, *International Journal of Systems Science*, 47:1280-1295..

# Contents

# Chapter 1

# Mathematical preliminaries

Here, we introduce ideas from information theory that prove useful in describing both machine and biological cognition, imposing necessary conditions on the transmission of signals that carry meaning. The Data Rate Theorem further relates information and control theories, and we examine as well the implications of Feynman's (2000) (and Bennett's) identification of information as a form of free energy. We close with a striking example of the hidden symmetries to be found in cognitive systems – natural or artificial.

## 1.1   The Shannon-McMillan Theorem

According to the structure of the underlying language of which a message is a particular expression, some messages are more 'meaningful' than others, that is, are in accord with the grammar and syntax of the language. The Shannon-McMillan or Asymptotic Equipartition Theorem, describes how messages themselves are to be classified.

Suppose a long sequence of symbols is chosen, using the output of a random variable $X$, so that an output sequence of length n, with the form $x_n = (\alpha_0, \alpha_1, ..., \alpha_{n-1})$ has joint and conditional probabilities

$$P(X_0 = \alpha_0, X_1 = \alpha_1, ..., X_{n-1} = \alpha_{n-1})$$
$$P(X_n = \alpha_n | X_0 = \alpha_0, ..., X_{n-1} = \alpha_{n-1}). \tag{1.1}$$

Using these probabilities we may calculate the conditional uncertainty $H(X_n | X_0, X_1, ..., X_{n-1})$ using sums of the form $-\sum_j P_j \log[P_j]$. See Cover and Thomas (2006) for detailed expressions.

The uncertainty of the *information source*, $H[\mathbf{X}]$, is defined as

$$H[\mathbf{X}] \equiv \lim_{n \to \infty} H(X_n | X_0, X_1, ..., X_{n-1}). \tag{1.2}$$

In general $H(X_n|X_0, X_1, ..., X_{n-1}) \leq H(X_n)$.

Only if the random variables $X_j$ are all stochastically independent does equality hold. If there is a maximum $n$ such that, for all $m > 0$,

$$H(X_{n+m}|X_0, ..., X_{n+m-1}) = H(X_n|X_0, ..., X_{n-1})$$

then the source is said to be of *order n*. It is easy to show that

$$H[\mathbf{X}] = \lim_{n \to \infty} \frac{H(X_0, ...X_n)}{n+1}.$$

In general the outputs of the $X_j, j = 0, 1, ..., n$ are *dependent*. That is, the output of the communication process at step $n$ depends on previous steps. Such serial correlation, in fact, is the very structure which enables most of what is done in this book.

Here, however, the processes are all assumed stationary in time, that is, the serial correlations do not change in time, and the system is *stationary*.

A very broad class of such self-correlated, stationary, information sources, the so-called *ergodic* sources for which the long-run relative frequency of a sequence converges stochastically to the probability assigned to it, have a particularly interesting property. It is possible, in the limit of large $n$, to divide all sequences of outputs of an ergodic information source into two distinct sets, $S_1$ and $S_2$, having, respectively, very high and vanishingly low probabilities of occurrence, with the source uncertainty providing the splitting criterion. In particular the Shannon-McMillan Theorem states that, for a (long) sequence having $n$ (serially correlated) elements, the number of 'meaningful' sequences, $N(n)$ – those belonging to set $S_1$ – will satisfy the relation

$$\frac{\log[N(n)]}{n} \approx H[\mathbf{X}]. \tag{1.3}$$

More formally,

$$\lim_{n \to \infty} \frac{\log[N(n)]}{n} = H[\mathbf{X}]$$
$$= \lim_{n \to \infty} H(X_n|X_0, ..., X_{n-1})$$
$$= \lim_{n \to \infty} \frac{H(X_0, ..., X_n)}{n+1}. \tag{1.4}$$

Using the internal structures of the information source permits *limiting attention only to high probability 'meaningful' sequences of symbols.*

## 1.2 The Rate Distortion Theorem

The Shannon-McMillan Theorem can be expressed as the 'zero error limit' of the Rate Distortion Theorem, which defines a splitting criterion that identifies high probability pairs of sequences. We follow closely the treatment of Cover and Thomas (2006).

The origin of the problem is the question of representing one information source by a simpler one in such a way that the least information is lost. For example we might have a continuous variate between 0 and 100, and wish to represent it in terms of a small set of integers in a way that minimizes the inevitable distortion that process creates. Typically, for example, an analog audio signal will be replaced by a 'digital' one. The problem is to do this in a way which least distorts the reconstructed audio waveform.

Suppose the original stationary, ergodic information source $Y$ with output from a particular alphabet generates sequences of the form $y^n = y_1, ..., y_n$.

These are 'digitized,' in some sense, producing a chain of 'digitized values' $b^n = b_1, ..., b_n$, where the $b$-alphabet is much more restricted than the $y$-alphabet.

$b^n$ is, in turn, *deterministically retranslated* into a reproduction of the original signal $y^n$. That is, each $b^m$ is mapped on to a unique n-length y-sequence in the alphabet of the information source $Y$: $b^m \rightarrow \hat{y}^n = \hat{y}_1, ..., \hat{y}_n$.

Note, however, that many $y^n$ sequences may be mapped onto the *same* retranslation sequence $\hat{y}^n$, so that information will, in general, be lost.

The central problem is to explicitly minimize that loss.

The retranslation process defines a new stationary, ergodic information source, $\hat{Y}$.

The next step is to define a *distortion measure*, $d(y, \hat{y})$, which compares the original to the retranslated path. For example the *Hamming distortion* is

$$d(y, \hat{y}) = 1, y \neq \hat{y}$$
$$d(y, \hat{y}) = 0, y = \hat{y}. \tag{1.5}$$

For continuous variates the *Squared error distortion* is

$$d(y, \hat{y}) = (y - \hat{y})^2. \tag{1.6}$$

There are many possibilities.

The distortion between paths $y^n$ and $\hat{y}^n$ is defined as

$$d(y^n, \hat{y}^n) = \frac{1}{n} \sum_{j=1}^{n} d(y_j, \hat{y}_j). \tag{1.7}$$

Suppose that with each path $y^n$ and $b^n$-path retranslation into the $y$-language and denoted $y^n$, there are associated individual, joint, and conditional probability distributions $p(y^n), p(\hat{y}^n), p(y^n|\hat{y}^n)$.

The *average distortion* is defined as

$$D = \sum_{y^n} p(y^n)d(y^n, \hat{y}^n). \tag{1.8}$$

It is possible, using the distributions given above, to define the information transmitted from the incoming $Y$ to the outgoing $\hat{Y}$ process in the usual manner, using the Shannon source uncertainty of the strings:
$$I(Y, \hat{Y}) \equiv H(Y) - H(Y|\hat{Y}) = H(Y) + H(\hat{Y}) - H(Y, \hat{Y}).$$

If there is no uncertainty in $Y$ given the retranslation $\hat{Y}$, then no information is lost. In general, this will not be true.

The *information rate distortion function* $R(D)$ for a source $Y$ with a distortion measure $d(y, \hat{y})$ is defined as

$$R(D) = \min_{p(y,\hat{y}); \sum_{(y,\hat{y})} p(y)p(y|\hat{y})d(y,\hat{y}) \leq D} I(Y, \hat{Y}). \tag{1.9}$$

The minimization is over all conditional distributions $p(y|\hat{y})$ for which the joint distribution $p(y, \hat{y}) = p(y)p(y|\hat{y})$ satisfies the average distortion constraint (i.e., average distortion $\leq D$).

The *Rate Distortion Theorem* states that $R(D)$ *is the maximum achievable rate of information transmission which does not exceed the average distortion* $D$. Another way of saying this is that $R(D)$ is the minimum channel capacity permitting message transmission with average distortion less than or equal to $D$. Cover and Thomas (2006) provide details.

More to the point, however, is the following: Pairs of sequences $(y^n, \hat{y}^n)$ can be defined as *distortion typical*; that is, for a given average distortion $D$, defined in terms of a particular measure, pairs of sequences can be divided into two sets, a high probability one containing a relatively small number of (matched) pairs with $d(y^n, \hat{y}^n) \leq D$, and a low probability one containing most pairs. As $n \to \infty$, the smaller set approaches unit probability, and, for those pairs,

$$p(y^n) \geq p(\hat{y}^n|y^n) \exp[-nI(Y, \hat{Y})].$$

Thus, roughly speaking, $I(Y, \hat{Y})$ embodies the splitting criterion between high and low probability pairs of paths.

For the theory of interacting information sources, then, $I(Y, \hat{Y})$ can play the role of $H$ in subsequent dynamic treatments.

The rate distortion function can actually be calculated in many cases by using a Lagrange multiplier method. See Cover and Thomas (2006) for details.

For a Gaussian channel under the squared distortion measure, $R(D) = 1/2 \log[\sigma^2/D]$, where $\sigma^2$ is the noise variance, assuming a zero mean.

## 1.3 The Data Rate Theorem

The Data-rate Theorem (DRT), a generalization of the classic Bode Integral Theorem for linear control systems, describes the stability of feedback control under data rate constraints (Nair et al. 2007). Given a noise-free data link between a discrete linear plant and its controller, unstable modes can be stabilized only if the feedback data rate $\mathcal{H}$ is greater than the rate of 'topological information' generated by the unstable system. For the simplest incarnation, if the linear matrix equation of the plant is of the form $x_{t+1} = \mathbf{A}x_t + ...$, where $x_t$ is the n-dimensional state vector at time $t$, then the necessary condition for stabilizability is

$$\mathcal{H} > \log[|det\mathbf{A}^u|] \tag{1.10}$$

where $det$ is the determinant and $\mathbf{A}^u$ is the decoupled unstable component of $\mathbf{A}$, i.e., the part having eigenvalues $\geq 1$. The determinant represents a generalized volume. Thus there is a critical positive data rate below which there does not exist any quantization and control scheme able to stabilize an unstable system (Nair et al. 2007).

This result, and its variations and extensions, relate control theory to information theory and are as fundamental as the Shannon Coding and Source Coding Theorems, and the Rate Distortion Theorem for understanding complex cognitive machines and biological phenomena.

We will extend the DRT, using new approaches from cognitive theory to explore a variety of failure modes that can be examined under data-rate constraints, but are not limited to explicitly unstable behaviors. Thus we are concerned with relatively subtle failures of real-time systems under 'fog-of-war' data-rate constraints.

## 1.4 The Mean Field Model

Wallace and Wallace (1998, 1999) ask how a language, in a large sense, 'spoken' on a network structure, responds as properties of the underlying network change. The language might be speech, pattern recognition, or cognition. The network might be social, chemical, or neural. The properties of interest were the magnitude of 'strong' or 'weak' ties which, respectively, either disjointly partitioned the network or linked it across such partitioning. These would be analogous to local and mean-field couplings in physical systems.

Fix the magnitude of strong ties – again, those which disjointly partition the underlying network into cognitive or other submodules – but vary the index of nondisjunctive weak ties, $P$, between components, taking $K = 1/P$.

Assume the piecewise, adiabatically stationary ergodic information source (or sources) dual to cognitive process depends on three parameters, two explicit and one implicit. The explicit are $K$ as above and, as a calculational device, an 'external field strength' analog $J$, which gives a 'direction' to the system. We will, in the limit, set $J = 0$. Note that many other approaches may well be possible, since renormalization techniques are more philosophy than prescription.

The implicit parameter, $r$, is an inherent generalized 'length' characteristic of the phenomenon, on which $J$ and $K$ are defined. That is, $J$ and $K$ are written as functions of averages of the parameter $r$, which may be quite complex, having nothing at all to do with conventional ideas of space. For example $r$ may be defined by the degree of niche partitioning in ecosystems or separation in social structures.

For a given generalized language of interest having a well defined (adiabatically, piecewise stationary) ergodic source uncertainty, $H = H[K, J, \mathbf{X}]$.

To summarize a long train of standard argument (Wilson 1971; Binney et al. 1986), imposition of invariance of $H$ under a renormalization transform in the implicit parameter $r$ leads to expectation of both a critical point in $K$, written $K_C$, reflecting a phase transition to or from collective behavior across the entire array, and of power laws for system behavior near $K_C$. Addition of other parameters to the system results in a 'critical line' or surface.

Let $\kappa \equiv (K_C - K)/K_C$ and take $\chi$ as the 'correlation length' defining the average domain in $r$-space for which the information source is primarily dominated by 'strong' ties. The first step is to average across $r$-space in terms of 'clumps' of length $R = <r>$. Then $H[J, K, \mathbf{X}] \rightarrow H[J_R, K_R, \mathbf{X}]$.

Taking Wilson's (1971) analysis as a starting point – not the only way to proceed – the 'renormalization relations' used here are:

$$H[K_R, J_R, \mathbf{X}] = f(R)H[K, J, \mathbf{X}]$$
$$\chi(K_R, J_R) = \frac{\chi(K, J)}{R} \tag{1.11}$$

with $f(1) = 1$ and $J_1 = J, K_1 = K$. The first equation significantly extends Wilson's treatment. It states that 'processing capacity,' as indexed by the source uncertainty of the system, representing the 'richness' of the generalized language, grows monotonically as $f(R)$, which must itself be a dimensionless function in $R$, since both $H[K_R, J_R]$ and $H[K, J]$ are themselves dimensionless. Most simply, this requires replacing $R$ by $R/R_0$, where $R_0$ is the 'characteristic length' for the system over which renormalization procedures are reasonable, then setting $R_0 \equiv 1$, hence measuring length in units of $R_0$.

Wilson's original analysis focused on free energy density. Under 'clumping,' densities must remain the same, so that if $F[K_R, J_R]$ is the free energy of the clumped system, and $F[K, J]$ is the free energy density before clumping, then Wilson's (1971) equation (4) is $F[K, J] = R^{-3}F[K_R, J_R]$,

$$F[K_R, J_R] = R^3 F[K, J].$$

Remarkably, the renormalization equations are solvable for a broad class of functions $f(R)$, or more precisely, $f(R/R_0), R_0 \equiv 1$.

The second equation just states that the correlation length simply scales as $R$.

Again, the central feature of renormalization in this context is the assumption that, at criticality, the system looks the same at all scales, that is, it is *invariant under renormalization* at the critical point. All else follows from this.

There is no unique renormalization procedure for information sources: other, very subtle, symmetry relations – not necessarily based on the elementary physical analog we use here – may well be possible. For example, McCauley (1993, p.168) describes the highly counterintuitive renormalizations needed to understand phase transition in simple 'chaotic' systems. This is important, since biological or social systems may well alter their renormalization properties – equivalent to tuning their phase transition dynamics – in response to external signals. We will make much use of a simple version of this possibility, termed 'universality class tuning,' below.

To begin, following Wilson, take $f(R) = R^d$, $d$ some real number $d > 0$, and restrict $K$ to near the 'critical value' $K_C$. If $J \to 0$, a simple series expansion and some clever algebra gives

$$H = H_0 \kappa^\alpha$$
$$\chi = \frac{\chi_0}{\kappa^s} \tag{1.12}$$

where $\alpha, s$ are positive constants. More biologically relevant examples appear below.

Further from the critical point, matters are more complicated, appearing to involve Generalized Onsager Relations, 'dynamical groupoids', and a kind of thermodynamics associated with a Legendre transform of $H$: $S \equiv H - KdH/dK$. Although this extension is quite important to describing behaviors away from criticality, the mathematical detail is cumbersome.

An essential insight is that *regardless of the particular renormalization properties, sudden critical point transition is possible in the opposite direction for this model.* That is, going from a number of independent, isolated and fragmented systems operating individually and more or less at random, into a single large, interlocked, coherent structure, once the parameter $K$, the inverse strength of weak ties, falls below threshold, or, conversely, once the strength of weak ties parameter $P = 1/K$ becomes large enough.

Thus, increasing nondisjunctive weak ties between them can bind several different cognitive 'language' functions into a single, embedding hierarchical metalanguage containing each as a linked subdialect, and do so in an inherently punctuated manner. This could be a dynamic process, creating a shifting, ever-changing pattern of linked cognitive submodules, according to the challenges or opportunities faced by the system of interest.

This can be made more exact using a rate distortion argument (or, more generally, using the Joint Asymptotic Equipartition Theorem) as follows:

Suppose that two ergodic information sources $\mathbf{Y}$ and $\mathbf{B}$ begin to interact, to 'talk' to each other, to influence each other in some way so that it is possible, for example, to look at the output of $\mathbf{B}$ – strings $b$ – and infer something about the behavior of $\mathbf{Y}$ from it – strings $y$. We suppose it possible to define a retranslation from the B-language into the Y-language through a deterministic code book, and call $\hat{\mathbf{Y}}$ the translated information source, as mirrored by $\mathbf{B}$.

Define some distortion measure comparing paths $y$ to paths $\hat{y}$, $d(y, \hat{y})$. Invoke the Rate Distortion Theorem's mutual information $I(Y, \hat{Y})$, which is the splitting criterion between high and low probability pairs of paths. Impose, now, a parameterization by an inverse coupling strength $K$, and a renormalization representing the global structure of the system coupling. This may be much different from the renormalization behavior of the individual components. If $K < K_C$, where $K_C$ is a critical point (or surface), the two information sources will be closely coupled enough to be characterized as condensed.

In the absence of a distortion measure, the Joint Asymptotic Equipartition Theorem gives a similar result.

Detailed coupling mechanisms will be sharply constrained through regularities of grammar and syntax imposed by limit theorems associated with phase transition.

**Biological renormalization**

Next the mathematical detail concealed by the invocation of the asymptotic limit theorems emerges with a vengeance. Equation (1.11) states that the information source and the correlation length, the degree of coherence on the underlying network, scale under renormalization clustering in chunks of size $R$ as

$$H[K_R, J_R]/f(R) = H[J, K]$$

$$\chi[K_R, J_R]R = \chi(K, J),$$

with $f(1) = 1, K_1 = K, J_1 = J$, where we have slightly rearranged terms.

Differentiating these two equations with respect to $R$, so that the right hand sides are zero, and solving for $dK_R/dR$ and $dJ_R/dR$ gives, after some consolidation, expressions of the form

$$dK_R/dR = u_1 d\log(f)/dR + u_2/R$$
$$dJ_R/dR = v_1 J_R d\log(f)/dR + \frac{v_2}{R} J_R. \tag{1.13}$$

The $u_i, v_i, i = 1, 2$ are functions of $K_R, J_R$, but not explicitly of $R$ itself.

We expand these equations about the critical value $K_R = K_C$ and about $J_R = 0$, obtaining

$$dK_R/dR = (K_R - K_C)yd\log(f)/dR + (K_R - K_C)z/R$$
$$dJ_R/dR = wJ_R d\log(f)/dR + xJ_R/R. \tag{1.14}$$

The terms $y = du_1/dK_R|_{K_R=K_C}, z = du_2/dK_R|_{K_R=K_C}, w = v_1(K_C, 0), x = v_2(K_C, 0)$ are constants.

Solving the first of these equations gives

$$K_R = K_C + (K - K_C)R^z f(R)^y \tag{1.15}$$

again remembering that $K_1 = K, J_1 = J, f(1) = 1$.

Wilson's essential trick is to iterate on this relation, which is supposed to converge rapidly near the critical point, assuming that for $K_R$ near $K_C$, we have

$$K_C/2 \approx K_C + (K - K_C)R^z f(R)^y. \tag{1.16}$$

Now iterate in two steps, first solving this for $f(R)$ in terms of known values, and then solving for $R$, finding a value $R_C$ that we then substitute into the first of equations (1.11) to obtain an expression for $H[K, 0]$ in terms of known functions and parameter values.

The first step gives the general result

$$f(R_C) \approx \frac{[K_C/(K_C - K)]^{1/y}}{2^{1/y}R_C^{z/y}}. \tag{1.17}$$

Solving this for $R_C$ and substituting into the first expression of equation (1.11) gives, as a first iteration of a far more general procedure (Shirkov and Kovalev 2001), the result

$$H[K, 0] \approx \frac{H[K_C/2, 0]}{f(R_C)} = \frac{H_0}{f(R_C)}$$
$$\chi(K, 0) \approx \chi(K_C/2, 0)R_C = \chi_0 R_C \tag{1.18}$$

which are the essential relationships.

Note that a power law of the form $f(R) = R^m, m = 3$, which is the direct physical analog, may not be reasonable, since it says that 'language richness' can grow very rapidly as a function of increased network size. Such rapid growth is simply not observed.

Taking the more realistic example of non-integral 'fractal' exponential growth,

$$f(R) = R^\delta \tag{1.19}$$

where $\delta > 0$ is a real number which may be quite small, equation (1.18) can be solved for $R_C$, obtaining

$$R_C = \frac{[K_C/(K_C - K)]^{[1/(\delta y+z)]}}{2^{1/(\delta y+z)}} \tag{1.20}$$

for $K$ near $K_C$. Note that, for a given value of $y$, one might characterize the relation $\alpha \equiv \delta y + z = $ constant as a 'tunable universality class relation' in the sense of Albert and Barabasi (2002).

Substituting this value for $R_C$ back into equation (1.17) gives a complex expression for $H$, having three parameters: $\delta, y, z$.

A more biologically interesting choice for $f(R)$ is a logarithmic curve that 'tops out', for example

$$f(R) = m \log(R) + 1. \tag{1.21}$$

Again $f(1) = 1$.

Using Mathematica 4.2 or above to solve equation (1.17) for $R_C$ gives

$$R_C = \left[ \frac{Q}{W[Q \exp(z/my)]} \right]^{y/z} \tag{1.22}$$

where

$$Q \equiv (z/my)2^{-1/y}[K_C/(K_C - K)]^{1/y}.$$

The transcendental function $W(x)$ is defined by the relation $W(x)\exp(W(x)) = x$.

Called the Lambert W-function (or, in Mathematica the ProductLog), it arises in the theory of random networks and in renormalization strategies for quantum field theories.

An asymptotic relation for $f(R)$ would be of particular biological interest, implying that 'language richness' increases to a limiting value with population growth.

Taking

$$f(R) = \exp[m(R - 1)/R] \tag{1.23}$$

gives a system which begins at 1 when $R = 1$, and approaches the asymptotic limit $\exp(m)$ as $R \to \infty$. Mathematica 4.2 or above finds

$$R_C = \frac{my/z}{W[A]} \tag{1.24}$$

where $A \equiv (my/z)\exp(my/z)[2^{1/y}[K_C/(K_C - K)]^{-1/y}]^{y/z}$.

These developments indicate the possibility of taking the theory significantly beyond arguments by abduction from simple physical models, although the notorious difficulty of implementing information theory existence arguments will undoubtedly persist.

**Universality class distribution**

Physical systems undergoing phase transition usually have relatively pure renormalization properties, with quite different systems clumped into the same 'universality class,' having fixed exponents at transition (Binney et al. 1986). Biological and social phenomena, as well as machine dynamics, may be far more complicated:

If the system of interest is a mix of subgroups with different values of some significant renormalization parameter $m$ in the expression for $f(R, m)$, according to a distribution $\rho(m)$, then the first expression in equation (1.11) should generalize, at least to first order, as

$$H[K_R, J_R] = < f(R, m) > H[K, J]$$
$$\equiv H[K, J] \int f(R, m)\rho(m)dm. \qquad (1.25)$$

If $f(R) = 1 + m \log(R)$ then, given any distribution for $m$,

$$< f(R) > = 1+ < m > \log(R), \qquad (1.26)$$

where $< m >$ is simply the mean of $m$ over that distribution.

Other forms of $f(R)$ having more complicated dependencies on the distributed parameter or parameters, like the power law $R^\delta$, do not produce such a simple result. Taking $\rho(\delta)$ as a normal distribution, for example, gives

$$< R^\delta > = R^{<\delta>} \exp[(1/2)(\log(R^\sigma))^2] \qquad (1.27)$$

where $\sigma^2$ is the distribution variance. The renormalization properties of this function can be determined from equation (1.17), and the calculation is left to the reader as an exercise, best done in Mathematica 4.2 or above.

Thus the information dynamic phase transition properties of mixed systems will not in general be simply related to those of a single subcomponent, a matter of possible empirical importance: If sets of relevant parameters defining renormalization universality classes are indeed distributed, experiments observing pure phase changes may be very difficult. Tuning among different possible renormalization strategies in response to external signals would result in even greater ambiguity in recognizing and classifying information dynamic phase transitions.

Important aspects of mechanism may be reflected in the combination of renormalization properties and the details of their distribution across subsystems.

In sum, real biological, social, machine, or mixed hybrid systems are likely to have very rich patterns of phase transition which may not display the simplistic, indeed, literally elemental, purity familiar to physicists. Overall mechanisms will, however, still remain significantly constrained by the theory, in the general sense of probability limit theorems.

**Punctuated universality class tuning**

The next step is to iterate the general argument onto the process of phase transition itself, producing a model of high order cognition as a tunable global workspace subject to inherent punctuated detection of external events.

As described above, an essential character of physical systems subject to phase transition is that they belong to particular 'universality classes'. Again, this means that the exponents of power laws describing behavior at phase transition will be the same for large groups of markedly different systems, with 'natural' aggregations representing fundamental class properties (Binney et al. 1986).

It appears that cognitive systems undergoing phase transition analogs need not be constrained to such classes, and that 'universality class tuning', meaning the strategic alteration of parameters characterizing the renormalization properties of punctuation, might well be possible. Here we focus on the tuning of parameters within a single, given, renormalization relation. Clearly, however, wholesale shifts of renormalization properties must ultimately be considered as well, a matter for future work.

Universality class tuning has been observed in models of 'real world' networks. To quote Albert and Barabasi (2002),

> The inseparability of the topology and dynamics of evolving networks is shown by the fact that [the exponents defining universality class] are related by [a] scaling relation..., underlying the fact that a network's assembly uniquely determines its topology. However, in no case are these exponents unique. They can be tuned continuously...

Suppose that a structured external environment, itself an appropriately regular information source $\mathbf{Y}$, 'engages' a modifiable cognitive system. The environment begins to write an image of itself on the cognitive system in a distorted manner permitting definition of a mutual information $I[K]$ splitting criterion according to the Rate Distortion or Joint Asymptotic Equipartition Theorems. $K$ is an inverse coupling parameter between system and environment. At punctuation – near some critical point $K_C$ – the systems begin to interact very strongly indeed, and, near $K_C$, using the simple physical model of equation (1.12),

$$I[K] \approx I_0 [\frac{K_C - K}{K_C}]^\alpha.$$

For a physical system $\alpha$ is fixed, determined by the underlying 'universality class.' Here we will allow $\alpha$ to vary, and, in the section below, to itself respond explicitly to signals.

Normalizing $K_C$ and $I_0$ to 1,

$$I[K] \approx (1 - K)^\alpha. \tag{1.28}$$

The horizontal line $I[K] = 1$ corresponds to $\alpha = 0$, while $\alpha = 1$ gives a declining straight line with unit slope which passes through 0 at $K = 1$. Consideration shows there are progressively sharper transitions between the necessary zero value at $K = 1$ and the values defined by this relation for $0 < K, \alpha < 1$. The rapidly rising slope of transition with declining $\alpha$ is of considerable significance:

The instability associated with the splitting criterion $I[K]$ is defined by

$$Q[K] \equiv -K dI[K]/dK = \alpha K(1 - K)^{\alpha - 1} \qquad (1.29)$$

and is singular at $K = K_C = 1$ for $0 < \alpha < 1$. We interpret this to mean that values of $0 < \alpha \ll 1$ are highly unlikely for real systems, since $Q[K]$, in this model, represents a kind of barrier for broadly 'social' information systems.

On the other hand, smaller values of $\alpha$ mean that the system is far more efficient at responding to the adaptive demands imposed by the embedding structured environment, since the mutual information which tracks the matching of internal response to external demands, $I[K]$, rises more and more quickly toward the maximum for smaller and smaller $\alpha$ as the inverse coupling parameter $K$ declines below $K_C = 1$. That is, systems able to attain smaller $\alpha$ are more responsive to external signals than those characterized by larger values, in this model, but smaller values will be harder to reach, probably only at some considerable physiological or opportunity costs. Focused action takes resources, of one form or another.

Wallace (2005a) makes these considerations explicit, modeling the role of contextual and energy constraints on the relations between $Q$, $I$, and other system properties.

The more realistic renormalization strategies given above produce sets of several parameters defining the universality class, whose tuning gives behavior much like that of $\alpha$ in this simple example.

Formal iteration of the phase transition argument on this calculation gives tunable high-order cognition, focusing on paths of universality class parameters.

Suppose the renormalization properties of a language-on-a network system at some 'time' $k$ are characterized by a set of parameters $A_k \equiv \alpha_1^k, ..., \alpha_m^k$. Fixed parameter values define a particular universality class for the renormalization. We suppose that, over a sequence of 'times,' the universality class properties can be characterized by a path $x_n = A_0, A_1, ..., A_{n-1}$ having significant serial correlations which, in fact, permit definition of an adiabatically piecewise stationary ergodic information source associated with the paths $x_n$. We call that source $\mathbf{X}$.

Suppose also, in the now-usual manner, that the set of external (or internal, systemic) signals impinging on the system of interest is also highly structured and forms another information source **Y** which interacts not only with that system globally, but specifically with its universality class properties as characterized by **X**. **Y** is necessarily associated with a set of paths $y_n$.

Pair the two sets of paths into a joint path, $z_n \equiv (x_n, y_y)$ and invoke an inverse coupling parameter, $K$, between the information sources and their paths. This leads, by the arguments above, to phase transition punctuation of $I[K]$, the mutual information between **X** and **Y**, under either the Joint Asymptotic Equipartition Theorem or under limitation by a distortion measure, through the Rate Distortion Theorem. The essential point is that $I[K]$ is a splitting criterion under these theorems, and thus partakes of the homology with free energy density, following the arguments of Feynman (2000), who identifies information in terms of the free energy needed to erase it.

Activation of universality class tuning, the mean field model's version of attentional focusing, then becomes itself a punctuated event in response to increasing linkage between the cognitive system and an external structured signal or some particular stream of internal events.

This iterated argument exactly parallels the extension of the General Linear Model to the Hierarchical Linear Model in regression theory (Byrk and Raudenbusch 2001).

Another path to the fluctuating dynamic threshold might be through a second order iteration similar to that just above, but focused on the parameters defining the universality class distributions given above.

## 1.5   Information Symmetries

A remarkable recent development has been the finding of a deep relation between information theory inequalities and a number of results in the theory of finite groups (e.g., Yeung 2008). That is, there are hidden symmetries in information theory:

Given two random variables $X_1$ and $X_2$ having Shannon uncertainties $H(X_1)$ and $H(X_2)$ defined in the usual manner, the information theory chain rule states that, for the joint uncertainty $H(X_1, X_2)$,

$$H(X_1) + H(X_2) \geq H(X_1, X_2). \tag{1.30}$$

Similarly, let $G$ be any finite group, and $G_1, G_2$ be subgroups of $G$. Let

$|G|$ represent the order of a group – the number of elements. Then the intersection $G_1 \cap G_2$ is also a subgroup, and

$$\log[\frac{|G|}{|G_1|}] + \log[\frac{|G|}{|G_2|}] \geq \log[\frac{|G|}{|G_1 \cap G_2|}]. \qquad (1.31)$$

Defining a probability for a 'random variate' associated with a group $G$ as $Pr\{X = a\} = 1/|G|$ permits construction of a group-characterized information source, noting that, in general, the joint uncertainty of a set of random variables in not necessarily the logarithm of a rational number. The surprising ultimate result, however, is that there is a one-to-one correspondence between unconstrained information inequalities and group inequalities. Indeed, unconstrained inequalities can be proved by techniques in group theory, and certain group-theoretic inequalities can be proven by techniques of information theory.

More generally, the theory of error-correcting codes, usually called algebraic coding theory (Pretzel 1996, Roman 1997; van Lint 1999), seeks particular redundancies in message coding over noisy channels that enable efficient reconstruction of lost or distorted information. The full-bore panoply of groups, ideals, rings, algebras, and finite fields is brought to bear on the problem to produce a spectrum of codes having different capabilities and complexities: BCH, Goppa, Hamming, Linear, Reed-Muller, Reed-Solomon, and so on.

Here, we will provide examples suggesting that the relations between groups, groupoids, and a broad spectrum of information related phenomena of interest in biology are, similarly, surprisingly intimate.

Group symmetries associated with an error-minimization coding scheme – as opposed to error correction coding – will dominate a necessary conditions statistical model of a 'spontaneous symmetry breaking' phase transition that drives the collapse of protein folding to pathological amyloid production (Wallace 2015b), and groupoids emerge as central in the study of a similar wide-ranging 'ground state' failure of cognitive process, adopting the Maturana/Varela (Maturana and Varela 1980) perspective on the necessity of cognition at every scale and level of organization of the living state. Here, we will implicitly extend the relation between information inequalities and finite group structures to a fundamental duality between an information theoretic characterization of cognition and *groupoids*, which are a generalization of group theory in which a product is not necessarily defined between every object. The simplest example is a disjoint union of groups. A more subtle example is the groupoid characterization of equivalence classes. See the Mathematical Appendix for details.

# Chapter 2

# Animal consciousness: a primer

Forthcoming generations of massively parallel 'Self-X' machines will be expected to program, repair, and protect themselves while managing a broad range of critical systems in real time. This is, far more than industry salesmen will openly admit, very much *terra incognita*: we simply do not know how to reliably supervise and stabilize such systems. Animal – and human – models can provide insights, albeit having had the relentless benefit of a half-billion years of evolutionary selection pressure acting on structure and function. This chapter presents an extended meditation on high level animal cognition that will provide a background for later descriptions of complex machine behaviors and pathologies.

## 2.1 Darwin's Rainbow

Evolution is littered with polyphyletic parallelism: many roads lead to functional Romes. Consciousness embodies one such example and we have elsewhere represented it with an equivalence class structure that factors the broad realm of information-theoretic realizations of Baars' global workspace model (Wallace 2005a, 2012b; Wallace and Fullilove 2008). The construction suggests many different physiological and machine systems can support rapidly shifting, highly tunable, and even simultaneous temporary assemblages of interacting unconscious cognitive modules. The discovery implies various animal taxa exhibiting behaviors we broadly recognize as conscious are, in fact, simply expressing different forms of the same underlying phenomenon. Slower versions of the basic structure can be mathematically derived, as a kind of paraconsciousness often ascribed to group phenomena. The variety of possibilities, a veritable rainbow, suggests minds today may be only a small surviving fraction of ancient evolutionary radiations

– bush phylogenies of consciousness and paraconsciousness. Under this scenario, the resulting diversity was subsequently pruned by selection and chance extinction. Although few traces of the radiation may be found in the direct fossil record, exaptations and vestiges are scattered across the living minds. Humans, for one, display an uncommonly profound synergism between consciousness, emotion, and the capacity for cultural transmission that enables efficient Lamarckian adaptation. These circumstances have implications for the design of Self-X cognitive machines, and for the spectrum of dysfunctions inevitably plaguing them.

High order mental function has long been suspected in animal species other than *Homo sapiens*. The *American Zoologist* (vol. 40, no. 6, 2000), for example, published the proceedings of a wide-ranging symposium on animal consciousness held by the Society for Integrative and Comparative Biology in January 1999. From that volume, Cartmill (2000) quotes Darwin (1889):

> ...The difference in mind between man and the higher animals, great as it is, certainly is one of degree and not of kind. We have seen that the senses and intuitions, the various emotions, attention, curiosity, imitation, reason etc., of which man boasts, may be found in an incipient, or even sometimes in a well-developed condition, in the lower animals...

In the same volume Griffin (2000) writes:

> A striking aspect of this symposium is that almost all the participants take it for granted that some animals *are* conscious – not all animals all the time, but at least some animals on some occasions... Instead of the resistance to considering such questions that used to be customary among behavioral scientists, there was stimulating and constructive discussion of the *content* of animal consciousness...
>
> This change in climate of opinion does not make the analysis of animal consciousness easy. All the difficulties and uncertainties which led behaviorists to ban the subject from scientific psychology remain in place. But difficulties are not impossibilities... Insofar as animals are conscious the content of their conscious experiences probably differs

in many ways from human consciousness, so that investigating it requires more than merely inquiring whether particular kinds of human awareness occur in other species...

Indeed, Griffin (1976, 1992) and Griffin and Speck (2004) review a vast range of ethological observations suggestive of consciousness in many animal species.

More recently, animal sentience was the topic of a full issue of *Applied Animal Behavior Science*, (Vol. 10, nos. 1-2, October, 2006), in which Pepperberg (2006) writes

...[D]ata... demonstrate that many species of animal posses cognitive capacities that we have until now considered unique to humans and other primates.

Simmonds (2006), in that same volume, states "...[V]arious complex behaviors and social structures ...support the notion that cetaceans should be regarded as intelligent animals."

A parallel perspective has even emerged within the academic consciousness industry, appearing in such journals as *Consciousness and Cognition* and at meetings of the Association for the Scientific Study of Consciousness (Edelman et al. 2005; Seth et al., 2005).

All in all, rapidly-operating consciousness appears to be an ancient, and highly effective, evolutionary adaptation. As Edelman et al. (2005) put the matter:

It is plausible that complex brains capable of rich and flexible behavioral repertoires began evolving in two very different radiations between 530 and 540 million years ago (Knoll and Carroll, 1999; Morris, 2000)....

Edelman et al. (2005) also point out, however, that mammals, birds, and cephalopods have very different neural anatomies. While an analog to the reentrant thalamocortical structure which seems to underlie human/mammal consciousness has been identified in birds, the cephalopod brain remains an enigma, in spite of striking ethological observations suggestive of consciousness.

Evolutionary psychologists have attempted to address the roles natural selection and phylogenetic constraints have played in generating multiple minds. Hayes (2003), for example, writes:

The task of evolutionary psychology is not to show that natural selection can influence cognitive processes but to establish exactly what kind of effects natural selection, and developmental selection, do and do not tend to have. Just as natural selection tends to be conservative with respect to respiratory pigments (e.g., hemoglobin) and revisionist with respect to respiratory structures (e.g., skin, gills, and lungs), it is likely that some properties of behavior-control systems are more susceptible than others to phylogenetic change and therefore that they show greater variation across species and in the course of development.

The widening recognition of a spectrum of minds is now extended into mathematical models of consciousness. There are several different formulations of Bernard Baars' (1988, 2005) treatment of consciousness, deriving a narrow variety of analytically tractable models from a far larger continuum of those possible (Wallace, 2005a, b, 2012b). The approach is analogous to developing empirical regression models, the grist for much science, based, however, on information theory's Rate Distortion and Shannon-McMillan Theorems rather than on the Central Limit Theorem.

Pielou's (1977, p. 102) caution on the use of mathematical models to describe biological phenomena is worth repeating in this context:

> ...[Mathematical models] are easy to devise; even though the assumptions of which they are constructed may be hard to justify, the magic phrase 'let us assume that...' overrides objections temporarily. One is then confronted with a much harder task: How is such a model to be tested? The correspondence between a model's predictions and observed events is sometimes gratifyingly close but this cannot be taken to imply the model's simplifying assumptions are reasonable in the sense that neglected complications are indeed negligible in their effects...
>
> In my opinion the usefulness of models is great... [however] it consists *not in answering questions but in raising them*. Models can be used to inspire new field investigations and these are the only real source of new knowledge as opposed to new speculation.

Despite repeated efforts to confound the two, mathematics is not evolution. Over the course of hundreds of millions of years, evolution has found many explicit solutions in intermediate phenotypes arising via idiosyncratic processes dependent on the locally available variation on which selection acts, internal physiological and genetic constraints that channel possible change, and history's stochastic contingencies (Gould 2002). The key questions orbit about which solutions evolution actually chose, however plausible various mathematical optima may be. The questions are ultimately matters for the empiricist. A good model, however, can help guide efforts at discovering evolution's course, with the caveats specific to the practice of modeling.

This introductory chapter reviews evidence for the parallel consciousnesses the spectrum of models of the Baars formalism suggests existed and have since passed and those that exist today. This will greatly illuminate subsequent address of high order machine cognition and its characteristic failure modes.

## 2.2   Basic Theory

The central ideas of the Baars consciousness model are (Baars and Franklin 2003):

(1) The brain can be viewed as a collection of distributed specialized networks (processors).

(2) Consciousness is associated with a global workspace in the brain – a fleeting memory capacity whose focal contents are widely distributed (broadcast) to many unconscious specialized networks.

(3) Conversely, a global workspace can also serve to integrate many competing and cooperating input networks.

(4) Some unconscious networks, called contexts, shape conscious contents. For example, unconscious parietal maps modulate visual feature cells that underlie the perception of color in the ventral stream.

(5) Such contexts work together jointly to constrain conscious events.

(6) Motives and emotions can be viewed as goal contexts.

(7) Executive functions work as hierarchies of goal contexts.

Although this basic approach has been the focus of many researchers for nearly over decades, academic consciousness studies, under the relentless pressure of a deluge of brain imaging results, have only recently begun digesting the perspective.

Currently popular agent-based and artificial neural network (ANN) treatments of cognition, consciousness and other higher order mental functions, taking Krebs' (2005) view, are little more than *sufficiency* arguments, mimicking mentality without providing real understanding of the underlying structure. *Necessary* conditions, as Dretske (1981, 1988, 1993, 1994) argues, give considerably more insight. They are the conditions to which evolving mental phenomena must assimilate.

Wallace (2005a, 2012b) addressed Baars' theme from Dretske's viewpoint, examining the necessary conditions which the asymptotic limit theorems of information theory impose on global broadcasts. A central outcome of this work has been the incorporation, in a mathematically clean manner, of constraints on individual consciousness – what Baars calls *contexts*.

Information theory methods, extended by a homology between information source uncertainty and the free energy density of a physical system, allow a formal account of the effects on individual consciousness of parallel physiological modules such as the immune system, embedding structures such as the local social network, and, most importantly, the cultural heritages that mark human biology (Richerson and Boyd 2006). This multi-layer embedding evades the mereological fallacy that fatally bedevils brain-only theories of human consciousness (Bennett and Hacker 2003). Neuron firing alone, although certainly a part of the whole, does not comprise the totality of mental function. Consciousness, a higher-order function, is the provenance of an entire animal, including, for many species, its social context.

Modeling the linkage of unconscious cognitive submodules involves the transference of phase change approaches from statistical physics to information theory via the homology between information source uncertainty and free energy density (Wallace 2005a, b, 2012b). The transfer, as we will demonstrate in the next chapters, cleanly generates a punctuated accession to consciousness. The necessary renormalization calculation focuses on a phase transition that arises from a change in the average strength of nondisjunctive weak ties (*sensu* Granovetter 1973) linking the unconscious submodules. A second-order universality class tuning, described in Chapter 1, allows for adaptation of conscious attention via rate distortion manifolds. A version of the Baars model (including contexts) emerges as an almost exact parallel to hierarchical regression, based, however, on the Shannon-McMillan Theorem rather than the Central Limit Theorem on which most modern-day modeling depends.

Wallace and colleagues (Wallace 2005b, 2006, 2007, 2012b; Wallace and Fullilove 2008) recently proposed a somewhat different approach that serves as the basis for another benchmark model against which empirical data can be compared. In fact there can be intermediate models as well as those acting at very slow rates. This suggests a broad equivalence class structure for global broadcast neural function models.

The essential point is that there are several analytically tractable models of the Baars general broadcast mechanism.

In one model, the average probability of information transfer linkages between cognitive modular components acts as a kind of temperature, so that an increase in probability of such contact raises the 'temperature' above a critical value, and the linked system suddenly 'evaporates' into a general broadcast. The characteristic 'universality class constants' of such a phase transition then become the subject of a second order treatment allowing tuning of that broadcast, according to constraints imposed by Baars' 'contexts'. These constrain the 'stream of consciousness' to realms useful to the animal.

A different perspective involves mean numbers of open information transfer linkages between cognitive modules having dual information sources, in a certain sense. If the average number of such linkages exceeds a threshold, depending on the abstract topology of the underlying cognitive modular network, then a single 'Giant Component' suddenly emerges linking most of the individual nodes into a single identifiable object that can transfer information across itself easily. Again, this is a form of Baars' general broadcast, as constrained by less rapidly acting contexts. The second order tuning is done here by varying the underlying topology, as opposed to the 'universality class tuning' of the mean field approximation.

The two perspectives produce essentially the same tunable broadcast comparable to the Baars global workspace model of consciousness. Less mathematically tractable structures seem possible. Evolution, however, does not seem particularly constrained by mathematical tractability, and thereupon hangs our tale.

## 2.3   Primitive Consciousness

Consciousness, then, may come in a vast Darwinian Rainbow of prover-
bial colors. If one views the basic phenomenon as arising from a shifting
structure of crosstalking unconscious cognitive modules operating in the
realm of a few hundred milliseconds, then, according to this development,
evolution will have had a vast playing field of possibilities, all producing
global broadcast behaviors – consciousness. Simple systems might well be
found in many insects, higher order iterations across a considerable range
of animal species. One clear conjecture is that such iterations will almost
always be susceptible to some form of inattentional blindness, as the syn-
tactic/grammatical bandpass of a tuned rate distortion manifold is always
limited (Wallace 2007; Glazebrook and Wallace 2009a, b). Another is that,
if simultaneous broadcast mechanisms operate, at the same or different
rates, there will be limits imposed by the Rate Distortion Theorem on
the uncorrupted transmission of information between them (Wallace and
Fullilove 2008).

Slowly acting general broadcast architectures linking unconscious cognitive modules might also be found in many living things as a kind of paraconsciousness. It may even be possible for conscious animals themselves to
entertain, as contexts, other global workspace processes operating on much
slower timescales than consciousness itself. Certainly human institutions,
in which we are all embedded, constitute structures having multiple global
broadcasts, albeit operating over very long times (Wallace and Fullilove
2008). Appropriate eusocial colonies may provide other examples.

What, then, is an alternative form of consciousness? An attempt to
flesh out an example might better ground the model for experimentalists.

Emotion in humans has often been viewed as a 'primitive' form of consciousness upon which later forms have been built. Panskepp (2003) has
argued that emotion represents a primary form of consciousness, based
in early-evolved brain structures, becoming convoluted with Baars' later-
developed broadcast mechanisms.

Thayer and Lane (2000) summarize the case for what can be described
as a cognitive emotional process. Emotions, in their view, are an integrative
index of individual adjustment to changing environmental demands, an organismal response to an environmental event that allows rapid mobilization
of multiple subsystems. Emotions are the moment-to-moment output of a
continuous sequence of behavior, organized around biologically important
functions.

Emotions are self-regulatory responses that allow the efficient coordination of the organism for goal-directed behavior. Specific emotions imply specific eliciting stimuli, specific action tendencies (including selective attention to relevant stimuli), and specific reinforcers. When the system works properly, it allows for flexible adaptation of the organism to changing environmental demands, so that an emotional response represents a *selection* of an appropriate response and the inhibition of other less appropriate responses from a more or less broad behavioral repertoire of possible responses. Such 'choices' lead directly to something closely analogous to Atlan and Cohen's cognition model discussed in later chapters.

Damasio (1989) concludes that emotion is the most complex expression of homeostatic regulatory systems. The results of emotion serve the purpose of survival even in nonminded organisms, operating along dimensions of approach or aversion, of appetition or withdrawal. Emotions protect the subject organism by avoiding predators or scaring them away, or by leading the organism to food and sex. Emotions often operate as a basic mechanism for making decisions without the labors of reason; that is, without resorting to deliberated considerations of facts, options, outcomes, and rules of logic. In humans, learning can pair emotion with facts which describe the premises of a situation, the option taken relative to solving the problems inherent in a situation, and, perhaps most importantly, the outcomes of choosing a certain option, both immediately and in the future.

The pairing of emotion and fact remains in memory in such a way that when the facts are considered deliberately under similar conditions, the paired emotion or some aspect of it can be reactivated. The recall, according to Damasio, allows emotion to exert its qualification, either as a conscious signal or as non-conscious bias, or both. In both types of action the emotions and the machinery underlying them play an important regulatory role in the life of the organism. This higher order role for emotion is still related to the needs of survival, albeit less apparently.

Thayer and Friedman (2002) argue, from a dynamic systems perspective, that failure of what they term 'inhibitory processes' that, among other things, direct emotional responses to environmental signals, is an important aspect of psychological disorders. Sensitization and inhibition, they claim, 'sculpt' the behavior of an organism to meet changing environmental demands. When these inhibitory processes are dysfunctional – and choice fails – pathology appears at numerous levels of system function, from the cellular to the cognitive.

Thayer and Lane (2000) also take a dynamic systems perspective on emotion and behavioral subsystems. In the service of goal-directed behavior and in the context of a behavioral system, they see these organized into coordinated assemblages that can be described by a small number of control parameters. These parameters are analogous to the factors of factor analysis, revealing the latent structure among a set of questionnaire items and reducing the higher dimensional item space into a lower dimensional factor space. In their view, emotions may represent preferred configurations in a larger 'state-space' of a possible behavioral repertoire of the organism.

From this perspective, disorders of affect represent a condition in which the individual is unable to select the appropriate response, or to inhibit the inappropriate response, so that the response selection mechanism inherent to emotional cognition is somehow corrupted. Gilbert (2001) suggests that a canonical form of such 'corruption' is the excitation of modes that, in better circumstances, represent 'normal' evolutionary adaptations.

Later chapters explore in some detail how separate global broadcast mechanisms can coexist and interact, and the difficulties inherent to their proper coordination. For example the sometimes ambiguous relation between emotion and higher order cognition in humans – traditionally the conflict between heart and mind – has long been a subject of commentary (Timberlake 1990).

We will revisit some of these mechanisms as 'rate distortion manifolds' (Glazebrook and Wallace 2009a, b) and as 'generalized autoimmune disorders'.

## 2.4   Polyphyletic Parallelisms

If evolutionary history is any indication, emotion is unlikely the sole plesiomorphic consciousness. Evolution is littered with innovative flux. Multicellularity began among the Ediacara 650 million years ago and arose again in the Tommotian phase of the Cambrian Explosion, with a diversity of body plans unrivaled since. The Tetrapoda's late Devonian land invasion included more than one multiple-digit plan. *Ichthyostega*, *Acanthostega*, and *Tulerpeton* emerged with six, seven, even eight digits on each limb. Varieties of great apes far outnumbering present-day remnants brachiated through the Miocene.

We hypothesize similar evolutionary radiations of mind, wherein bouts of divergent innovations in consciousness and paraconsciousness arose together. In all likelihood, multiple attempts were made at building limbic-like systems and, subsequently, cortex-like functionalities atop the reptilian brain. There are even now a variety of ways to interconnect the three.

Holloway (1996) reviewed several examples of brain reorganization over the course of primate evolution, including this prime example of reorganization:

> ...[I]n the [human] visual system, i.e., the primary visual striate cortex and the lateral geniculate nuclei, differences (-121 per cent and -146 per cent respectively) *are* significant, and these reductions signal a *relative increase* in the volume of parietal 'association' cortex, which is usually related to complex cognitive activities such as visuo-spatial integration.

Holloway, among others, argued such reorganization could include the development of new interconnections, including, in humans in particular, an increasing number of maturing fibre systems linking different cortical regions via the corpus callosum. Striedter (2004) cites the evolution of the human brain as an example of Devon's rule that 'large equals well-connected' – evolutionarily enlarging brain regions will often innervate phylogenetically independent regions. The neocortex seems to have unusually extensive projections to the medulla. This, in turn, is likely to explain (at least in part) why humans are so remarkably dexterous in their hand, eye, mouth, and vocal-fold movements.

In addition to, or because of, reorganization, out-and-out novel structures have also evolved. Striedter offers a few examples, among them the electronsensory lateral line lobe in teleosts, the torus longitudinalis in ray-finned fish, and the mammalian neocortex. We imagine such phylogenetic proliferation in newly discovered extinct taxa will represent the paleoneurologist's equivalent of a lost city found.

The key point here is that plentiful data indicate evolution has long experimented with the means and modes by which unconscious modules are interconnected. The resulting referential experiences the organisms partake are likely quite different even as the underlying brains are phylogenetically related. At this point, however, we can only surmise what a consciousness feels like with a lateral line lobe in tow.

In any scenario of the evolution of consciousness, however, the resulting phylogenetic bushes of mind were subsequently pruned by some combination of blind chance and failure to adapt to changing circumstances. If so, it seems we are left with little recourse in excavating the resulting mental fossils. The Cretaceous meteorite left no dinosaur minds behind.

Still, CNS endocasts may offer a few clues (Holloway 1996) and the brain of the occasional hominid or mastodon found in ice may be preserved well enough for dissection. Alternatively, living mammalian and other heads are likely filled with evolutionary artifacts and exaptations jury-rigged together by selection and historical accident (Gould 1991). The epistemological criteria by which one can identify the mental equivalents of the whale hip bone are available for experimental tests (Skoyles 1999). As stated, one possibility is Panskepp's (2003) argument that emotion was an early form of general broadcast consciousness now operating in synchrony with higher order forms in humans and other animals.

Another possibility is human-specific and, as a study subject, less exposed to the travails of the mereological fallacy. Human consciousness and emotions, unlike those of most animals, are strongly, if not uniquely, synergistic with the rich dual heritage system of embedding culture (Richerson and Boyd 2006). This suggests, in addition to more complex failure modes, a culturally dictated plasticity (Heine 2001) that may have enabled us to readily adapt to changing circumstances and the vicissitudes of socioecological chance (Wallace and Wallace 1999). Indeed, exaptation of basic animal consciousness – phenomenal, access, or otherwise – to such a synergism may well constitute the unique late hominid advantage that has enabled small, highly disciplined bands to become the most fearsome predators on the planet.

The synergism may come at a cost (Wallace 2005b, summarized in Chapter 3). Some of the most common psychopathologies may arise at evo-devo interfaces, where consciousness' historical sources – phylogenetic innovation, exaptation, cultural heritages – have the most difficulty developmentally meshing even in the healthiest among us. The paradigm has implications for patient care and offers a testable alternative to mismatch theories of psychological disorder caught in Pleistocene amber (Baron-Chon 1997; McGuire and Troisi 1998). Treatment protocols that ignore the effects human history over the past 10,000 years has had, and continues to have, on psychological ontogeny appear, at best, of distinctly limited clinical value (Wallace 2005b).

Pathologies in human integration and reorganization may hark further back, eons before. Oliver Sacks has proposed some human diseases may induce mockeries of ancient mental functions. Parkinson's impairs motor flexibility. The resulting symptoms include a 'reptilian' stare and "alterations of extreme immobility with sudden almost explosive motion, which are reminiscent of some reptiles". Brain lesions can lead to a variety of encephalitic syndromes, including, rarely, branchial myoclonus. The resulting rhythmic movements in the palate, middle ear and neck occur in what are the vestiges of the gill arches, releasing our inner fish. Here, a disease that strips phylogenetic innovation releases an impossible reversion.

## 2.5   Implications

The development here carries the burden of seeming a 'theory of everything', in that the different equivalence classes of general broadcast models appear to cover a vast swath of higher level cognitive phenomena across a considerable range of organisms and their assemblages. Taking Pielou's viewpoint, the 'let us assume that...' of the requirement in later chapters that an asymptotically piecewise stationary ergodic information source be 'dual' to a given cognitive process, overrides objections temporarily and allows construction of this grand castle-in-air. Regarding such assumptions, two points:

First, few cognitive phenomena are likely to be ergodic in this sense, and development of a quasi-ergodic version of the theory is a starkly nontrivial mathematical enterprise. Absent the mathematical smoke-and-mirrors, what remains – again in Pielou's sense (Pielou 1977, p. 102) – is the set of questions these models raise regarding the ubiquity of conscious and paraconscious phenomena across many organisms and their natural groupings. In this spirit, the apparent ease with which cognitive modules may link together to form shifting, or even tunable, giant components, or engage in information dynamic phase transitions, suggests that individual consciousness in animals, and individual or group paraconsciousness for organisms and their assemblies, may have been quite common over a very long period, as far back as the early mind.

Second, the development is most fundamentally a statistical model based on the Rate Distortion Theorem, in much the same sense that the General Linear Model is a statistical model based on the Central Limit Theorem. It is no more a theory of everything than is a fitted regression equation. The primary scientific utility of such things, as always, lies in empirical comparisons between models fitted to different systems under similar conditions, or the same system under different conditions, and in the structure of model residuals.

Statistical and mathematical models best serve as subordinate partners in the ongoing scientific conversation among theory, observation, and experiment. This work is no exception. The trick now is to operationalize the formalism into measurable variables of consciousness, whatever they may be. Information theory is notorious, however, for providing 'existence theorems' whose application is arduous indeed. While the Shannon Coding Theorem implied the possibility of very efficient coding schemes as early as 1949, it took more than forty years for practical 'turbo codes' to be created. The adaptation here is unlikely to be less difficult.

The discovery of large equivalence classes of mathematical models exhibiting global broadcast behaviors, some that may operate simultaneously within an individual animal or colony, suggests it would be fruitful to widen our perspectives on animal and machine consciousness beyond even the liberal limits laid down by the Society for Integrative and Comparative Biology. The road to a paleontology of consciousness, a rainbow on the horizon, is wide open and likely characterized by strange switchbacks and cul-de-sacs.

The models presented here, abstract as they may seem, offer one of the first analytic road maps for understanding the development and varieties of consciousness. In the context of the constraints of an information topology surrounding the Rate Distortion Theorem, as much a part of our intellectual bedrock as central limits and relativity, the evolution or construction of parallel modes of consciousness appears a real possibility.

Implications for machine design are both profound and starkly conflicting. First, if present forms of animal consciousness are indeed highly pruned survivors of the interaction between selection and chance extinction, then there is no need to blindly follow current biological patterns. A better strategy is to let the equivalence classes of problem types impose their structures onto high level machine cognition as contexts and/or selection pressures, allowing design to follow demand, as it were. Second, while there is little real insight into how high level mental function is stabilized and regulated in surviving taxa of conscious animals, it is at least possible to do experiments and make observations on them. The stabilization and regulation of other designs, in particular those selected by problem structure and market pressures alone, seems completely beyond us.

# Chapter 3

# Psychiatric disorders

## 3.1 Introduction

The most powerful 'autonomic' systems we can observe involve individual human minds and the institutions and larger social structures that humans create. This chapter applies ideas from the Baars model of consciousness to an exploration of human mental disorders. The exercise will prove useful in subsequent discussions of failure modes in large-scale critical real time control systems.

Mental disorders in humans are not well understood. Indeed, such classifications as the *Diagnostic and Statistical Manual of Mental Disorders - fourth edition* (DSMIV, 1994), the standard descriptive nosology in the US, were openly characterized as 'prescientific' by Gilbert (2001) and others. Recent revisions – 'DSM-V'– have received a similarly scathing response. Arguments from genetic determinism fail, in part because of an apparently draconian population bottleneck that, early in our species' history, resulted in an overall genetic diversity less than observed within and between contemporary chimpanzee subgroups. Arguments from psychosocial stress fare better, but are affected by the apparently complex and contingent developmental paths determining the onset of schizophrenia – one of the most prevalent serious mental disorders – dementias, psychoses, and so forth, some of which may be triggered in utero by exposure to infection, low birthweight, or other stressors, at critical periods of gestation or subsequent development.

Gilbert suggests an extended evolutionary perspective, in which evolved mechanisms like the 'flight-or-fight' response are inappropriately excited or suppressed, resulting in such conditions as anxiety or post traumatic stress disorders. Nesse (2000) suggests that depression may represent the dysfunction of an evolutionary adaptation down-regulating foraging activity in the face of unattainable goals.

Kleinman and Good, however, (1985, p. 492) have outlined some of the cross cultural subtleties affecting the study of depression, seeming to argue against any simple evolutionary interpretation:

> When culture is treated as a constant (as is common when studies are conducted in our own society), it is relatively easy to view depression as a biological disorder, triggered by social stressors in the presence of ineffective support, and reflected in a set of symptoms or complaints that map back onto the biological substrate of the disorder... However, when culture is treated as a significant variable, for example, when the researcher seriously confronts the world of meaning and experience of members of non-Western societies, many of our assumptions about the nature of emotions and illness are cast in sharp relief. Dramatic differences are found across cultures in the social organization, personal experience, and consequences of such emotions as sadness, grief, and anger, of behaviors such as withdrawal or aggression, and of psychological characteristics such as passivity and helplessness or the resort to altered states of consciousness. They are organized differently as psychological realities, communicated in a wide range of idioms, related to quite varied local contexts of power relations, and are interpreted, evaluated, and responded to as fundamentally different meaningful realities... Depressive illness and dysphoria are thus not only interpreted differently in non-Western societies and across cultures; they are *constituted* as fundamentally different forms of social reality.

More generally, Kleinman and Cohen (1997) find that:

> [S]everal myths... have become central to psychiatry... The first is that the forms of mental illness everywhere display similar degrees of prevalence... [Second is] an excessive adherence to a principle known as the pathogenic/pathoplastic dichotomy, which holds that biology is responsible for the underlying structure of a malaise,

whereas cultural beliefs shape the specific ways in which a person experiences it. The third myth maintains that various unusual culture-specific disorders whose biological bases are uncertain occur only in exotic places outside the West... In an effort to base psychiatry in 'hard' science and thus raise its status to that of other medical disciplines, psychiatrists have narrowly focused on the biological underpinnings of mental disorders while discounting the importance of such 'soft' variables as culture and socioeconomic status...

Further, serious mental disorders in humans are often comorbid among themselves – depression and anxiety, compulsive behaviors, psychotic ideation, etc. – and with serious chronic physical conditions such as coronary heart disease, atherosclerosis, diabetes, hypertension, dyslipidemia, and so on. These too are increasingly recognized as developmental in nature (Wallace 2004, 2005a), and are frequently compounded by behavioral problems like violence or substance use and abuse. Indeed, smoking, alcohol and drug addiction, compulsive eating, and the like, are often done as self-medication for the impacts of psychosocial and other stressors, constituting socially-induced 'risk behaviors' synergistically accelerating a broad spectrum of mental and physical problems.

Recent research on schizophrenia, dyslexia, and autism, supports a 'brain connectivity' model for these disorders that is of considerable interest from a global broadcast perspective, since large-scale brain connectivity is essential for the operation of consciousness.

Burns et al. (2003), on the basis of sophisticated diffusion tensor magnetic resonance imaging studies, find that schizophrenia is a disorder of large-scale neurocognitive networks rather than specific regions, and that pathological changes in the disorder should be sought at the supra-regional level. Both structural and functional abnormalities in frontoparietal networks have been described and may constitute a basis for the wide range of cognitive functions impaired in the disorder, such as selective attention, language processing and attribution of agency.

Silani et al. (2005) find that, for dyslexia, altered activation observed within the reading system is associated with altered density of grey and white matter of specific brain regions, such as the left middle and inferior temporal gyri and left arcuate fasciculus. This supports the view that dyslexia is associated with both local grey matter dysfunction and with altered larger scale connectivity among phonological/reading areas.

Villalobos et al. (2005) explore the hypothesis that large-scale abnormalities of the dorsal stream and possibly the mirror neuron system, may be responsible for impairments of joint attention, imitation, and secondarily for language delays in autism. Their empirical study showed that those with autism had significantly reduced connectivity with bilateral inferior frontal area 44, which is compatible with the hypothesis of mirror neuron defects in autism. More generally, their results suggest that dorsal stream connectivity in autism may not be fully functional.

Courchesne and Pierce (2005) suggest that, for autism, connectivity within the frontal lobe is excessive, disorganized, and inadequately selective, whereas connectivity between frontal cortex and other systems is poorly synchronized, weakly responsive and information impoverished. Increased local but reduced long-distance cortical-cortical reciprocal activity and coupling would impair the fundamental frontal function of integrating information from widespread and diverse systems and providing complex context-rich feedback, guidance and control to lower-level systems.

Coplan (2005) has observed a striking pattern of excessive frontal lobe self-connectivity in certain cases of anxiety disorder, and Coplan et al. (2005) find that maternal stress can affect long-term hippocampal neurodevelopment in a primate model.

As stated, brain connectivity is the sine qua non of the global broadcast models of consciousness, and further analysis suggests that these disorders cannot be fully understood in the absence of a functional theory of consciousness, and in particular, of a detailed understanding of the elaborate regulatory mechanisms which must have evolved over the past half billion years to ensure the stability of that most central and most powerful of adaptations.

Distortion of consciousness is not simply an epiphenomenon of the emotional dysregulation that many see as the 'real' cause of mental disorder. Like the pervasive effects of culture, distortion of consciousness lies at the heart of both the individual experience of mental disorder and the effect of it on the embedding of the individual within both social relationships and cultural or environmental milieu. Distortion of consciousness in mental disorders inhibits both routine social interaction and the ability to meet internalized or expected cultural norms, a potentially destabilizing positive feedback. Distortion of consciousness profoundly affects the ability to learn new, or change old, skills in the face of changing patterns of threat or opportunity, perhaps the most critical purpose of the adaptation itself.

Distortion of consciousness, particularly any decoupling from social and cultural context, is usually a threat to long-term individual survival, and those with mental disorders significantly affecting consciousness typically face shortened lifespans.

This chapter will review some recent advances in consciousness theory, briefly described previously, focusing on the role of that adaptation in mental disorders. The approach uses an information theory formalism that is in some contrast to neural network studies of mental disorder. As Krebs (2005) has argued, neural network models of mental function fall victim to a 'sufficiency indeterminacy' in the same sense that the Ptolemaic system of astronomy, with its endless epicycle-upon-epicycle Fourier series expansion of planetary dynamics, fails in comparison with the Newtonian analysis of central gravitational motion. That is, as Krebs puts it, neural possibility does not imply neural plausibility, and neural network computer models of mental phenomena can be constructed to do literally whatever one wants, in the same sense that a Fourier series can be constructed to approximate any function over a fixed interval without providing much basic understanding of that function.

Recent resumption of scientific research on consciousness in humans has followed Bernard Baars' pioneering restatement of the problem, as described in Section 2.2.

The Baars model has received increasing experimental verification over the last two decades (e.g., Dehaene and Naccache 2001; Massimini et al. 2005). Since it particularly attempts to properly represent the matter of embedding and interpenetrating contexts, it provides a basis for understanding the synergism of consciousness and mental disorders in humans. In particular it addresses the role of embedding social and cultural contexts, and, as argued below, allows a parallel with the initiation and progression of cancer as a disorder of information, more fully discussed in Wallace et al. (2003).

Wallace (2005a) provides a rigorous mathematical formulation of the Baars model, in terms of an iterated, second-order, contextually embedded, hierarchical General Cognitive Model (GCM) crudely analogous to hierarchical regression. It is, however, based on the Shannon-McMillan rather than on the Central Limit Theorem, and is strongly supplemented by methodologies from topological manifold theory and differential geometry (Glazebrook and Wallace 2009a, b).

By contrast, the approach here focuses on modular networks of interacting cognitive substructures, and particularly study of their embedding in progressively larger systems. While the two methods do translate into each other, they provide somewhat different perspectives, something like the 'matrix' and 'wave function' interpretations of early quantum mechanics.

## 3.2   A Modular Network Model

**Cognition as 'language'**

Cognition is not consciousness. Indeed, most mental, and many physiological, functions, while cognitive in a particular formal sense, hardly ever become entrained into consciousness. For example, one seldom is able to consciously regulate immune function, blood pressure, or the details of binocular tracking and bipedal motion, except to decide 'what shall I look at', 'where shall I walk'. Nonetheless, many cognitive processes, conscious or unconscious, appear intimately related to 'language', broadly speaking. The construction is surprisingly straightforward.

Atlan and Cohen (1998), and Cohen (2000), argue, in the context of immune cognition, that the essence of cognitive function involves comparison of a perceived signal with an internal, learned picture of the world, and then, upon that comparison, choice of one response from a much larger repertoire of possible responses.

Cognitive pattern recognition-and-response, from this view, proceeds by functionally combining an incoming 'external sensory signal' with an internal 'ongoing activity', incorporating the learned picture of the world, and triggering some appropriate action based on a decision that the pattern of sensory activity requires a response. Two explicit neural network examples will be given below.

More formally, a pattern of sensory input is mixed in an unspecified but systematic manner with a pattern of internal ongoing activity to create a path of combined signals $x = (a_0, a_1, ..., a_n, ...)$. Each $a_k$ thus represents some algorithmic composition of internal and external signals.

This path is fed into a similarly unspecified decision function generating an output $h(x)$ that is an element of one of two disjoint sets $B_0$ and $B_1$ of possible system responses.

Let $B_0 \equiv \{b_0, ..., b_k\}$, and $B_1 \equiv \{b_{k+1}, ..., b_m\}$.

Assume a graded response, supposing that if $h(x) \in B_0$, the pattern is not recognized, and if $h(x) \in B_1$, the pattern is recognized, and some action $b_j, k + 1 \leq j \leq m$ takes place.

The principal objects of interest are paths $x$ which trigger pattern recognition and response. That is, given a fixed initial state $a_0$, such that $h(a_0) \in B_0$, examine all possible subsequent paths $x$ beginning with $a_0$ and leading to the event $h(x) \in B_1$. Thus $h(a_0, ..., a_j) \in B_0$ for all $j < m$, but $h(a_0, ..., a_m) \in B_1$. More complicated schemes are possible but shed little further light.

For each positive integer $n$, let $N(n)$ be the number of high probability 'grammatical' and 'syntactical' paths of length $n$ beginning with some particular $a_0$ having $h(a_0) \in B_0$ and lead to the condition $h(x) \in B_1$. Call such high probability paths 'meaningful', assuming, not unreasonably, that $N(n)$ will be considerably less than the number of all possible paths of length $n$ leading from $a_0$ to the condition $h(x) \in B_1$.

While combining algorithm, the form of $h$, and the details of grammar and syntax, can all remain unspecified in this model, the critical mathematical assumption permitting inference on necessary conditions is that the finite limit

$$H \equiv \lim_{n \to \infty} \frac{\log[N(n)]}{n} \qquad (3.1)$$

both exists and is independent of the path $x$.

Call such a pattern recognition-and-response cognitive process *ergodic*. Not all cognitive processes are likely to be ergodic, implying that $H$, if it indeed exists at all, is path dependent, although extension to 'nearly' ergodic processes is possible (Wallace 2005a; Wallace and Fullilove 2008).

Invoking the spirit of the Shannon-McMillan Theorem, as described in the first chapter, it is possible to define an adiabatically, piecewise stationary, ergodic (APSE) information source $\mathbf{X}$ associated with stochastic variates $X_j$ having joint and conditional probabilities $P(a_0, ..., a_n)$ and $P(a_n|a_0, ..., a_{n-1})$ such that appropriate joint and conditional Shannon uncertainties satisfy the classic relations (Cover and Thomas, 2006)

$$H[\mathbf{X}] = \lim_{n \to \infty} \frac{\log[N(n)]}{n} = \lim_{n \to \infty} H(X_n|X_0, ..., X_{n-1}) = \lim_{n \to \infty} \frac{H(X_0, ..., X_n)}{n}.$$

This information source is defined as *dual* to the underlying ergodic cognitive process.

The essence of adiabatic is that, when the information source is parameterized according to some appropriate scheme, within continuous 'pieces' of that parameterization, changes in parameter values take place slowly enough so that the information source remains as close to stationary and ergodic as needed to make the fundamental limit theorems work. Stationary means that probabilities do not change in time, and ergodic (roughly) that cross-sectional means converge to long-time averages. Between 'pieces' one invokes various kinds of phase change formalism, for example renormalization theory in cases where a mean field approximation holds, or variants of random network theory where a mean number approximation is applied. Some of this is outlined in the first chapter.

The Shannon uncertainties $H(...)$ are cross-sectional law-of-large-numbers sums of the form $-\sum_k P_k \log[P_k]$, where the $P_k$ constitute a probability distribution. See Ash (1990), Khinchin (1957) or Cover and Thomas (2006) for the details, which are standard.

**Two neural network examples**

First, the simple Hopfield/Hebb stochastic neuron. A series of inputs $y_i^j, i = 1...m$ from $m$ nearby neurons at time $j$ is convoluted with 'weights' $w_i^j, i = 1...m$, using an inner product

$$a_j = \mathbf{y}^j \cdot \mathbf{w}^j = \sum_{i=1}^m y_i^j w_i^j \qquad (3.2)$$

given a 'transfer function' $f(\mathbf{y}^j \cdot \mathbf{w}^j)$ such that the probability of the neuron firing and having a discrete output $z^j = 1$ is $P(z^j = 1) = f(\mathbf{y}^j \cdot \mathbf{w}^j)$. Thus the probability that the neuron does not fire at time $j$ is $1 - f(\mathbf{y}^j \cdot \mathbf{w}^j)$.

The $m$ values $y_i^j$ constitute 'sensory activity' and the $m$ weights $w_i^j$ the 'ongoing activity' at time $j$, with $a_j = \mathbf{y}^j \cdot \mathbf{w}^j$ and $x = a_0, a_1, ...a_n, ...$

This approach generates a standard neural network model in which the network is trained by appropriately varying the $\mathbf{w}$ through least squares or other error minimization feedback.

Park et al. (2000) treat the stochastic neural network in terms of a space of related probability density functions $[p(\mathbf{x}, \mathbf{y}; \mathbf{w})|\mathbf{w} \in \mathcal{R}^m]$, where $\mathbf{x}$ is the input, $\mathbf{y}$ the output and $\mathbf{w}$ the parameter vector. The learning goal is to find an optimum $\mathbf{w}^*$ maximizing the log likelihood function. They define a loss function of learning as

$$L(\mathbf{x}, \mathbf{y}; \mathbf{w}) \equiv -\log p(\mathbf{x}, \mathbf{y}; \mathbf{w}) \qquad (3.3)$$

and one can take as a learning paradigm the gradient relation

$$\mathbf{w}_{t+1} = \mathbf{w}_t - \eta_t \partial L(\mathbf{x}, \mathbf{y}; \mathbf{w})/\partial \mathbf{w} \qquad (3.4)$$

where $\eta_t$ is a learning rate.

Park et al. attack this optimization problem by recognizing that the space of $p(\mathbf{x}, \mathbf{y}; \mathbf{w})$ is Riemannian with a metric given by the Fisher information matrix

$$G(\mathbf{w}) = \int \int \partial \log p/\partial \mathbf{w}[\partial \log p/\partial \mathbf{w}]^T p(\mathbf{x}, \mathbf{y}; \mathbf{w})dydx \qquad (3.5)$$

where $T$ is the transpose operation. A Fisher-efficient on-line estimator is then obtained by using the 'natural' gradient algorithm

$$\mathbf{w}_{t+1} = \mathbf{w}_t - \eta_t G^{-1} \partial L(\mathbf{x}, \mathbf{y}; \mathbf{w})/\partial \mathbf{w}. \tag{3.6}$$

Through the synergistic family of probability distributions $p(\mathbf{x}, \mathbf{y}; \mathbf{w})$, this can be viewed as a special case of the general 'convolution argument' given above.

**The giant component**

A formal equivalence class algebra can be constructed by choosing different origin points $a_0$ and defining the equivalence of two states $a_m, a_n$ by the existence of high probability meaningful paths connecting them to the same origin point. Disjoint partition by equivalence class, analogous to orbit equivalence classes for dynamical systems, defines the vertices of the proposed network of cognitive dual languages. Each vertex then represents a different information source dual to a cognitive process.

Suppose, now, that linkages can fleetingly occur between the ordinarily disjoint cognitive modules defined by this algebra. This is represented by establishment of a non-zero mutual information measure between them: cross-talk.

Wallace (2005a) describes this structure in terms of fixed magnitude disjunctive strong ties giving the equivalence class partitioning of modules, and nondisjunctive weak ties linking modules across the partition, and parameterizes the overall structure by the average strength of the weak ties, to use Granovetter's (1973) term. By contrast the approach here, initially, is to simply look at the average number of fixed-strength nondisjunctive links in a random topology. These are two analytically tractable limits of a much more complicated regime.

Since nothing is known about how the cross-talk connections can occur – for purposes of illustration only – assume they are random and construct a random graph in the classic Erdos/Renyi manner. Suppose there are $M$ disjoint cognitive modules – $M$ elements of the equivalence class algebra of languages dual to some cognitive process – now taken to be the vertices of a possible graph.

As Corless et al. (1996) discuss, when a graph with $M$ vertices has $m = (1/2)aM$ edges chosen at random, for $a > 1$ it almost surely has a giant connected component having approximately $gM$ vertices, with

$$g(a) = 1 + W(-a\exp(-a))/a \tag{3.7}$$

where $W$ is the Lambert-W function defined implicitly by the relation

$$W(x)\exp(W(x)) = x. \tag{3.8}$$

Figure 3.1 shows $g(a)$, displaying what is clearly a sharp phase transition at $a = 1$.

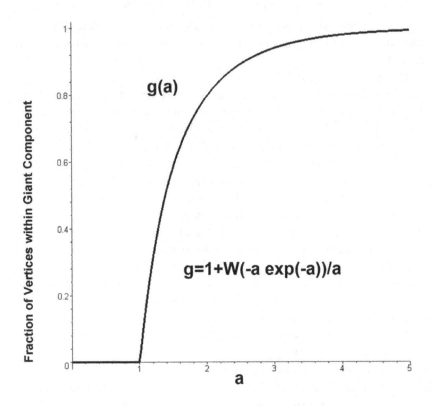

g(a)

g=1+W(-a exp(-a))/a

Fig. 3.1 Relative size of the largest connected component of a random graph, as a function of 2× the average number of fixed-strength connections between vertices. $W$ is the Lambert-W function, or the ProductLog in Mathematica, solving the relation $W(x)\exp[W(x)] = x$. Note the sharp threshold at $a = 1$, and the subsequent topping-out.'Tuning' the giant component by changing network topology generally leads to a family of similar curves, those having progressively higher threshold having correspondingly lower asymptotic limits (e.g., Newman et al. 2001, fig. 4).

Such a phase transition initiates a new, collective, shifting, cognitive phenomenon: a tunable broadcast defined by a set of cross-talk mutual information measures between interacting unconscious cognitive submodules. The source uncertainty, $H$, of the language dual to the collective cognitive process, defining the richness of the cognitive language of the global broadcast, will grow as some function of $g$, as more and more unconscious processes are incorporated into it. Wallace (2005a) examines what, in effect, are the functional forms $H \propto \exp(\alpha g), \alpha \ln[1/(1-g)], (1/(1-g))^\delta$, letting $R = 1/1 - g$ define a 'characteristic length' in the renormalization scheme. See the first chapter for details. While these all have explicit solutions for the renormalization calculation (mostly in terms of the Lambert-W function), other, less tractable, expressions are certainly plausible, for example $H \propto g^\gamma, \gamma > 0, \gamma$ real. Given a particular $H(g)$, the approach of Wallace (2005a), summarized in Chapter 1, involves adjusting universality class parameters of the phase transition, a matter requiring much mathematical development.

By contrast, in this new class of models, the degree of clustering of the graph of cognitive modules might, itself, be tunable, producing a variable threshold for consciousness: a topological shift, that should be observable from brain-imaging studies. Second order iteration would lead to an analog of the hierarchical cognitive model of Wallace (2005a).

The Wallace model focuses on changing the average strength of weak ties between unconscious submodules rather than the average number of fixed-strength weak ties as is done here, and tunes the universality class exponents of the phase transition, that may also imply subtle shifts in underlying topology.

Following Albert and Barabasi (2002, Section V), note that real networks differ from random graphs in that their degree distribution, the probability of $k$ linkages between vertices, often follows a power law $P(k) \approx k^{-\gamma}$ rather than the Poisson distribution of random networks, $P(k) = a^k \exp(-a)/k!, k \geq 0$. Since power law networks do not have any characteristic scale, they consequently termed scale-free.

It is possible to extend the Erdos/Renyi threshold results to such 'semi-random' graphs. For example, Luczak (1990) has shown that almost all random graphs with a fixed degree smaller than 2 have a unique giant cluster. Molloy and Reed (1995, 1998) proved that, for a random graph with degree distribution $P(k)$, an infinite cluster emerges almost surely when

$$Q \equiv \sum_{k \geq 1} k(k-2)P(k) > 0. \tag{3.9}$$

Following Volz (2004), cluster tuning of random networks leads to a counterintuitive result. Define the clustering coefficient $C$ as the proportion of triads in a network out of the total number of potential triads, i.e.,

$$C = \frac{3N_\Delta}{N_3} \tag{3.10}$$

where $N_\Delta$ is the number of triads in the network and $N_3$ is the number of connected triples of nodes, noting that in every triad there are three connected nodes. Taking the approach of Molloy and Reed (1998), Volz shows quite directly that, for a random network with parameter $a$, at cluster value $C$, there is a critical value given by

$$a_C = \frac{1}{1 - C - C^2}. \tag{3.11}$$

If $C = 0$, i.e., no clustering, then the giant component forms when $a = 1$. Increasing $C$ *raises* the average number of edges that must be present for a giant component to form. For $C \geq \sqrt{5}/2 - 1/2$, which is precisely the Golden Section, where the denominator in this expression vanishes, no giant component can form, regardless of $a$. Not all network topologies, then, can actually support a giant component, and hence, in this model, consciousness. This is of some importance, having obvious and deep implications ranging from the evolutionary history of consciousness to the nature of sleep.

A more complete exploration of the giant component can be found, e.g., in Newman et al. (2001), especially the discussion leading to their figure 4. In general, 'tuning' of the GC will generate a family of curves similar to figure 3.1, but with those having threshold to the right of that in the plot 'topping out' at limits progressively less than 1: higher thresholds seem usually to imply smaller giant components. In sum, the giant component is itself highly tunable, replicating, in this model, the fundamental stream of consciousness.

Note that the formalism presented here does not address the essential matter of how the system of interacting cognitive modules behaves away from critical points, particularly in the presence of 'external gradients'. Answering this question requires the imposition of generalized empirical Onsager equations, introducing complications of topological 'rate distortion manifolds', metric structures, and the like.

**Mutual and reciprocal interaction**

Just as a higher order information source, associated with the GC of a random or semirandom graph, can be constructed out of the interlinking of unconscious cognitive modules by mutual information, so too external information sources, for example in humans the cognitive immune and other physiological systems, and embedding sociocultural structures, can be represented as slower-acting information sources whose influence on the GC can be felt in a collective mutual information measure. The measure will, through the Joint Asymptotic Equipartition Theorem generalizing the

Shannon-McMillan Theorem, be the splitting criterion for high and low probability joint paths across the entire system.

The tool for this is network information theory (Cover and Thomas, 2006). Given three interacting information sources, $Y_1, Y_2, Z$, the splitting criterion, taking $Z$ as the 'external context', is given by

$$I(Y_1, Y_2|Z) = H(Z) + H(Y_1|Z) - H(Y_1, Y_2, Z) \tag{3.12}$$

where $H(..|..)$ and $H(..,..,..)$ represent conditional and joint uncertainties (Cover and Thomas, 2006).

This generalizes to

$$I(Y_1, ...Y_n|Z) = H(Z) + \sum_{j=1}^{n} H(Y_j|Z) - H(Y_1, ..., Y_n, Z). \tag{3.13}$$

Assuming the global broadcast to involve a very rapidly shifting, and indeed highly tunable, dual information source $X$, embedding contextual cognitive modules like the immune system will have a set of significantly slower-responding sources $Y_j, j = 1..m$, and external social, cultural and other 'environmental' processes will be characterized by even more slowly-acting sources $Z_k, k = 1..n$. Mathematical induction on equation (3.13) gives a complicated expression for a mutual information splitting criterion between high and low probability joint paths written as

$$I(X|Y_1, .., Y_m|Z_1, .., Z_n). \tag{3.14}$$

This encompasses a fully interpenetrating 'biopsychosociocultural' structure for individual consciousness, one in which Baars' contexts act as important, but flexible, boundary conditions, defining the underlying topology available to the far more rapidly shifting global broadcast of linked unconscious cognitive modules.

This result does not commit the mereological fallacy Bennett and Hacker (2003) impute to excessively neurocentric perspectives on consciousness in humans, that is, the mistake of imputing to a part of a system the characteristics which require completeness.

## 3.3 Punctuation

As many have noted (e.g., Feynman 2000), equation (3.1), $H \equiv \lim_{n \to \infty} \log[N(n)]/n$, is homologous to the thermodynamic limit in the definition of the free energy density of a physical system. This has the form

$$F(K) = \lim_{V \to \infty} -K \frac{\log[Z(K)]}{V} \equiv \frac{\log[\hat{Z}(K)]}{V} \tag{3.15}$$

where $F$ is the free energy density, $K$ the normalized temperature, $V$ the system volume, and $Z(K)$ is the partition function defined by the system Hamiltonian.

The homology permits a natural transfer of renormalization methods from statistical mechanics to information theory, as shown in Chapter 1. In the spirit of the Large Deviations Program of applied probability theory, this produces phase transitions and analogs to evolutionary punctuation in systems characterized by piecewise, adiabatically stationary, ergodic information sources. These 'biological' phase changes appear to be ubiquitous in natural systems and can be expected to dominate machine behaviors as well, particularly those which seek to emulate biological paradigms. Wallace (2002) uses these arguments to explore the differences and similarities between evolutionary punctuation in genetic and learning plateaus in neural systems. Punctuated phenomena will emerge as important in the discussions below of subtle information system malfunctions, be those systems biological, social, *in silico*, or hybrid.

## 3.4   A 'Cancer' Model

What is missing from this picture so far, and indeed will prove central, is description of the elaborate control mechanisms that must exist to ensure the integrity of the relation defined by the expression of equation (3.14), so that the information source $X$, representing the global broadcast of consciousness, remains confined to the topological structures defined by the external contexts represented by the set of information sources $Z(k), k = 1...n$. As a reviewer has noted, some mental disorders, at least, might be identified with the failure of these (social, cultural, and emotional) goal contexts to successfully constrain conscious events. Others may act by affecting the basic ability of the brain to engage in important large-scale coordinated activities.

More generally, the expression of equation (3.14), informed by the homology with equation (3.15), permits general discussion of the failure modes of global broadcast systems of all kinds, in particular of their second order iteration that appears to be the analog to consciousness in higher animals.

The foundation for this lies in the Rate Distortion Theorem. Under the conditions of that theorem, equation (3.14) is the splitting criterion between high and low probability joint paths defining the maximum rate at which an external information source can write an image of itself having a given maximum of distortion, according to some defined measure (Cover and Thomas 2006; Dembo and Zeitouni 1998). Inverting the argument, equation (3.14) suggests that an external information source can, if given enough time, write an image of itself upon consciousness. That is, structures in $Z$-space can write images of themselves on $X$. If that external source is pathogenic, then, given sufficient exposure, some measure of consciousness dysfunction becomes inevitable.

This may not, in fact, be fully separate from the question of the pathological decoupling of $X$ from the $Z$, as pathologies in $Z$-space may write an image of themselves onto the very containment mechanisms supposed to confine consciousness to the topology defined by cultural, social, and emotional goal contexts, ensuring the integrity of the expression in equation (3.14).

A more general discussion of comorbid mind/body disorders in humans emerges quite naturally (Wallace 2004). The picture, in humans, then, is of a multifactorial and broadly interpenetrating mind/body sociocultural dysfunction, often having early onset and insidious, irregular, developmental progression. These disorders are, broadly speaking, distorted images of pathogenic external environments literally written upon the developing embryo, on the growing child, and on the maturing adult (Wallace 2005a, Ch. 6; Wallace and Wallace 2010). The expression of equation (3.14) suggests that, in similar form, these images will be inevitably written upon consciousness as well, possibly through the failure of the mechanisms supposed to constrain it to the embedding goal contexts (Wallace 2015c).

Further consideration implies significant parallels with the initiation and progression of cancer in multicellular organisms, a quintessential disorder of information transmission. The analogy requires some development, condensed from Wallace et al. (2003).

Nunney (1999) suggests that in larger animals, whose lifespans are proportional to about the 4/10 power of their cell count, prevention of cancer in rapidly proliferating tissues becomes more difficult in proportion to their size. Cancer control requires the development of additional mechanisms and systems with increasing cell count to address tumorigenesis as body size increases – a synergistic effect of cell number and organism longevity.

As Nunney puts it:

> This pattern may represent a real barrier to the evo-
> lution of large, long-lived animals and predicts that those
> that do evolve... have recruited additional controls [over

those of smaller animals] to prevent cancer.

In particular, different tissues may have evolved markedly different tumor control strategies. All of these, however, are likely to be energetically expensive, permeated with different complex signaling strategies, and subject to a multiplicity of reactions to signals.

Work by Thaler (1999) and Tenaillion et al. (2001) suggests that the mutagenic effects associated with a cell sensing its environment and history could be as exquisitely regulated as transcription. Invocation of the Rate Distortion or Joint Asymptotic Equipartition Theorems in address of the mutator necessarily means that mutational variation comes to significantly reflect the grammar, syntax, and higher order structures of embedding environmental processes. This involves far more than simple stochastic excursions about a deterministic 'spine', and most certainly implies the need for exquisite regulation. Thus there are deep information and control theory arguments in favor of Thaler's speculation.

Thaler further argues that the immune system provides an example of a biological system that ignores conceptual boundaries between development and evolution.

Thaler specifically examines the meaning of the mutator for the biology of cancer, which, like the immune system it defies, is seen as involving both development and evolution.

Thus Thaler, in essence, looks at the effect of structured external stress on tumorigenesis and describes the 'local evolution' of cancer within a tissue in terms of a 'punctuated interpenetration' between a tumorigenic mutator mechanism and an embedding cognitive process of mutation control, including but transcending immune function.

The mutation control process constitutes the Darwinian selection pressure determining the fate of the (path dependent) output of a mutator mechanism. Externally-imposed and appropriately structured environmental signals then jointly increase mutation rate while decreasing mutation control effectiveness through an additional level of punctuated interpenetration. This is envisioned as a single, interlinked biological process.

Various authors have argued for 'non-reductionist' approaches to tumorigenesis (Baverstock 2000; Waliszewski et al. 1998), including psychosocial stressors as inherent to the process (Forlenza and Baum 2000). What is clear is that, once a mutation has occurred, multiple systems must fail for tumorigenesis to proceed. It is well known that processes of DNA repair (Snow 1997), programmed cell death – apoptosis (Evans and Littlewood 1998), and immune surveillance (Herberman 1995) all act to redress cell mutation. The immune system is increasingly viewed as cognitive, and is known to be equipped with an array of possible remediations (Atlan and Cohen 1998; Cohen 2000).

It is, then, possible to infer a larger, jointly-acting 'mutation control' process incorporating these and other cellular, systemic, and, in higher animals, social mechanisms. This clearly must involve comparison of developing cells with some internal model of what constitutes a 'normal' pattern, followed by a choice of response: none, repair, programmed cell death, or full-blown immune attack. The comparison with an internal picture of the world, with a subsequent choice from a response repertoire, is, as Atlan and Cohen (1998) point out, the essence of cognition.

One is led to propose, in the sense of the expression of equation (3.14), that a mutual information may be defined characterizing the interaction of a structured system of external selection pressures with the 'language' of cellular cognition effecting mutation control. Under the Joint Asymptotic Equipartition or Rate Distortion Theorems, that mutual information constitutes a splitting criterion for pairwise linked paths that may itself be punctuated and subject to sudden phase transitions.

Pathologically structured external environmental signals can become jointly and synergistically linked both with cell mutation and with the cognitive process which attempts to redress cell mutation, enhancing the former, degrading the latter, and significantly raising the probability of successful tumorigenesis.

Raised rates of cellular mutation that quite literally reflect environmental pressure through selection's distorted mirror do not fit a cognitive paradigm: The adaptive mutator may propose, but selection disposes. However, the effect of structured environmental stress on both the mutator and on the mutation control constituting the selection pressure facing a clone of mutated cells connects the mechanisms. Subsequent multiple evolutionary 'learning plateaus' (Wallace 2002) representing the punctuated interpenetration between mutation control and clones of mutated cells constitute the stages of disease. Such stages arise in the context of an embedding system of environmental signals that, to use a Rate Distortion argument, literally writes an image of itself on all aspects of the disease.

These speculations are consistent with, but suggest extension of, a growing body of research. Kiecolt-Glaser et al. (2002), for example, discuss how chronic inflammation related to chronic stress has been linked with a spectrum of conditions associated with aging, including cardiovascular disease, osteoporosis, arthritis, type II diabetes, certain cancers, and other conditions. Dalgleish (2001, 2002) and others (O'Byrne and Dalgleish 2001; Ridley 1996) have argued at length that chronic immune activation and inflammation are closely related to the etiology of cancer and other diseases. As Balkwill and Mantovani (2001) put the matter, "If genetic damage is the 'match that lights the fire' of cancer, some types of inflammation may provide 'fuel that feeds the flames' ".

Dalgleish (1991) has suggested application of non-linear mathematics to examine the role of immune response in cancer etiology, viewing different phenotypic modes of the immune system – the Th1/Th2 dichotomy – as 'attractors' for chaotic processes related to tumorigenesis, and suggests therapeutic intervention to shift from Th2 to Th1. Such a shift in phenotype might well be viewed as a phase transition.

This analysis implies a complicated and subtle biology for cancer in higher animals, one in which external environmental 'messages' become convoluted with both pathogenic clone mutation and with an opposing, and possibly organ-specific, variety of tumor control strategies. In the face of such a biology, anti-inflammants (Coussens and Werb 2002) and other 'magic bullet' interventions appear inadequate, a circumstance having implications for control of the aging of conscious systems that can be inferred from these examples.

Although chronic inflammation, related certainly to structured environmental stress, is likely to be a contributor to the enhancement of pathological mutation and the degradation of corrective response, it is unlikely to be the only such trigger. The constant cross-talk between central nervous, hormonal, immune, and tumor control systems in higher animals guarantees that the 'message' of the external environment will write itself upon the full realm of individual physiology in a highly plieotropic, punctuated, manner, with multifactorial impact on both cell clone mutation and tumor control.

## 3.5   Implications

These examples, particularly the model of cancer as an information disorder (Wallace et al. 2003), suggest that consciousness in higher animals, perhaps the essence of information processing, is necessarily accompanied by elaborate regulatory and corrective processes, both internal and external, to ensure both the integrity of large-scale brain connectivity and that the dynamics of the global broadcast are confined to the topology determined by embedding goal contexts. Only a few are well known: Sleep enables the consolidation and fixation in memory and semiautomatic mechanism of what has been consciously learned, and proper social interaction enhances mental fitness in humans. Other long-evolved, but currently poorly understood, mechanisms probably act as correctives to keep Gilbert's evolutionary structures from going off the rails, e.g., attempting to limit flight-or-fight HPA responses to 'real' threats, and so on.

Consciousness, a very old adaptation central to the survival of higher animals, has had the benefit of several hundred million years of evolution to develop the corrective and compensatory structures for its stability and efficiency over the life course. Although these are currently not well characterized, it seems clear that the synergism between culture and depression that Kleinman and others see as particularly characteristic of the disorder emerges 'naturally' from the relation of equation (3.14). Wallace (2015c) extends the argument.

The explicit inference, then, is that human consciousness can suffer interpenetrating dysfunctions of mutual and reciprocal interaction with embedding environments having early onset and often insidious staged developmental progression, possibly according to a cancer model. These may affect general brain connectivity or act to degrade the linkage between consciousness and goal contexts, thus decoupling their topologies. There will be no simple, reductionist brain chemical 'bug in the program' whose 'fix' can fully correct such problems. On the contrary, the growth of an individual over the life course, and contact with toxic features of the outside world, can be expected to initiate developmental disorders that will become more intrusive over time, most obviously following some damage accumulation model, but likely according to far more subtle schemes, perhaps analogous to punctuated equilibrium in evolutionary context (Wallace 2002).

The obvious rate distortion argument suggests that, if an external information source is pathogenic, then sufficient exposure to it, especially during critical developmental periods, is sure to write a sufficiently accurate image of it on mind and body in a punctuated manner so as to initiate or promote similarly progressively punctuated developmental dysfunction. Critical periods include, but are surely not limited to, the uterine environment and early childhood. Sufficient trauma, particularly when exacerbated by post-traumatic secondary victimization, may be expected to trigger subsequent developmental dysfunction at any time.

To reiterate, these considerations suggest strongly that, in parallel with consciousness, an elaborate system of correction and control must have evolved as well, quite analogous to the elaborate tumor control mechanisms that necessarily accompany multicellularity.

As is the case with many cancers, the key health intervention, at the population level, is clearly to limit pathogenic exposures, a matter of proper environmental sanitation, in a broad sense, largely a question of social justice long understood to be primarily determined by the interactions of cultural trajectory, group power relations, and economic structure with public policy (Fanon 1966; Farmer 2003; Fullilove 2004; Gandy and Zumla 2003; D. Wallace and R. Wallace 1998).

At the individual level, intervention against mental disorders is likely to be far more problematic, just as it is in the treatment of cancer, and for analogous reasons. This analysis suggests that one does not often cure developmental disorders once they have begun, indeed, a good analogy seems to be with the onset of chronic organic disease. It is not at all easy to turn back the developmental clock, and the parallels with punctuated equilibrium in evolutionary process suggests a one-way street.

The best that can often be achieved is to trigger or extend remission, either by encouraging or strengthening mechanisms of natural control and recovery, or through direct chemical or other intervention. That is, proper treatment can sometimes induce long-lasting remission, but this is subject to the determinants of medical failure, often precisely the factors of cultural trajectory, group power relations, economic structure, and public policy at the base of many population-level disease patterns. For an extended discussion see, for example, Wallace and Wallace (2004), who find that structured psychosocial stress can write a literal image of itself onto the success or failure of individual-level therapeutic intervention, drug-related or not, just as it can on the development and functioning of human intelligence and consciousness.

Some of the ambiguities of 'treatment' under such circumstances will be addressed in Chapter 7.

Although one may argue, as with the immune system, that exposure to 'adverse environments' is necessary to develop resistance to induction of mental disorders, it seems likely that this depends on the degree of adversity and whether that adversity occurs at a developmental critical point in life history. Failure of maternal attachment in infancy due to external socioeconomic stressors has proven to have long-term consequences for hippocampal neurodevelopment in animal models (Coplan et al. 2003).

This chapter outlines something of a consciousness-centered perspective on mental disorders, both those determined by defects in large-scale brain connectivity, and possibly by related failures of embedding goal contexts to constrain the topological dynamics of the global workspace. Further work in this direction might well focus on characterizing specific disorders from this viewpoint, and designing experiments to test such characterizations.

The relation of equation (3.14) and the arguments surrounding it, however, already provide, in the context of mental disorders, quite a 'hard science' basis for the evolutionary anthropologist Robert Boyd's oft-repeated assertion that culture is as much a part of human biology as the enamel on our teeth.

Not only culture and socioeconomic status, but historical trajectory, power relations between individuals and groups, and the effects of public policy, will write images of themselves onto the fundamental topology of individual consciousness, too frequently defining paths of debilitating developmental disorder that can blight lives.

Subsequent chapters will examine the implications of this model of human psychopathology for the stability and reliability of the complex machines that are being developed to control a vast array of critical processes. The evolutionary selection necessary to ensure their correct function under real-time, fog-of-war stresses has yet to take place. Given the limited abilities of evolutionarily developed regulatory structures to prevent mental disorders in humans and other higher animals, the prognosis for complex cognitive machines is not good.

# Chapter 4

# Models of machine cognition

## 4.1 Introduction

The heat barrier in single-core chip technology creates a powerful, hardware-driven, impetus toward highly parallel computing (e.g., Asanovic et al. 2006; Butler 2007). Programming single core machines has long been a nightmare, and the challenges presented by chips having hundreds or thousands of cores assembled into machines having millions of chips may require draconian solutions. Asanovic et al. suggest that:

> Since real world applications are naturally parallel and hardware is naturally parallel, what we need is a programming model, system software, and a supporting architecture that are naturally parallel.

There is a recently formalized, massively parallel, natural 'computation' model that may be adaptable to the coming generation of highly parallel machines, as well as to other large networks of intelligent devices. It is the model of distributed cognition encompassing humans, their cultural artifacts, and their institutions (Wallace and Fullilove 2008).

For nearly a half-million years, hominids in small, disciplined, groups have been the most efficient and fearsome predators on Earth. More recently, humans, in large-scale organization, have recast the surface features and ecological dynamics of the entire planet. Human organizations, at all scales, are cognitive, taking the perspective of Atlan and Cohen (1998), in that they perceive patterns of threat or opportunity, compare those patterns with some internal, learned or inherited, picture of the world, and then choose one or a small number of responses from a vastly larger set of what is possible to them. Human institutions are now the subject of intense study from the perspectives of distributed cognition (Cohen et al. 2006; Laxmisan et al. 2007; Patel 1998; Wallace and Fullilove 2008).

Hollan et al. (2000), expanding on previous work by Hutchins and collaborators (1994) describe these matters as follows:

> The theory of distributed cognition, like any cognitive theory, seeks to understand the organization of cognitive systems. Unlike traditional theories, however, it extends the reach of what is considered *cognitive* beyond the individual to encompass interactions between people and with resources and materials in the environment. It is important from the outset to understand that distributed cognition refers to a perspective on *all of cognition*, rather than a particular kind of cognition... Distributed cognition looks for cognitive processes, wherever they may occur, on the basis of the functional relationships of elements that participate together in the process. A process is not cognitive simply because it happens in a brain, nor is a process noncognitive simply because it happens in the interactions between many brains... In distributed cognition one expects to find a system that can dynamically configure itself to bring subsystems into coordination to accomplish various functions. A cognitive process is delimited by the functional relationships among the elements that participate in it, rather than by the spatial colocation of the elements... Whereas traditional views look for cognitive events in the manipulation of symbols inside individual actors, distributed cognition looks for a broader class of cognitive events and does not expect all such events to be encompassed by the skin or skull of an individual...
>
> –Cognitive processes may be distributed across members of a social group.
>
> –Cognitive processes may involve coordination between internal and external (material or environmental) structures.
>
> –Processes may be distributed through time in such a way that the products of earlier events can transform nature of later events.

As previous chapters describe, the study of individual consciousness has again become academically respectable, after nearly a century of ideologically enforced silence, and Baars' Global Workspace Theory (GWT) is the present front runner in the Darwinian competition between theoretical approaches (Dehaene and Naccache 2001). Wallace and colleagues (Wallace 2005a, 2012b, Wallace and Fullilove 2008) have developed a fairly detailed mathematical model of GWT, using a Dretske-like information theory formalism (Dretske 1994), extended by tools from statistical physics, the Large Deviations Program of applied probability, and the topological theory of highly parallel computation.

Institutional cognition – involving simultaneous, multiple global workspaces – is, however, a significantly more complex and varied phenomenon that is less constrained by biological evolution, and far more efficient in many important respects (Wallace and Fullilove 2008).

As the cultural anthropologists will attest, the structures, functions, and innate character of institutional cognition are greatly variable and highly adaptable across social and physical geography, and across history. Individual human consciousness, by contrast, remains constrained by the primary biological necessity of single-tasking, leading to the striking phenomenon of inattentional blindness (IAB) when consciousness becomes necessarily focused on one primary process to the virtual exclusion of others (Wallace 2007).

Generalizing a second order mathematical treatment of Baars' model of individual consciousness to organizational structures, Wallace and Fullilove (2008) suggest the contrasting possibility of collective multitasking, although that is mathematically a far more complicated process to analyze and describe. That work uncovered an institutional analog to individual inattentional blindness, and additional failure modes specific to the complication of multiple global broadcast systems, particularly distortion in the transmission of information between them.

Here we will recapitulate that analysis from the perspective of machine design, specifically invoking devices having as many global broadcast mechanisms as a large, highly capable human institution, but operating with characteristic times similar to individual consciousness – a few hundred milliseconds.

By contrast, small, disciplined human groups involved in hunting, combat, firefighting, sports, or emergency medicine, may function in realms of a few seconds to a few minutes. They are adaptive and 'self programming' in the face of dynamic challenge.

Similarly designed fast, self-programming, highly adaptive, multiple global broadcast, machines could be expected to do far more than just play variants of Chess or Go well, although their canonical and idiosyncratic failure modes would not be stabilized by the tens of thousands of years of cultural and 'market' selection pressures that have structured the various cognitive human institutions. Creating an 'ethical' stabilizing context for them seems a difficult challenge.

Recent work on emergent behavior in networked computing systems by Richter et al. (2006) provides another perspective on system stability:

> In 1850 more than 700 French soldiers marched lock-step over the rope bridge of Angers. The bridge began to vibrate, collapsed, and 226 soldiers died... This tragedy is often quoted as an example of a resonance catastrophe... Similar phenomena increasingly occur also in informatics... [which is] becoming more and more complex and unmanageable. Our daily life provides various situations where we are surrounded by self-organizing, interacting systems showing unknown or emergent behavior... [where] the global behavior of a system appears more coherent and directed than the behavior of individual parts... [T]he question is not whether complexity increases or informatics is confronted with emergence, but how we will design new systems that..[can] cope with the emerging global behavior of self-organizing systems by adequate control actions...
>
> [W]e shall be surrounded by large systems of intelligent devices interacting and cooperating in potentially unlimited networks. The design complexity of these systems calls for new design paradigms, and due to the effects of interaction in dynamically changing environments the global behavior of these systems might be unexpected... In particular, to some degree, these systems will organize themselves, independently of initial designs or external interventions.

This perspective has been greatly elaborated by a number of German researchers, who have established a formal research program in Organic Computing. Mnif and Muller-Scholler (2006), in particular, use a Shannon entropy formalism to characterize emergence, and our approach can be considered parallel to that work.

Somewhat ominously, one of the most spectacular examples of self organization in networked devices is the occurrence of widely-propagating power
grid blackouts. Kinney et al. (2005) describe the phenomenon as follows:

> Today the North American power grid is one of the
> most complex and interconnected systems of our time, and
> about one half of all domestic generation is sold over ever-
> increasing distances on the wholesale market before it is
> delivered to customers... Unfortunately the same capa-
> bilities that allow power to be transferred over hundreds
> of miles also enable the propagation of local failures into
> grid-wide events... It is increasingly recognized that under-
> standing the complex emergent behaviors of the power grid
> can only be understood from a systems perspective, tak-
> ing advantage of the recent advances in complex network
> theory...

Dobson (2007) states:

> [P]robabalistic models of cascading failure and power
> system simulations suggest that there is a critical loading
> at which expected blackout size sharply increases and there
> is a power law in the distribution of blackout size... There
> are two attributes of the critical loading: 1. A sharp change
> in gradient of some quantity such as expected blackout size
> as one passes through the critical loading. 2. A power law
> region in probability distribution of blackout size at the
> critical loading. We use the terminology 'critical' because
> this behavior is analogous to a critical phase transition in
> statistical physics.

Analogous 'emergent' high-level behaviors in linked cognitive modules
become inevitable once thresholds of information transfer between them
– crosstalk – are exceeded. The challenge is to stabilize and harness this
simple phenomenon to do useful work.

Here the focus is on percolation-like modular network models taken to
second order, subject to a topological tuning making them even more flexible. The first chapter shows that a similar model can be constructed using
thermodynamic phase transition formalism provided one permits a second
order universality class tuning. The two approaches thus emerge as exactly
solvable approximate models in an apparent continuum of possibilities, each

of which might well serve as a basis for machine design, tuned to the class
of problem to be solved.

The term 'universality class' arises from simple physical theory in which
the phase transition behavior of large classes of different materials can often
be scaled to match a single, relatively simple, algebraic expression (Binney
et al. 1986). Tuning the exponents defining such an expression provides
another degree of freedom for network structures that seems unavailable to
simple physical systems.

Phase transition is only one behavior of interest in second order models,
and the characteristics of such systems away from phase change regimes will
prove to be of central importance. In subsequent chapters this will require
development of empirical equations analogous to Onsager's treatment of
nonequilibrium thermodynamics (de Groot and Mazur 1984).

We review recent research on individual consciousness, as a kind of
second order iteration of simple cognition, and then examine the nontrivial extensions needed to describe highly parallel machines having multiple
workspaces. This development will then suggest adaptations of the approach applicable to programming high-level, real-time, cognitive machines,
and clarify the problems of stabilizing such devices.


## 4.2   The Baars Model

Recall the central ideas of Baars' Global Workspace Theory of individual
consciousness from Section 2.2.

The first step in constructing an explicit mathematical model of that
theoretical construct is to argue for the existence of a network of loosely
linked cognitive unconscious modules, and to characterize each of them by
the richness of the canonical language – information source – associated
with it. This is in some contrast to attempts to explicitly model neural
structures themselves using network theory, e.g., the neuropercolation approach of Kozma et al. (2004, 2005), which nonetheless uses many similar
mathematical techniques.

Here, rather, the focus is on the necessary conditions imposed by the
asymptotic limits of information theory on any realization of a cognitive
process, be it biological wetware, silicon dryware, or some direct or systems-
level hybrid. All cognitive processes, in this formulation, are to be associated with a canonical dual information source necessarily constrained by
the Rate Distortion Theorem, or, in the zero-error limit, the Shannon-

McMillan Theorem (Cover and Thomas 2006). It is interactions between nodes in this abstractly defined network that will be of interest here, rather than whatever mechanisms, social or biological system, or mixture of them, actually constitute the underlying cognitive modules.

The second step is to examine the conditions under which a giant component (GC) suddenly emerges as a kind of phase transition in a network of such linked cognitive modules, to determine how large that component is, and to define the relation between the size of the component and the richness of the cognitive language associated with it. This is the candidate for Baars' shifting, tunable, general broadcast of consciousness.

While Wallace (2005a) examines the effect of changing the average strength of nondisjunctive weak ties acting across linked unconscious modules, the previous chapter focused on changing the average *number* of such ties having a fixed strength, a complementary perspective whose extension via a kind of 'renormalization' leads to a far more general approach.

The third step is to tune the threshold at which the giant component comes into being, and to tune vigilance, the threshold for accession to consciousness.

This modular network treatment can be enriched by introducing a groupoid formalism roughly similar to that used in recent analyses of linked dynamic networks described by differential equation models (Golubitsky and Stewart 2006; Stewart et al. 2003, 2004). Internal and external linkages between information sources break the underlying groupoid symmetry, and introduce *more structures*, the global broadcast and the effect of contexts, respectively. The analysis provides a foundation for further mathematical exploration of linked cognitive processes.

The generalization of interest here is to examine the conditions under which cognitive modules may multitask, engaging in more than one giant component at the same time, i.e., synchronously. This is something individual consciousness does not permit under normal circumstances. The obvious trade off, of course, is the very rapid flow of individual consciousness, a matter of a few hundred milliseconds, as opposed to the much slower, if considerably more comprehensive, operations of institutional cognition. The conjecture, of course, is that machines can be built that would carry out complex processes of multiple global broadcast cognition at rates approaching those of individual conscious animals.

## 4.3 Cognition as Language

Recall the arguments of Section 3.2.

Atlan and Cohen (1998) define the essence of cognitive function as comparison of a perceived signal with an internal, learned picture of the world, and, upon comparison, choice of one response from a much larger repertoire of those possible.

Sensory input is mixed in an unspecified but systematic algorithmic manner with internal ongoing activity to create a path of combined signals $x = \{a_0, a_1, ..., a_n, ...\}$. Each $a_k$ can be associated with appropriate joint and conditional probabilities leading to definition of a dual Shannon information source, $H$, that satisfies the relation

$$H = \lim_{n \to \infty} \frac{\log[N(n)]}{n} \tag{4.1}$$

where $N(n)$ is the number of 'meaningful' paths of length $n$, independent of path.

## 4.4 The Cognition Groupoid

According to the arguments of Section 3.2, a formal equivalence class algebra can be constructed by choosing different origin points $a_0$ and defining equivalence of two states $a_k, a_j$ by the existence of high probability meaningful paths connecting them with the same origin. Disjoint partition by equivalence class, analogous to orbit equivalence classes for dynamical systems, defines the vertices of the proposed network of cognitive dual languages. Each vertex then represents a different information source dual to a cognitive process. This is not a representation of a neural network as such, or of some circuit in silicon. It is, rather, an abstract set of 'languages' dual to the cognitive processes instantiated by biological structures, social process, machines, or their hybrids.

This structure generates a groupoid, in the sense of Weinstein (1996). States $a_j, a_k$ in a set $A$ are related by the groupoid morphism if and only if there exists a high probability grammatical path connecting them to the same base point, and tuning across the various possible ways in which that can happen – the different cognitive languages – parameterizes the set of equivalence relations and creates the groupoid.

Not all possible pairs of states $(a_j, a_k)$ can be connected by such a morphism. Those that can, however, define the groupoid element, a morphism

$g = (a_j, a_k)$ having the natural inverse $g^{-1} = (a_k, a_j)$. See the Mathematical Appendix for details.

It appears that the equivalence class structure which Asanovic et al. (2006) identify for problem types can be recast in groupoid language, and may serve as a model for projecting structure onto potential hyperparallel architectures.

The groupoid approach has become quite popular in the study of networks of coupled dynamical systems defined by differential equation models. Here we have outlined how to extend the technique to networks of interacting information sources that, in a dual sense, characterize cognitive processes, and cannot at all be described by the usual differential equation models. These latter, it seems, are much the spiritual offspring of 18th Century mechanical clock models. Cognitive or conscious processes in higher animals involve neither computers nor clocks, but remain constrained by the limit theorems of information theory, and these permit scientific inference on necessary conditions. Extension of the approach to artificial systems provides a powerful new perspective.

Next we will attempt to create a 'biopsychosociocultural' model for single global broadcast systems, using a nested hierarchy splitting the simple groupoid modular network into a much more complicated structure.

## 4.5 Internal Symmetry Change

The symmetry groupoid constructed for cognitive modules in a kind of information space, is parameterized across that space by the possible ways in which states $a_j, a_k$ can be equivalent, i.e., connected to some origin by a meaningful path of an information source dual to a cognitive process. These are different, and in this approximation, non-interacting cognitive processes. But symmetry groupoids, like symmetry groups, can be made or broken: by internal cross-talk akin to spin-orbit interactions within a symmetric atom, and by cross-talk with slower, external, information sources, akin to putting a symmetric atom in a powerful magnetic or electric field.

As to the first process, suppose that linkages can fleetingly occur between the ordinarily disjoint cognitive modules defined by the network groupoid. This is represented by establishment of a non-zero mutual information measure between them: a rising cross-talk 'temperature' extending the strict groupoid symmetry developed above to a larger, 'more symmetric' groupoid.

Wallace (2005a) describes this structure in terms of fixed magnitude disjunctive strong ties that give the equivalence class partitioning of modules, and nondisjunctive weak ties linking modules across the partition, and parameterizes the overall structure by the average strength of the weak ties, to use Granovetter's (1973) term. By contrast, the approach here is to simply look at the average number of fixed-strength nondisjunctive links in a random topology.

Since we know nothing about how the cross-talk connections can occur, we will – at first – again assume they are random and construct a random graph in the classic Erdos/Renyi manner. Suppose there are $M$ disjoint cognitive modules – $M$ elements of the equivalence class algebra of languages dual to some cognitive process – which can now be taken as the vertices of a possible graph.

Recall, again, the results of Section 3.2.

For $M$ very large, following Savante et al. (1993), when edges (defined by establishment of a fixed-strength mutual information measure between the graph vertices) are added at random to $M$ initially disconnected vertices, a remarkable transition occurs when the number of edges becomes approximately $M/2$. Erdos and Renyi (1960) studied random graphs with $M$ vertices and $(M/2)(1 + \mu)$ edges as $M \to \infty$, and discovered that such graphs almost surely have the following properties:

1. If $\mu < 0$, only small trees and unicyclic components are present, where a unicyclic component is a tree with one additional edge; moreover, the size of the largest tree component is $(\mu - \ln(1 + \mu))^{-1} + \mathcal{O}(\log \log n)$.

2. If $\mu = 0$, however, the largest component has size of order $M^{2/3}$.

3. If $\mu > 0$, there is a unique giant component (GC) whose size is of order $M$; in fact, the size of this component is asymptotically $\alpha M$, where $\mu = -\alpha^{-1}[\ln(1-\alpha)-1]$, having an explicit solution for $\alpha$ in terms of the Lambert W-function. Thus, for example, a random graph with approximately $M \ln(2)$ edges will have a giant component containing $\approx M/2$ vertices.

Such a phase transition initiates a new, collective, cognitive phenomenon. At the level of the individual mind, unconscious cognitive modules link up to become the global broadcast of consciousness, emergently defined by a set of cross-talk mutual information measures between interacting unconscious cognitive submodules. The source uncertainty, $H$, of the language dual to the collective cognitive process characterizing the richness of the cognitive language of the broadcast, will grow as some monotonic function of the size of the GC, as more and more unconscious processes are incorporated into it.

Others have taken similar network phase transition approaches to assemblies of neurons, e.g., neuropercolation (Kozma et al. 2004, 2005), but their work has not focused explicitly on modular networks of cognitive processes, that may or may not be instantiated by neurons. Restricting analysis to such modular networks finesses much of the underlying conceptual difficulty, and permits use of the asymptotic limit theorems of information theory and the import of techniques from statistical physics.

## 4.6 External Symmetry Change

Just as a higher order information source, associated with the GC of a random or semirandom graph, can be constructed out of the interlinking of unconscious cognitive modules by mutual information, so too external information sources, for example in humans the cognitive immune and other physiological systems, and embedding sociocultural structures, can be represented as slower-acting information sources whose influence on the GC can be felt in a collective mutual information measure. For machines or institutions these would be the onion-like 'structured environment', to be viewed as among Baars' contexts. The collective mutual information measure will, through the Joint Asymptotic Equipartition Theorem that generalizes the Shannon-McMillan Theorem, be the splitting criterion for high and low probability joint paths across the entire system.

The tool for this is – again – network information theory (Cover and Thomas 2006). Given three interacting information sources, $Y_1, Y_2, Z$, the splitting criterion, taking $Z$ as the 'external context', is given by

$$I(Y_1, Y_2|Z) = H(Z) + H(Y_1|Z) + H(Y_2|Z) - H(Y_1, Y_2, Z) \qquad (4.2)$$

where $H(..|..)$ and $H(.., .., ..)$ represent conditional and joint uncertainties (Cover and Thomas, 2006).

Following the arguments of Section 3.2, this becomes

$$I(Y_1, ... Y_n|Z) = H(Z) + \sum_{j=1}^{n} H(Y_j|Z) - H(Y_1, ..., Y_n, Z). \qquad (4.3)$$

If the global broadcast/giant component involves a very rapidly shifting, and indeed highly tunable, dual information source $X$, embedding contextual cognitive modules will have a set of significantly slower-responding sources $Y_j, j = 1..m$, and external processes will be characterized by even more slowly-acting sources $Z_k, k = 1..n$. Mathematical induction on equation (3.13) gives a complicated expression for a mutual information splitting criterion that again can be written as

$$I(X|Y_1, .., Y_m|Z_1, .., Z_n). \tag{4.4}$$

Again, following the arguments leading to equation (3.14), Baars' 'contexts' become flexible, boundary conditions, defining the underlying topology available to the far more rapidly shifting global broadcast.

Again, this result evades the mereological fallacy Bennett and Hacker (2003) impute to excessively neurocentric perspectives on consciousness in humans. The underlying concept of this fallacy should extend to machines interacting with their environments.

The next section explores how rich local symmetries can be produced by invoking a global embedding, explicitly in terms of the groupoid formalism. The mereological fallacy, from this perspective, profoundly limits understanding of the possible richness of individual and multiple-workspace structures.

## 4.7   Emergence

Recall the argument of Section 3.3. Again, equation (4.1),

$$H \equiv \lim_{n \to \infty} \log[N(n)]/n,$$

is homologous to the thermodynamic limit in the definition of the free energy density of a physical system. This has the form

$$F(K) = \lim_{V \to \infty} -K \frac{\log[Z(K, V)]}{V} \equiv \frac{\log[\hat{Z}(K, V)}{V} \tag{4.5}$$

where $F$ is the free energy density, $K$ the normalized temperature, $V$ the system volume, and $Z(K)$ is the partition function defined by the system Hamiltonian.

The first chapter shows at some length how this homology permits the natural transfer of renormalization methods from statistical mechanics to information theory, producing phase transitions and analogs to evolutionary punctuation in systems characterized by piecewise, adiabatically stationary, ergodic information sources. These 'biological' phase changes can be expected to dominate information machine behaviors, particularly those seeking to emulate biological paradigms.

The approach uses a 'mean field' approximation in which average strength (or probability) of nondisjunctive linkages between cognitive nodes serves as a kind of temperature parameter. Phase transitions can then be described using various 'biological' renormalization strategies, in which 'universality class tuning' becomes the principal second order mechanism.

The argument above suggests that there is another analytically tractable limit, the giant component, implying the possibility of intermediate cases. The next section extends the giant component paradigm, so that the mean number of such linkages, above some variable threshold, is the parameter of central interest, and the second order tuning involves topological mechanisms.

Whatever scheme is chosen, however, the homology between equations (4.1) and (4.5) ensures that some form of emergent behavior, akin to a physical phase transition, is inevitable for networks of cognitive devices coupled by crosstalk, however instantiated.

## 4.8 Multiple Workspaces

The random network development above is predicated on there being a variable average number of fixed-strength linkages between components. Clearly, the mutual information measure of cross-talk is not inherently fixed, but can continuously vary in magnitude. This we address by a parameterized renormalization. In essence, the modular network structure linked by mutual information interactions has a topology depending on the degree of interaction of interest.

Define an interaction parameter $\omega$, a real positive number, and look at geometric structures defined in terms of linkages set to zero if mutual information is less than, and 'renormalized' to unity if greater than, $\omega$. Any given $\omega$ will define a regime of giant components of network elements linked by mutual information greater than or equal to it.

*The fundamental conceptual trick is to invert the argument*: a given topology for the giant component will, in turn, define some critical value, $\omega_C$, so that network elements interacting by mutual information less than that value will be unable to participate, i.e., will be locked out and not be consciously perceived.

Thus $\omega$ is a tunable, syntactically-dependent, detection limit that depends critically on the instantaneous topology of the giant component defining, for the human mind, the global broadcast of consciousness. That topology is, fundamentally, the basic tunable syntactic filter across the underlying modular symmetry groupoid, and variation in $\omega$ is only one aspect of a much more general topological shift. More detailed analysis is given below in terms of a topological rate distortion manifold.

There is considerable empirical evidence from fMRI brain imaging experiments to show that individual human consciousness involves a single global broadcast, leading necessarily to the phenomenon of inattentional blindness. Cognitive submodules within institutions, – individuals, departments, formal and informal workgroups – by contrast, can do more than one thing, and indeed, are usually required to multitask. One intent of this work is to suggest the possibility of constructing machines that work on similar principles, but much more rapidly.

Clearly, multiple global broadcast mechanisms would lessen the probability of inattentional blindness, but, we will find, do not eliminate it, and introduce other failure modes examined in more detail later.

Now postulate a set of crosstalk information measures between cognitive submodules, each associated with its own tunable giant component having its own special topology.

Suppose the set of giant components at some 'time' $k$ is characterized by a set of parameters $\Omega_k \equiv (\omega_1^k, ..., \omega_m^k)$. Fixed parameter values define a particular giant component set having a particular set of topological structures. Suppose that, over a sequence of 'times' the set of giant components can be characterized by a (possibly coarse-grained) path $x_n = \Omega_0, \Omega_1, ..., \Omega_{n-1}$ having significant serial correlations permitting definition of an adiabatically, piecewise stationary, ergodic (APSE) information source in the sense of Section 3.2. Call that information source **X**.

Suppose that a set of (external or internal) signals impinging on the set of giant components, is also highly structured and forms another APSE information source **Y** interacting not only with the system of interest globally, but specifically with the tuning parameters of the set of giant components characterized by **X**. **Y** is necessarily associated with a set of paths $y_n$.

Pair the two sets of paths into a joint path $z_n \equiv (x_n, y_n)$, and invoke some coupling parameter, $K$, between the information sources and their paths. This leads to phase transition punctuation of $I[K]$, the mutual information between **X** and **Y**, under either the Joint Asymptotic Equipartition Theorem, or, given a distortion measure, under the Rate Distortion Theorem.

$I[K]$ is a splitting criterion between high and low probability pairs of paths, and partakes of the homology with free energy density. Attentional focusing by the institution or machine then itself becomes a punctuated event in response to increasing linkage between the structure of interest and an external signal, or some particular system of internal events. This iterated argument parallels the extension of the General Linear Model into the Hierarchical Linear Model of regression theory.

Call this the Multitasking Hierarchical Cognitive Model (MHCM). For individual consciousness, there is only one giant component. For an institution, there will be a larger, and often very large, set of them. For a useful machine, the giant components must operate much more rapidly than is possible for an institution.

This requirement leads to the possibility of new failure modes related to impaired communication between giant components.

That is, a complication specific to high order institutional cognition or machine distributed cognition lies in the necessity of information transfer between giant components. The form and function of such interactions will, of course, be determined by the nature of the particular institution or machine, but, synchronous or asynchronous, contact between giant components is circumscribed by the Rate Distortion Theorem. To reiterate, the theorem states that, for a given maximum acceptable critical average signal distortion, there is a limiting maximum information transmission rate, such that messages sent at less than that limit are guaranteed to have average distortion less than the critical maximum. Too rapid transmission between parallel global workspaces – information overload – violates that condition, and guarantees large signal distortion. This is a likely failure mode apparently unique to multiple workspace systems that may otherwise have a lessened probability of inattentional blindness.

This can be formally addressed by an iteration of the basic model. That is, the phase transitions inherent to global broadcasts, as indexed by the $\omega_i$, must be iterated when multiple, simultaneous broadcasts occur: renormalize the interlinking information sources constituting a single broadcast down onto a single 'point' each representing a joint information source, and now examine the crosstalk between individual global broadcasts in terms of a 'higher' $\hat{\omega}$-measure. That is, $\hat{\omega}$ represents crosstalk between global broadcasts in which individual submodules are multitasking, engaging in more than one broadcast at a time. For example, in a physiological context, the immune system simultaneously engages in routine tissue maintenance, pathogen surveillance and attack, and neuroimmuno dialog. Such a global

broadcast of global broadcasts represents, in this model, the integrity of
the full system. If the $\hat{\omega}$ of this larger structure falls below some critical
value, the firm/machine/cockpit hybrid cannot function.

Iterating this model even further generates patterns of 'social' interaction between the system of interest and its embedding environment.

It should be clear, however, that $\omega$-measures are only part of the story.
The networks, and networks-of-networks linking internal subsystems by
crosstalk are *topologically structured*, not at all random, and seldom similar.
The internal topology of a system may critically determine the ability to
respond to environmental changes in a timely and effective manner.


## 4.9   The Dynamical Groupoid

A fundamental homology between the information source uncertainty dual
to a cognitive process and the free energy density of a physical system
arises, in part, from the formal similarity between their definitions in the
asymptotic limit. Information source uncertainty can be defined as in equation (4.1). This is quite analogous to the free energy density of a physical
system, equation (4.5).

Feynman (2000) provides a series of physical examples, based on Bennett's work, where this homology is, in fact, an identity, at least for very
simple systems. Bennett argues, in terms of idealized irreducibly elementary computing machines, that the information contained in a message can
be viewed as the work saved by not needing to recompute what has been
transmitted.

Feynman explores in some detail Bennett's ideal microscopic machine
designed to extract useful work from a transmitted message. The essential argument is that computing, in any form, takes work. Thus the more
complicated a cognitive process, measured by its information source uncertainty, the greater its energy consumption, and our ability to provide
energy to the brain is limited: Typically a unit of brain tissue consumes
an order of magnitude more energy than a unit of any other tissue. Inattentional blindness, Wallace (2007) argues, emerges as a thermodynamic
limit on processing capacity in a topologically-fixed global workspace, i.e.,
one which has been strongly configured about a particular task. Institutional and machine generalizations seem obvious, in the context of enor-
mous entropic losses through the physical instantiation of information and
its transmission.

Understanding the time dynamics of cognitive systems away from phase transition critical points requires a phenomenology similar to Onsager's empirical treatment of nonequilibrium thermodynamics. If the dual source uncertainty of a cognitive process, $H$, is parameterized by some vector of quantities $\mathbf{K} \equiv (K_1, ..., K_m)$, then, in analogy with nonequilibrium thermodynamics, gradients in the $K_j$ of the *disorder*, defined as the Legendre transform (Pettini, 2007)

$$S \equiv H(\mathbf{K}) - \sum_{j=1}^{m} K_j \partial H / \partial K_j \qquad (4.6)$$

become of central interest.

equation (4.6) is similar to the definition of entropy in terms of the free energy density of a physical system, as suggested by the homology between free energy density and information source uncertainty described above.

Pursuing the homology further, the generalized empirical Onsager equations defining temporal dynamics become

$$dK_j / dt = \sum_i L_{j,i} \partial S / \partial K_i \qquad (4.7)$$

where the $L_{j,i}$ are, in first order, constants reflecting the nature of the underlying cognitive phenomena. Note that, since information sources are not locally reversible, $L_{i,j} \neq L_{j,i}$. Even very short palindromes are rare for information sources, as opposed to simple physical systems.

The L-matrix is to be viewed empirically, in the same spirit as the slope and intercept of a regression model, and may have structure far different than familiar from more simple chemical or physical processes. The gradients $\partial S / \partial K$ are analogous to thermodynamic forces in a chemical system, and may be subject to override by external driving mechanisms.

Equations (4.6) and (4.7) can be derived in a simple parameter-free covariant manner that relies on the underlying topology of the information source space implicit to the development. Different cognitive phenomena have different dual information sources, and we are interested in the local properties of the system near a particular reference state. Impose a topology on the system, so that, near a particular 'language' $A$, dual to an underlying cognitive process, there is (in some sense) an open set $U$ of closely similar languages $\hat{A}$, such that $\{A, \hat{A}\} \subset U$. Note that it may be necessary to coarse-grain the system's responses to define these information sources. The problem is to proceed in such a way as to preserve the underlying essential topology, while eliminating 'high frequency noise'. The formal tools for this can be found, e.g., in Chapter 8 of Burago et al. (2001).

Since the information sources dual to the cognitive processes are similar, for all pairs of languages $A, \hat{A}$ in $U$, it is possible to:

1. Create an embedding alphabet including all symbols allowed to both of them.

2. Define an information-theoretic distortion measure in that extended, joint alphabet between any high probability (i.e. grammatical and syntactical) paths in $A$ and $\hat{A}$, which we write as $d(Ax, \hat{A}x)$. Note that these languages do not interact, in this approximation.

3. Define a metric on $U$, for example,

$$\mathcal{M}(A, \hat{A}) = |\lim \frac{\int_{A,\hat{A}} d(Ax, \hat{A}x)}{\int_{A,A} d(Ax, A\hat{x})} - 1| \qquad (4.8)$$

using an appropriate integration limit argument over the high probability paths. Note that the integration in the denominator is over different paths within $A$ itself, while in the numerator it is between different paths in $A$ and $\hat{A}$.

Consideration suggests $\mathcal{M}$ is a formal metric, having

$$\mathcal{M}(A, B) \geq 0, \mathcal{M}(A, A) = 0, \mathcal{M}(A, B) = \mathcal{M}(B, A),$$

$$\mathcal{M}(A, C) \leq \mathcal{M}(A, B) + \mathcal{M}(B, C).$$

Other approaches to metric construction on $U$ seem possible.

Structures weaker than a conventional metric would be of more general utility, but the mathematical complications are formidable (Glazebrook and Wallace 2009a, b).

These conditions can be used to define equivalence classes of *languages*, where previously we defined equivalence classes of *states* that could be linked by high probability, grammatical and syntactical, paths to some base point. This led to the characterization of different information sources. Here we construct an entity, formally a topological manifold, *which is an equivalence class of information sources*. This is, provided $\mathcal{M}$ is a conventional metric, a classic differentiable manifold.

The set of such equivalence classes generates the *dynamical groupoid*, and questions arise regarding mechanisms, internal or external, affecting that groupoid symmetry, as in the previous example. In particular imposition of a metric structure on this groupoid, and on its base set, would permit a nontrivial interaction between orbit equivalence relations and isotropy groups, leading to interesting algebraic structures.

Since $H$ and $\mathcal{M}$ are both scalars, a 'covariant' derivative can be defined directly as

$$dH/d\mathcal{M} = \lim_{\hat{A} \to A} \frac{H(A) - H(\hat{A})}{\mathcal{M}(A, \hat{A})} \qquad (4.9)$$

where $H(A)$ is the source uncertainty of language $A$.

Suppose the system to be set in some reference configuration $A_0$.

To obtain the unperturbed dynamics of that state, impose a Legendre transform using this derivative, defining another scalar via the Legendre transform

$$S \equiv H - \mathcal{M}dH/d\mathcal{M} \qquad (4.10)$$

The simplest possible Onsager equation – here seen as an empirical, fitted, relationship like a regression model – in this case becomes

$$d\mathcal{M}/dt = LdS/d\mathcal{M} \qquad (4.11)$$

where $t$ is the time and $dS/d\mathcal{M}$ represents an analog to the thermodynamic force in a chemical system. This is seen as acting on the reference state $A_0$. For

$$dS/d\mathcal{M}|_{A_0} = 0\,,$$
$$d^2S/d\mathcal{M}^2|_{A_0} > 0 \qquad (4.12)$$

the system is quasistable, a Black hole, if you will, and externally imposed forcing mechanisms will be needed to effect a transition to a different state. We shall explore this circumstance below in terms of topological considerations analogous to the concept of ecosystem resilience.

Conversely, changing the direction of the second condition, so that

$$dS^2/d\mathcal{M}^2|_{A_0} < 0,$$

leads to a repulsive peak, a White hole, representing a possibly unattainable realm of states.

Explicit parameterization of $\mathcal{M}$ introduces standard – and quite considerable – notational complications (e.g., Burago et al. 2001): imposing a metric for different cognitive dual languages parameterized by $\mathbf{K}$ leads to Riemannian, or even Finsler, geometries, including the usual geodesics.

The dynamics, so far, have been noiseless, while neural systems, from which we are abducting theory, are well known to be very noisy, and indeed may be subject to mechanisms of stochastic resonance. Equation (4.11) might be rewritten as

$$d\mathcal{M}/dt = LdS/d\mathcal{M} + \sigma W(t)$$

where $\sigma$ is a constant and $W(t)$ represents white noise. Again, $S$ is seen as a function of the parameter $\mathcal{M}$. This leads directly to a family of classic stochastic differential equations having the form

$$dM_t = L(t, M_t)dt + \sigma(t, M_t)dB_t \qquad (4.13)$$

where $L$ and $\sigma$ are appropriately regular functions of $t$ and $\mathcal{M}_t$. $dB_t$ represents noise which may not be 'white', i.e., may have quadratic variation that is not simply proportional to $t$. See the Mathematical Appendix for summary material on stochastic differential equations.

In the sense of Emery (1989), this leads into deep realms of stochastic differential geometry and related topics. The obvious inference is that noise, which needs not be 'white', can serve as a tool to shift the system between various equivalence classes, i.e., as a kind of crosstalk and the source of a generalized stochastic resonance.

We have defined a groupoid based on a particular set of equivalence classes of information sources dual to cognitive processes. That groupoid parsimoniously characterizes the available dynamical manifolds, and, in precisely the sense of the earlier development, altering of the groupoid symmetry creates different objects of interest, to be studied below.

This leads to the possibility, indeed, the necessity, of *Deus ex Machina* mechanisms – programming – to force transitions between the different possible modes within and across dynamic manifolds. In one model the programmer creates the manifold structure, and the machine hunts within that structure for the 'solution' to the problem according to equivalence classes of paths on the manifold. Noise, as with random mutation in evolutionary algorithms, might well be needed to guarantee convergence.

Equivalence classes of *states* gave dual information sources. Equivalence classes of *information sources* give different characteristic system dynamics, representing different programs. Later we will examine equivalence classes of *paths*, producing different directed homotopy topologies characterizing those dynamical manifolds. This introduces the possibility of having different quasi-stable resilience modes *within* individual dynamic manifolds. One set of these can be characterized as leading to 'solutions' of the underlying computing problem, while others may simply be pathological absorbing states, illustrating the inherent conflict/duality between programming and stability in massively parallel and inherently coevolutionary systems, a recurring theme. Pink or white noise, or more highly structured 'large deviations', might be imposed as a tunable means of creating crosstalk between different topological states within a dynamical manifold, or between different dynamical manifolds altogether.

Parenthetically, the arguments of Section 4.8 can be reframed in something like these terms, using the $\omega$-parameters in an equation similar to (4.13). Defining an embedding operator whose trace is given by setting that equation to zero gives an index theorem in the sense of Hazewinkel, (2002). That is, the topological structures of Section 4.8 are then defined in terms of the solutions of an analytic equation. Noise precludes unstable nonequilibrium steady state.

The next important structural iteration, however, is, in some respects, significantly more complicated than stochastic differential geometry.

## 4.10 The Rate Distortion Manifold

The second order iteration above – analogous to expanding the General Linear Model to the Hierarchical Linear Model – involving paths in parameter space, can itself be significantly extended. This produces a generalized tunable retina model that can be interpreted as a 'Rate Distortion manifold', a concept further opening the way for import of a vast array of tools from geometry and topology (Glazebrook and Wallace 2009a, b).

Suppose, now, that threshold behavior for system reaction requires some elaborate system of nonlinear relationships defining a set of renormalization parameters represented as a vector $\Omega_k \equiv (\omega_1^k, ..., \omega_m^k)$, in the sense of Section 4.8. The critical assumption is that there is a tunable zero order state, and that changes about that state are, in first order, relatively small, although their effects on punctuated process may not be at all small. Thus, given an initial $m$-dimensional vector $\Omega_k$, the parameter vector at time $k+1$, $\Omega_{k+1}$, can, in first order, be written as

$$\Omega_{k+1} \approx \mathbf{R}_{k+1}\Omega_k \tag{4.14}$$

where $\mathbf{R}_{t+1}$ is an $m \times m$ matrix, having $m^2$ components.

If the initial parameter vector at time $k = 0$ is $\Omega_0$, then at time $k$

$$\Omega_k = \mathbf{R}_k\mathbf{R}_{k-1}...\mathbf{R}_1\Omega_0. \tag{4.15}$$

The interesting correlates of high order system cognition are, in this development, *now represented by an information-theoretic path defined by the sequence of operators* $\mathbf{R}_k$, each member having $m^2$ components. The grammar and syntax of the path defined by these operators are associated with a dual information source, in the usual manner.

The effect of an information source of external signals, $\mathbf{Y}$, is now seen in terms of more complex joint paths in $Y$ and $R$-space whose behavior is, again, governed by a mutual information splitting criterion according to the JAEPT.

The complex sequence in $m^2$-dimensional $R$-space has, by this construction, been projected down onto a parallel path, the smaller set of $m$-dimensional $\omega$-parameter vectors $\Omega_0, ..., \Omega_k$.

If the punctuated tuning of system attention is now characterized by a 'higher' dual information source – an embedding generalized language – so that the paths of the operators $\mathbf{R}_k$ are autocorrelated, then the autocorrelated paths in $\Omega_k$ represent output of a parallel information source that is, given Rate Distortion limitations, apparently a grossly simplified, and hence highly distorted, picture of the 'higher' cognitive process represented by the $R$-operators, having $m$ as opposed to $m \times m$ components.

High levels of distortion may not necessarily be the case for such a structure, *provided it is properly tuned to the incoming signal*. If it is inappropriately tuned, however, then distortion may be extraordinary.

Let us examine a single iteration in more detail, assuming now there is a (tunable) zero reference state, $\mathbf{R}_0$, for the sequence of operators $\mathbf{R}_k$, and that

$$\Omega_{k+1} = (\mathbf{R}_0 + \delta\mathbf{R}_{k+1})\Omega_k \qquad (4.16)$$

where $\delta\mathbf{R}_k$ is 'small' in some sense compared to $\mathbf{R}_0$.

Note that in this analysis the operators $\mathbf{R}_k$ are, implicitly, determined by linear regression. We thus can invoke a quasi-diagonalization in terms of $\mathbf{R}_0$. Let $\mathbf{Q}$ be the matrix of eigenvectors which Jordan-block-diagonalizes $\mathbf{R}_0$. Then

$$\mathbf{Q}\Omega_{k+1} = (\mathbf{Q}\mathbf{R}_0\mathbf{Q}^{-1} + \mathbf{Q}\delta\mathbf{R}_{k+1}\mathbf{Q}^{-1})\mathbf{Q}\Omega_k \qquad (4.17)$$

If $\mathbf{Q}\Omega_k$ is an eigenvector of $\mathbf{J}_0 = \mathbf{Q}\mathbf{R}_0\mathbf{Q}^{-1}$, say $Y_j$ with eigenvalue $\lambda_j$, it is possible to rewrite this equation as a generalized spectral expansion

$$Y_{k+1} = (\mathbf{J}_0 + \delta\mathbf{J}_{k+1})Y_j \equiv \lambda_j Y_j + \delta Y_{k+1}$$

$$= \lambda_j Y_j + \sum_{i=1}^{n} a_i Y_i. \qquad (4.18)$$

$\mathbf{J}_0$ is a block-diagonal matrix, $\delta\mathbf{J}_{k+1} \equiv \mathbf{Q}\mathbf{R}_{k+1}\mathbf{Q}^{-1}$, and $\delta Y_{k+1}$ *has been expanded in terms of a spectrum of the eigenvectors of* $\mathbf{J}_0$, with

$$|a_i| \ll |\lambda_j|, |a_{i+1}| \ll |a_i|. \qquad (4.19)$$

The point is that, provided $\mathbf{R}_0$ has been tuned so that this condition is true, the first few terms in the spectrum of this iteration of the eigenstate will contain most of the essential information about $\delta\mathbf{R}_{k+1}$.

This appears quite similar to the detection of color in the retina, where three overlapping non-orthogonal eigenmodes of response are sufficient to characterize a huge plethora of color sensation. Here, if such a tuned spectral expansion is possible, a very small number of observed eigenmodes would suffice to permit identification of a vast range of changes, so that the rate-distortion constraints become quite modest. That is, there will not be much distortion in the reduction from paths in $R$-space to paths in $\Omega$-space. Inappropriate tuning, however, can produce very marked distortion, even inattentional blindness, in spite of multitasking. The approach is, essentially, a familiar, if dynamic, form of factor analysis.

Note that higher order Rate Distortion Manifolds are likely to give better approximations than lower ones, in the same sense that second order tangent structures give better, if more complicated, approximations in conventional differentiable manifolds (Pohl 1962).

Indeed, Rate Distortion Manifolds can be quite formally described using standard techniques from topological manifold theory (Glazebrook and Wallace 2009a, b). The essential point is that a rate distortion manifold is a topological structure constraining the multifactorial stream of high order system cognition, as well as the pattern of communication between giant components, much the way a riverbank constrains the flow of the river it contains. This is a fundamental insight.

The Rate Distortion Manifold can, however, also be described in purely information theoretic terms using a 'tuning theorem' variant of the Shannon Coding Theorem, as follows.

Messages from an information source, seen as symbols $x_j$ from some alphabet, each having probabilities $P_j$ associated with a random variable $X$, are 'encoded' into the language of a 'transmission channel', a random variable $Y$ with symbols $y_k$, having probabilities $P_k$, possibly with error. Someone receiving the symbol $y_k$ then retranslates it (without error) into some $x_k$, which may or may not be the same as the $x_j$ that was sent.

More formally, the message sent along the channel is characterized by a random variable $X$ having the distribution $P(X = x_j) = P_j, j = 1, ..., M$.

The channel through which the message is sent is characterized by a second random variable $Y$ having the distribution $P(Y = y_k) = P_k, k = 1, ..., L$.

Let the joint probability distribution of $X$ and $Y$ be defined as $P(X = x_j, Y = y_k) = P(x_j, y_k) = P_{j,k}$, and the conditional probability of $Y$ given $X$ as $P(Y = y_k | X = x_j) = P(y_k | x_j)$.

Recall that the Shannon uncertainty of $X$ and $Y$ independently and the joint uncertainty of $X$ and $Y$ together are defined respectively as

$$H(X) = -\sum_{j=1}^{M} P_j \log(P_j)$$

$$H(Y) = -\sum_{k=1}^{L} P_k \log(P_k)$$

$$H(X,Y) = -\sum_{j=1}^{M}\sum_{k=1}^{L} P_{j,k} \log(P_{j,k}). \qquad (4.20)$$

The *conditional uncertainty* of $Y$ given $X$ is defined as

$$H(Y|X) = -\sum_{j=1}^{M}\sum_{k=1}^{L} P_{j,k} \log[P(y_k|x_j)]. \qquad (4.21)$$

For any two stochastic variates $X$ and $Y$, $H(Y) \geq H(Y|X)$, as knowledge of $X$ generally gives some knowledge of $Y$. Equality occurs only in the case of stochastic independence.

Since $P(x_j, y_k) = P(x_j)P(y_k|x_j)$, then $H(X|Y) = H(X,Y) - H(Y)$.

The information transmitted by translating the variable $X$ into the channel transmission variable $Y$ – possibly with error – and then retranslating without error the transmitted $Y$ back into $X$ is defined as

$$I(X|Y) \equiv H(X) - H(X|Y) = H(X) + H(Y) - H(X,Y). \qquad (4.22)$$

See Cover and Thomas (2006) for details. The essential point is that if there is no uncertainty in $X$ given the channel $Y$, then there is no loss of information through transmission. In general this will not be true, and herein lies the essence of the theory.

Given a fixed vocabulary for the transmitted variable $X$, and a fixed vocabulary and probability distribution for the channel $Y$, we may vary the probability distribution of $X$ in such a way as to maximize the information sent. The capacity of the channel is defined as

$$C \equiv \max_{P(X)} I(X|Y) \qquad (4.23)$$

subject to the subsidiary condition that $\sum P(X) = 1$.

The critical trick of the Shannon Coding Theorem for sending a message with arbitrarily small error along the channel $Y$ at any rate $R < C$ is to encode it in longer and longer 'typical' sequences of the variable $X$; that is, those sequences whose distribution of symbols approximates the probability distribution $P(X)$ above which maximizes $C$.

If $S(n)$ is the number of such 'typical' sequences of length $n$, then $\log[S(n)] \approx nH(X)$, where $H(X)$ is the uncertainty of the stochastic variable defined above. Some consideration shows that $S(n)$ is much less than the total number of possible messages of length $n$. Thus, as $n \to \infty$, only a vanishingly small fraction of all possible messages is meaningful in this sense. This observation, after some considerable development, is what allows the Coding Theorem to work so well. In sum, the prescription is to encode messages in typical sequences, which are sent at very nearly the capacity of the channel. As the encoded messages become longer and longer, their maximum possible rate of transmission without error approaches channel capacity as a limit. Again, Cover and Thomas (2006) provide details.

This approach can be, in a sense, inverted to give a tuning theorem parsimoniously describing the essence of the Rate Distortion Manifold.

Telephone lines, optical wave guides and the tenuous plasma through which a planetary probe transmits data to earth may all be viewed in traditional information-theoretic terms as a *noisy channel* around which we must structure a message so as to attain an optimal error-free transmission rate.

Telephone lines, wave guides and interplanetary plasmas are, relatively speaking, fixed on the timescale of most messages. Indeed, the capacity of a channel, is defined by varying the probability distribution of the 'message' process $X$ so as to maximize $I(X|Y)$.

Suppose there is some message $X$ so critical that its probability distribution must remain fixed. The trick is to fix the distribution $P(x)$ but *modify the channel* – i.e. tune it – so as to maximize $I(X|Y)$. The *dual* channel capacity $C^*$ can be defined as

$$C^* \equiv \max_{P(Y),P(Y|X)} I(X|Y). \tag{4.24}$$

But $C^* = \max_{P(Y),P(Y|X)} I(Y|X)$, since $I(X|Y) = H(X) + H(Y) - H(X,Y) = I(Y|X)$.

Thus, in a purely formal mathematical sense, *the message transmits the channel*, and there will indeed be, according to the Coding Theorem, a channel distribution $P(Y)$ which maximizes $C^*$.

One may do better than this, however, by modifying the channel matrix $P(Y|X)$. Since

$$P(y_j) = \sum_{i=1}^{M} P(x_i)P(y_j|x_i),$$

$P(Y)$ is entirely defined by the channel matrix $P(Y|X)$ for fixed $P(X)$ and

$$C^* = \max_{P(Y),P(Y|X)} I(Y|X) = \max_{P(Y|X)} I(Y|X).$$

Calculating $C^*$ requires maximizing the complicated expression $I(X|Y) = H(X) + H(Y) - H(X,Y)$, containing products of terms and their logs, subject to constraints that the sums of probabilities are 1 and each probability is itself between 0 and 1. Maximization is done by varying the channel matrix terms $P(y_j|x_i)$ within the constraints. This is a difficult problem in nonlinear optimization. However, for the special case $M = L$, $C^*$ may be found by inspection:

If $M = L$, then choose $P(y_j|x_i) = \delta_{j,i}$, where $\delta_{i,j}$ is 1 if $i = j$ and 0 otherwise. For this special case, $C^* \equiv H(X)$, with $P(y_k) = P(x_k)$ for all $k$. *Information is thus transmitted without error when the channel becomes 'typical' with respect to the fixed message distribution $P(X)$.*

If $M < L$ matters reduce to this case, but for $L < M$ information must be lost, leading to Rate Distortion limitations.

Thus modifying the channel may be a far more efficient means of ensuring transmission of an important message than encoding that message in a 'natural' language maximizing the rate of transmission of information on a fixed channel.

This argument examines the two limits in which either the distributions of $P(Y)$ or of $P(X)$ are kept fixed. The first provides the usual Shannon Coding Theorem, and the second, a tuning theorem variant, i.e., a tunable, retina-like, Rate Distortion Manifold. It seems likely, however, than for many important systems $P(X)$ and $P(Y)$ will interpenetrate, to use Richard Levins' terminology. That is, $P(X)$ and $P(Y)$ will affect each other in characteristic ways, so that some form of mutual tuning may be the most effective strategy.

Versions of this result have been known for some time. Shannon (1959) writes:

> There is a curious and provocative duality between the properties of a source with a distortion measure and those of a channel. This duality is enhanced if we consider channels in which there is a cost associated with the different input letters... Solving this problem corresponds, in a sense, to finding a source that is right for the channel and the desired cost... In a somewhat dual way, evaluating the rate distortion function for a source... corresponds to find-

ing a channel that is just right for the source and allowed distortion level.

## 4.11 No Free Lunch

The previous results can be used to give yet another perspective on the famous 'no free lunch' theorem of Wolpert and Macready (1995, 1997, 2005). As English (1996) states the matter:

> ...Wolpert and Macready... have established that there exists no generally superior function optimizer. There is no 'free lunch' in the sense that an optimizer 'pays' for superior performance on some functions with inferior performance on others... if the distribution of functions is uniform, then gains and losses balance precisely, and all optimizers have identical average performance... [A]n optimizer has to 'pay' for its superiority on one subset of functions with inferiority on the complementary subset...
>
> Anyone slightly familiar with the [evolutionary computing] literature recognizes the paper template 'Algorithm $X$ was treated with modification $Y$ to obtain the best known results for problems $P_1$ and $P_2$.' Anyone who has tried to find subsequent reports on 'promising' algorithms knows that they are extremely rare. Why should this be?
>
> A claim that an algorithm is the very best for two functions is a claim that it is the very worst, on average, for all but two functions.... It is due to the diversity of the benchmark set [of test problems] that the 'promise' is rarely realized. Boosting performance for one subset of the problems usually detracts from performance for the complement...
>
> Hammers contain information about the distribution of nail-driving problems. Screwdrivers contain information about the distribution of screw-driving problems. Swiss army knives contain information about a broad distribution of survival problems. Swiss army knives do many jobs, but none particularly well. When the many jobs must be done under primitive conditions, Swiss army knives are ideal.
>
> The tool literally carries information about the task...

> optimizers are literally tools – an algorithm implemented
> by a computing device is a physical entity...

Another way of stating this conundrum is to say that a computed solution is simply the product of the information processing of a problem, and, by a very famous argument, information can never be gained simply by processing. Thus a problem $X$ is transmitted as a message by an information processing channel, $Y$, a computing device, and recoded as an answer. By the 'dual' argument of the previous section there will be a channel coding of $Y$ which, when properly tuned, is most efficiently transmitted by the problem. In general, then, the most efficient coding of the transmission channel, that is, the best algorithm turning a problem into a solution, will necessarily be highly problem-specific. Thus there can be no best algorithm for all sets of problems, although there may well be an optimal algorithm for any given set.

Rate distortion, however, occurs when the problem is collapsed into a smaller, simplified version and then solved. Then there must be a tradeoff between allowed average distortion and the rate of solution: the retina effect. In a very fundamental sense, then, Rate Distortion Manifolds present a generalization of the converse of the Wolpert/Macready no free lunch arguments.

An important point is that this development says nothing about the efficiency of channel tuning. Another iteration of theory would be required to determine, say, the full width at half maximum (FWHM) of a particular system. The peak in dual channel capacity may be very broad in any given case, so that although one algorithm (or equivalence class of them) may be 'best', very many others may be nearly as good. One suspects that for a Rate Distortion Manifold/retina system tunability might sometimes be more critical.

## 4.12   Directed Homotopy

To reiterate, the groupoid treatment of modular cognitive networks above defined equivalence classes of states according to whether they could be linked by grammatical/syntactical high probability 'meaningful' paths to the same origin. The dynamical groupoid is based on identification of equivalence classes of languages. Next comes the precisely complementary question regarding paths on dynamical manifolds: for any two particular given states, is there some sense in which it is possible to define equivalence classes across the set of meaningful paths linking them? The assumption is that the system has been 'tuned' (i.e., programmed) using the rate distortion manifold approach above, so that the problem to be solved is more tractable, in a sense.

This is of particular interest to the second order hierarchical model that, in effect, describes a universality class tuning of the renormalization parameters characterizing the dancing, flowing, tunably punctuated accession to high order cognitive function.

A closely similar question is central to recent algebraic geometry approaches to concurrent, i.e., highly parallel, computing (Goubault and Raussen 2002; Goubault 2003; Pratt 1991).

For the moment, restrict the analysis to a giant component system characterized by two renormalization parameters, say $\omega_1$ and $\omega_2$, and consider the set of meaningful paths connecting two particular points, say $a$ and $b$, in the two dimensional $\omega$-space plane of figures 4.1 and 4.2. The arguments surrounding equations (4.6), (4.7) and (4.12) suggests that there may be regions of fatal attraction and strong repulsion, Black holes and White holes, that can either trap or deflect the path of institutional or multitasking machine cognition.

Figures 4.1 and 4.2 show two possible configurations for a Black and a White hole, diagonal and cross-diagonal. If one requires path monotonicity – always increasing or remaining the same – then, following Goubault (2003, figs. 6,7), there are, intuitively, two direct ways, without switchbacks, that one can get from $a$ to $b$ in the diagonal geometry of figure 4.1, without crossing a Black or White hole, but there are three in the cross-diagonal structure of figure 4.2.

Elements of each 'way' can be transformed into each other by continuous deformation without crossing either the Black or White hole. Figure 4.1 has two additional possible monotonic ways, involving over/under switchbacks, that are not drawn. Relaxing the monotonicity requirement generates a plethora of other possibilities, e.g., loopings and backwards switchbacks. It is not clear under what circumstances such complex paths can be meaningful, a matter for further study.

These 'ways' are the equivalence classes defining the topological structure of the two different $\omega$-spaces, analogs to the fundamental homotopy groups in spaces admitting of loops (Lee 2000). The closed loops needed for classical homotopy theory are impossible for this kind of system because of the 'flow of time' defining the output of an information source – one goes from $a$ to $b$, although, for nonmonotonic paths, intermediate looping would

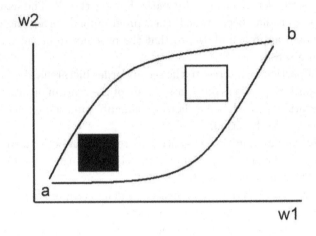

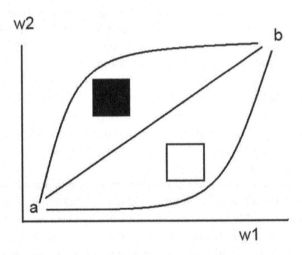

Fig. 4.1   Diagonal Black and White holes in the two dimensional $\omega$-plane. Only two direct paths can link points $a$ and $b$ that are continuously deformable into one another without crossing either hole. There are two additional monotonic switchback paths, not drawn.

Fig. 4.2   Cross-diagonal Black and White holes. Three direct equivalence classes of continuously deformable paths can link $a$ and $b$. Thus the two spaces are topologically distinct. Here, monotonic switchbacks are not possible, although relaxation of that condition can lead to 'backwards' switchbacks and intermediate loopings.

seem possible. The theory is thus one of directed homotopy, dihomotopy, and the central question revolves around the continuous deformation of paths in $\omega$-space into one another, without crossing Black or White holes. See Goubault and Rausssen (2002) for details.

These ideas can, of course, be applied to lower level cognitive modules as well as to the second order hierarchical cognitive model of institutional or machine cognition where they are, perhaps, of more central interest.

It seems likely that empirical study will show how the influence of cultural heritage or developmental history defines quite different dihomotopies of attentional focus in human organizations (Wallace and Fullilove 2008). That is, the topology of blind spots and their associated patterns of perceptual completion in human organizations will be culturally or developmentally modulated. It is this developmental cultural topology of multitasking organization attention that, acting in concert with the inherent limitations of the rate distortion manifold, generates the pattern of organizational inattentional blindness. Analogous developmental arguments should apply to real-time, high-level distributed machine cognition.

Such considerations, and indeed the Black Hole development of equation (4.12), suggest that a multitasking system becoming trapped in a particular pattern of behavior cannot, in general, expect to emerge from it in the absence of external forcing mechanisms.

A second perspective, perhaps more relevant to this work, is that the solution to a highly parallel computing problem might well be cast in terms of 'finding the right Black Hole'. That is, the machine begins at some starting point, and, if the problem has been used to properly constrain the shape of the underlying dynamic manifold, i.e., to act as a tuning 'goal context' in Baars' terminology, solution involves identifying the various topological modes possible to that complicated geometric object. Among those modes will be the absorbing singularities constituting problem solution. Evolutionary algorithms rear their heads as obvious potential tools, but some preliminary factoring, via topological analysis, might well be possible before they need be applied: using the 'fovea' of the retina.

Note particularly how the equivalence class structure to highly parallel problems that Asanovic et al. (2006) recognized can be used to define a groupoid symmetry that can then be imposed on the 'natural' groupoids underlying massively parallel computation, as characterized here.

This sort of behavior is central to ecosystem resilience theory (Holling 1973; Gunderson 2000), a matter which Wallace and Fullilove (2008) explore in more detail. The basic idea is that equivalence classes of dynamic manifolds, and the directed homotopy classes within those manifolds, each and together create domains of quasi-stability requiring action of some external executive – programmer, operating system, higher level adaptive cognitive module – for change. A self-dynamic, adaptive machine entering a pathological quasi-stable resilience mode will stay there until moved out of it by executive act.

The multi-level topology of institutional cognition provides a tool for study of resilience in human organizations or social systems, and probably for machines as well. Apparently, the set of dynamic manifolds, and its subsets of directed homotopy equivalence classes, formally classifies nonequilibrium steady states, and thus characterizes the different possible resilience modes. Some of these may be highly pathological. Others will represent solutions to the computing problem, according to this scheme. This suggests, yet again, that, for massively parallel cognitive systems, programming and stability are intimately dual conundrums.

## 4.13 Implications

The simple groupoid defined by a distributed cognition machine's basic cognitive modular structure can be altered by intrusion of (rapid) crosstalk within it, and by the imposition of (slower) crosstalk from without. The former, if strong enough, can initiate a set of topologically-determined giant component global broadcasts, in a punctuated manner, while the latter deform the underlying topology of the entire system. Altered symmetry – raised coupling 'temperature' – can create richer structure in systems characterized by groupoids, just as it does for those characterized by groups.

Equivalence classes of 'cognitive languages', in a certain sense, generate the dynamical groupoid of the system, and the associated dihomotopy groupoids the topologies of those individual manifolds, containing both 'solutions' to the computing problem and pathological or entrapment states, representing the necessary duality between programming and stability in massively parallel and thus inherently coevolutionary cognitive systems.

Multitasking machine attention – the program – acts through a Rate Distortion manifold, a kind of retina-like filter for grammatical and syntactical meaningful paths. Signals outside the topologically constrained tunable syntax/grammar bandpass of this manifold are subject to lessened probability of punctuated detection: inattentional blindness. Path-dependent machine developmental history will, according to this model, profoundly affect the phenomenon by imposing additional topological constraints defining the 'surface' along which this second order behavior can (and cannot) glide.

The key trick seems to be using the problem itself as a 'goal context' to define that 'surface', whose singularities or absorbing states constitute the solution to the problem. Characterizing the topology of the problem-constrained dynamic manifold would probably greatly simplify the use of evolutionary algorithms, stochastic resonance, or other techniques to actually identify the singularities, i.e., to 'find the solution'.

Glazebrook and Wallace (2009a, b) have suggested that, lurking in the background of this basic construction, is what Bak et al. (2006) call a groupoid atlas, an extension of topological manifold theory to groupoid mappings. Also lurking is identification and exploration of the natural groupoid convolution algebra that so often marks these structures (Connes 1994).

Consideration suggests, in fact, that a path may be meaningful according to the groupoid parametrization of all possible dual information sources, and that tuning is done across that parametrization via a rate distortion manifold.

Implicit, however, are the constraints imposed by machine history and/or problem definition, in a large sense, which may limit the properties of $\mathbf{R}_0$, i.e., hold the system to a developmentally determined topology leading to a solution as detection of a singularity.

Here we have attempted to reexpress this trade-off in terms of a syntactical/grammatical version of conventional signal theory as a 'tuned meaningful path' form of the classic balance between sensitivity and selectivity particularly constrained by the directed homotopy imposed by a machine experience that is itself the outcome a historical process involving interaction with an external environment defined by the problem to be solved.

Overall, this analysis is analogous to, but more complicated than, recent mathematical formulations of Baars' Global Workspace theory (Wallace 2005a). Intuitively, one suspects that the higher the dimension of the second order attentional Rate Distortion Manifold, that is, the greater the multitasking, the broader the effective bandwidth of attentional focus, and the less likely is inattentional blindness. For a conventional differentiable manifold, a second or higher order tangent space would give a better approximation to the local manifold structure than a simple plane (Pohl 1962).

Nonetheless, inattentional blindness, while constrained by multitasking, is not eliminated by it, suggesting that higher order institutional or machine cognition, the generalization of individual consciousness, is subject to canonical and idiosyncratic patterns of failure analogous to, but perhaps more subtle than, the kind of disorders described in the previous chapters. Indeed, while machines designed along these principles – multitasking Global Broadcast devices – could be spectacularly efficient at many complex tasks, ensuring their stability might be even more difficult than for institutions having the benefit of many centuries of cultural evolution.

The approach might be to use a well-defined 'problem groupoid' as an external goal context to stabilize the machine. Problem sets without well defined groupoid structures might well lead to very irregular system behaviors, in this model, a matter of possible interest to those concerned with computer security: confronting a machine with a properly 'ill defined' problem could paralyze it.

In addition, the necessity of interaction – synchronous or asynchronous – between internal giant components suggests the possibility of failures governed by the Rate Distortion Theorem. Forcing rapid communication between internal giant components ensures high error rates. Recent ethnographic work (Cohen et al., 2006; Laxmisan et al., 2007) regarding systematic medical error in emergency rooms focuses particularly on 'handover' problems at shift change, where incoming medical staff are rapidly briefed by outgoing staff. Systematic information overload in such circumstances seems almost routine, and is widely recognized as a potential error source within institutions.

A third failure mode involves the possibility of pathological resilience states defined by the dynamic groupoid, and the individual manifold dihomotopy groupoids. Address of such 'lock-in' seems to require action of an external executive to stabilize these highly parallel, self-programming, adaptive machines. This seems equivalent to 'apparently doing everything right but still getting the wrong answer'.

The 'non-pathological' set of topological resilience states appears to represent the solutions to the computing problem. There are some hints, in the stochastic differential equation model, that appropriate use of programmed 'large deviations' might help find such solutions. The next chapters will explore this insight.

The approach here generalizes recent formal analysis of individual consciousness to analogous second order treatments of distributed machine cognition, both the network model of the main text and the 'mean field' approximation given in the first chapter. This suggests, in particular, that

multiple workspace multitasking significantly reduces, but cannot eliminate, the likelihood of inattentional blindness, of overfocus on one task to
the exclusion of other relevant patterns. It further appears that rate distortion failure in communication between individual global workspaces will be
potentially a serious problem for such systems – synchronous or sequential
versions of the telephone game.

Thus the multitasking hierarchical cognitive model appropriate to institutional or distributed machine cognition is considerably more complicated than the equivalent for individual animal or human consciousness,
biologically limited to a single shifting, tunable giant component structure.
Human institutions, by contrast, appear able to entertain several, and perhaps many, such global broadcasts simultaneously, although these generally
operate at a much slower rate than is possible for individual consciousness.
Distributed cognition machines, according to this model, would be able to
function as efficiently as large institutions, but at or near the rate characteristic of individual consciousness.

Shared culture, however, seems to provide far more than merely a shared
language for the establishment of the human organizations enabling our
adaptation to, or alteration of, our varied environments. It also may provide the stabilizing mechanisms needed to overcome many of the canonical
and idiosyncratic failure modes inherent to such structures – the embedding
directives of law, tradition, and custom that have evolved over many centuries. Culture is truly as much a part of human biology as the enamel on
our teeth (Richerson and Boyd 2006). No such secondary heritage system
is available for machine stabilization. This point will emerge repeatedly
from markedly different perspectives in the following chapters.

In sum, this work contributes to a mathematical formalization of biologically inspired distributed machine cognition based on a necessary conditions communication theory model quite similar to Dretske's attempts at
understanding high level mental function for individuals. However, high
order, multiple global broadcast cognition seems not only far more complicated than is the case for individual animal consciousness, but appears
prone to particular collective errors whose minimization, for institutions operating along these principles, may have been the subject of a long period
of cultural development.

Absent a better understanding of institutional stabilization mechanisms,
and hence lacking an engineering strategy for the construction of 'ethical'
machines, reliable massively parallel real-time computing technology may
be exceedingly difficult, and uncontrolled emergent network behavior ever

more intrusive. Under such circumstances, analogs to developmental psychopathology, in which regulatory mechanisms for higher order processes fail under stress, and to inattentional blindness, where a system's narrow syntactic bandpass results in pathological fixation, seem inevitable. Computing devices or systems constructed on biological models will inevitably lack the elaborate, but poorly understood, systems of control mechanisms that have evolved to stabilize cognitive processes in animals and their social assemblages. Such systems will be prone to subtle degradation, and, ultimately, catastrophic failure, much like the rope bridge at Angers.

As will repeatedly emerge in subsequent chapters, under real time constraints – fog of war conditions – the deliberate induction of failure in such systems by unfriendly agencies should not be particularly difficult.

# Chapter 5

# Coevolutionary machines

## 5.1 Introduction

The previous chapter introduced a class of biologically inspired models of massively parallel machine cognition based on a spectrum of multiple global broadcast versions of the Baars model of animal consciousness. The essential features revolve around Dretske's (1994) fundamental insight that any instantiation of high level cognition – biological, social, machine, or their many possible hybrids – will necessarily be constrained by the asymptotic limit theorems of information theory. It is possible, at least in principle, to manipulate those constraints so as to 'program' highly coevolutionary machines.

It is a trivial but important observation that massively parallel machines are always coevolutionary in that their modules and/or hierarchical levels must necessarily interact and affect one another. In addition, real-time systems will inevitably engage in coevolutionary interaction with the embedding environments they are, in fact, designed to affect. This circumstance must, at sufficient scale, asymptotically dominate machine behaviors.

In many respects, what we propose is analogous to the liquid state machine (LSM) of Maass et al. (2002), seen as useful in modeling neural dynamics (e.g., Rabinovich et al. 2008):

    1. Several real time computations can be carried out in parallel within the same circuitry.

    2. 'Found' modules can come together to cooperate in computation.

    3. Continuing transient process without classical attractor states can produce useful results.

Similar properties arise in a 'natural' manner using our approach:

1.  Multiple (simultaneous or asynchronous) global broadcasts are possible in which individual cognitive modules can each participate.

2.  Sufficient crosstalk between individual cognitive modules can initiate a sudden phase transition linking them into a higher level structure.

3. Assuming information sources to be of finite order is analogous to the 'fading memory' requirement of the LSM.

4. Convergence in a 'programmed' system is to a particular dynamic, an information source dual to a cognitive process, rather than to some stable answer. This is more like a 'game strategy', as if one had to choose between playing chess, baseball, football, etc., analogous to the 'continuing transient process' of the LSM.

## 5.2   Cognition Redux

Recall the results of Section 3.2. Atlan and Cohen (1998) and Cohen (2000) argue that the essence of cognitive function involves comparison of a perceived signal with an internal (learned and/or inherited) picture of the world, and then, upon comparison, choosing a response from a much larger repertoire of possible responses.

Such choice, since it always generates a reduction in uncertainty (Ash 1990, p. 21), directly instantiates an information source.

This adiabatic, piecewise stationary, ergodic (APSE) information source is defined as *dual* to the underlying ergodic cognitive process.

*Adiabatic* means that the source has been parameterized according to some scheme, and that, over a certain range, along a particular piece, as the parameters vary, the source remains as close to stationary and ergodic as needed for information theory's central theorems to apply. *Stationary* means that the system's probabilities do not change in time, and *ergodic*, roughly, that the cross sectional means approximate long-time averages. Between pieces it is necessary to invoke various kinds of phase transition formalisms, as described more fully in the first chapter. Extension to non ergodic, non stationary sources is possible but involves significant mathematical overhead (Wallace 2005a; Wallace and Fullilove, 2008).

## 5.3 Global Broadcast

As described in Section 3.3, the relation

$$H \equiv \lim_{n \to \infty} \frac{\log[N(n)]}{n},$$

is homologous to the thermodynamic limit in the definition of the free energy density of a physical system. This has the form

$$F(K) = \lim_{V \to \infty} -K \frac{\log[Z(K,V)]}{V} \equiv \frac{\log[\hat{Z}(K,V)]}{V},$$

where $F$ is the free energy density, $K$ the normalized temperature, $V$ the system volume, and $Z(K,V)$ is the partition function defined by the system Hamiltonian – the function that defines the system's energy (Landau and Lifshitz 2007).

Chapter 1 shows at some length how this homology permits the natural transfer of renormalization methods from statistical mechanics to information theory. This produces phase transitions and analogs to evolutionary punctuation in systems characterized by APSE information sources. These biological phase changes appear to be ubiquitous in natural systems and can be expected to dominate constructed systems as well.

There are, then, a number of analytically tractable approaches to the general broadcast mechanism.

For a first model, the average probability of information transfer linkages between cognitive modular components acts as a kind of temperature analog, so that an increase in probability of such contact raises the 'temperature' above a critical value, and the linked system suddenly 'evaporates' into a General Broadcast. The characteristic 'universality class constants' of such a phase transition then become the subject of a second order treatment allowing tuning of that broadcast, according to constraints imposed by Bernard Baars' 'contexts'. These constrain the 'stream of consciousness' to realms useful to the system of interest.

A second perspective involves mean numbers of information transfer linkages between cognitive modules having dual information sources. If the average number of such linkages exceeds a threshold, depending on the abstract topology of the underlying cognitive modular network, then a single 'Giant Component' suddenly emerges. This links most of the individual nodes into a single identifiable object that can transfer information across itself easily. Again, this is a form of general broadcast constrained by less rapidly acting 'contexts'. The second order tuning is done here by varying the underlying topology, as opposed to the 'universality class tuning' of the mean field approximation above.

The two approaches produce tunable global broadcasts instantiating Baars' global workspace model of high order cognition. Less mathematically tractable structures seem possible. In a biological context, of course, evolution is not constrained by mathematical tractability.

The previous chapter shows that the mean number model permits a single cognitive module to participate in multiple global broadcasts, an important feature of the liquid state machine (Maas et al. 2002).


## 5.4   Coevolution

Recent work in the theory of coevolutionary biological systems seems adaptable to the analysis of multiple global broadcast cognition. The essential dynamics arise when workspaces become closely integrated with, and have reciprocal influence on, each other, or with a larger, embedding, environmental structures that they are, in fact, designed to regulate. Such reciprocation can trigger a coevolutionary ratchet as a tool for convergence of the system, a generalization of Nix/Vose and other (co)evolutionary algorithms.

To reiterate, an essential difference with the Nix/Vose and coevolutionary machine models is that convergence, if it occurs, is to an equivalence class of highly dynamic information sources rather than to some fixed 'solution'. That is, a complex cognitive real-time 'Self-X' control machine, in this model, converges to an ongoing behavior pattern rather than to a static 'answer'.

The convergence, however, may be either to a proper 'answer' or to a pathological absorbing state: the inherent duality between programming and stability for such machines.

The argument invokes the essential mutual interaction between subsystems of a highly parallel machine. Competition for such resources as bandwidth, memory access, and power, and collaboration in addressing the problem to be solved, leads toward a rough parallel with the kinds of difficulties Wiegand (2003) finds inherent to coevolutionary algorithms in which convergence is to some desired fixed result. This will be complicated by interaction with embedding environments that can themselves respond to intervention.

Natural systems subject to coevolutionary interaction may become enmeshed in the Red Queen dilemma of Alice in Wonderland (Van Valen

1973), in that they must undergo constant evolutionary change in order to avoid extinction – they must constantly run just to stay in the same place. Convergence is then to some ongoing, broadly repetitive, process. An example would be a competitive arms race between predator and prey. Each evolutionary advance in predation must be met with a coevolutionary adaptation allowing the prey to avoid the more efficient predator. Otherwise, the system will become extinct, since a highly specialized predator can literally eat itself out of existence. Similarly, each prey defense must be matched by a predator adaptation for the system to persist. For example, the Texas pronghorn antelope lives on in the absence of its chief predator, the now-extinct American cheetah.

While natural populations cannot transmit acquired characteristics, human cultures, organizations, and machines, are well able to do so, and can forget more easily than natural systems, which record a projection of their environments in their genetic structure (Ademi et al. 2000). This suggests the possibility of both a Red Queen coevolutionary process affecting a multiple-workspace machine, and of a rapid inverse, a form of race-to-the-bottom ratchet as well (Wallace 2015a, Ch.7).

The next section presents a fairly elaborate theory of such behavior, that appears to generalize to distributed cognition embedded in a context with which it interacts strongly, to engage in a powerful mutual information crosstalk, and hence to machine models based on this perspective. The theory also applies to systems in which individual workspaces become closely interlinked. These events can be highly punctuated. The closely related phenomenon is coevolutionary programming. Thus programming and stability, are, again, two sides of the same coin in this model, a result perhaps already inherent to much current work on coevolutionary algorithms (e.g., Ficici et al. 2005; Wiegand 2003).

## 5.5 Basic Model

The essence of coevolution is recursion. Cognitive information sources representing interacting subcomponents of a larger system, in the sense of the last chapter, interact *by becoming each other's principal environments.*

Consider an appropriately block-structured matrix of crosstalk between a set of information sources dual to cognitive processes, characterized by network information sources like equation (4.4),

$$I_m(X_1...X_i|Y_1...Y_j|Z_1...Z_k), m = 1, 2, \ldots .$$

Now use the $I_j, j \neq m$ *as parameters for each other*, writing

$$I_m = I_m(K_1...K_s, ...I_j...), j \neq m$$

where the $K_s$ represent other relevant parameters.

Next, segregate the $I_j$ according to their relative rates of change.

The dynamics of such a system, following the pattern of equations (4.6) and (4.13), becomes a recursive network of stochastic differential equations, similar to those used to study many other highly parallel dynamic structures.

Letting the $K_j$ and $I_m$ all be represented as parameters $Q_j$, (with the caveat that $I_m$ not depend on itself), one can define, via the usual Legendre transform, 'entropies' of the form

$$S_I^m \equiv I_m - \sum_i Q_i \partial I_m / \partial Q_i$$

as in the previous chapter to obtain a complicated recursive system of phenomenological 'Onsager' stochastic differential equations like equation (4.13). Thus the $\partial S^m / \partial Q_i$ are analogous to the thermodynamic forces of a nonequilibrium physical system.

Then

$$dQ_t^j = \sum_i [L_{j,i}(t, ...\partial S_I^m / \partial Q^i...)dt + \sigma_{j,i}(t, ...\partial S_I^m / \partial Q^i...)dB_t^i]$$

$$= L^j(\mathbf{Q}, t)dt + \sum_i \sigma^{j,i}(\mathbf{Q}, t)dB_t^i \quad (5.1)$$

where the second equation follows from the collection of terms, and $\mathbf{Q} \equiv (Q^1, ..., Q^m)$.

The Mathematical Appendix outlines some standard material on stochastic differential equations.

Different kinds of 'noise', the $dB_t^i$, have particular forms of quadratic variation that may, in fact, represent a projection of environmental factors under something like a rate distortion manifold, as described in the previous chapter.

Indeed, the $I_m$ and/or the derived $S^m$ might, in some circumstances, be combined into a Morse function, permitting application of Pettini's (2007) Topological Hypothesis.

The model rapidly becomes unwieldy, probably requiring some clever combinatorial or groupoid convolution algebra and related diagrams for concise expression, much as in the usual field theoretic perturbation expansions (Hopf algebras, for example). The virtual reaction method of Zhu et al. (2007) is another possible approach.

There will be, first, multiple quasi-stable nonequilibrium steady states (nss) within a given system's $I_m$, representing a class of generalized resilience modes accessible via punctuation.

Second, however, will be analogs to the fragmentation discussed in Wallace (2015a, 2005a), when the system exceeds the critical value for some essential parameter $K_c$. That is, the $K$-parameter structure will represent full-scale fragmentation of the entire system, and not just punctuation within it.

There are, then, two classes of punctuation possible here, although the latter kind would seem to be the far more dramatic.

There are other possible patterns:

1. Setting the expectation of the system of equations (5.1) equal to zero and solving for stationary points again gives attractor states since the noise terms preclude unstable equilibria.

2. This structure may converge to limit cycle or pseudorandom 'strange attractor' behavior in which the system repeats characteristic patterns or remains within a particular neighborhood.

3. Most critically, *what is converged to, in both cases, is not a simple state or limit cycle of states. Rather it is an equivalence class (or cycling set of them) of highly dynamic information sources coupled by mutual interaction through crosstalk.* Thus 'stability' now represents convergence to a particular dynamical pattern rather than to some fixed configuration, the nss.

4. The Ito chain rule can be used to determine the expectation of the variates $Q_j^2$, leading to variance estimates, providing stability measures explored in following chapters.

Other formulations may well be possible, but this pattern will recur frequently.

It is interesting to compare these results with the approach of Dieckmann and Law (1996), who invoke evolutionary game theory to study dynamic biological coevolution. They obtain a first order set of canonical equations having the form

$$ds_i/dt = K_i(s)\partial W_i(s_i', s)|_{s_i'=s_i}. \tag{5.2}$$

Dieckmann and Law describe this as follows:

> The $s_i$, with $i = 1, ..., N$ denote adaptive trait values
> in a community comprising $N$ species. The $W_i(s'_i, s)$ are
> measures of fitness of individuals with trait values $s'_i$ in the
> environment determined by the resident trait values $s$, and
> the $K_i(s)$ are non-negative coefficients, possibly distinct
> for each species, that scale the rate of evolutionary change.
> Adaptive dynamics [of this kind] have frequently been pos-
> tulated, based either on the notion of a hill-climbing pro-
> cess on an adaptive landscape or some other sort of plau-
> sibility argument...

When this set is made equal to zero, so there is no time dependence, one
obtains what are characterized as 'evolutionary singularities', stationary
points.

Dieckmann and Law contend that their formal derivation of this equation satisfies four critical requirements:

> 1. The evolutionary process needs to be considered in
> a coevolutionary context.
> 2. A proper mathematical theory of evolution should
> be dynamical.
> 3. The coevolutionary dynamics ought to be under-
> pinned by a microscopic theory.
> 4. The evolutionary process has important stochastic
> elements.

Our development seems clearly within this same ballpark, (also within
which Ficici et al. 2005, analyze coevolutionary algorithms), although it has
taken a much different route, producing elaborate patterns of phase transition punctuation in a highly natural manner. Champagnat et al. (2006),
in fact, derive a higher order canonical approximation extending equation
(5.2) in a manner very much closer to equation (5.1), that is, a set of
stochastic differential equations describing evolutionary dynamics. Champagnat et al. go even further, using a large deviations argument to analyze
dynamical coevolutionary paths, not merely evolutionary singularities:

> In general, the issue of evolutionary dynamics drifting
> away from trajectories predicted by the canonical equation
> can be investigated by considering the asymptotic of the

probability of 'rare events' for the sample paths of the diffusion. By 'rare events' we mean diffusion paths drifting far away from the canonical equation. The probability of such rare events is governed by a *large deviation principle*...: when [a critical parameter $\epsilon$] goes to zero, the probability that the sample path of the diffusion is close to a given rare path $\phi$ decreases exponentially to 0 with rate $I(\phi)$, where the 'rate function' $I$ can be expressed in terms of the parameters of the diffusion...

This result can be used to study long-time behavior of the diffusion process when there are multiple attractive evolutionary singularities... [under proper conditions] the most likely path followed by the diffusion when exiting [a basin of attraction] is the one minimizing the rate function $I$ over all the [appropriate] trajectories... The time needed to exit [the basin is] of the order [$\exp(H/\epsilon)$ where $H$ is a quasi-potential representing the minimum of the rate function $I$ over all possible trajectories]...

A central fact of large deviations theory is that the rate function $I$ Champagnat et al. invoke can almost always be expressed as a kind of uncertainty measure, that is, in the form $I = -\sum_j P_j \log(P_j)$ for some probability distribution. This result goes under a number of names; Sanov's Theorem, Cramer's Theorem, the Gartner-Ellis Theorem, the Shannon-McMillan Theorem, and so forth (Dembo and Zeitouni, 1998). This central fact suggests the possibility of second order effects in coevolutionary process: the fluctuational paths defined by the system of equations in (5.1) may, under some conditions, become serially correlated outputs of an information source, allowing the programming of a generalized Red Queen via imposed crosstalk.

The basic idea, then, is that the 'information' of the large deviation, $I$ above, can be *induced* by a highly patterned free energy signal representing a message sent from an external information source, i.e., the programmer.

## 5.6 Programming as 'Farming'

To paraphrase Luchinsky, (1997), large fluctuations, although infrequent, are fundamental in a broad range of processes, and it was recognized by Onsager and Machlup (1953) that insight into the problem could be gained from studying the distribution of fluctuational paths along which the system moves to a given state. This distribution is a fundamental characteristic of the fluctuational dynamics, and its understanding leads toward control of fluctuations. Fluctuational motion from the vicinity of a stable state may occur along different paths. For large fluctuations, the distribution of these paths peaks sharply along an optimal, most probable, path. In the theory of large fluctuations, the pattern of optimal paths plays a role similar to that of the phase portrait in nonlinear dynamics.

In our development, meaningful paths driven by cognitive process will play the role of optimal paths in the theory of large fluctuations Champagnat et al., (2006), invoke for biological coevolution.

Producing, and then limiting, a sufficiently broad repertoire of cognitive responses – programming a coevolutionary machine – leads to a model in which the high probability fluctuational paths defined by the system of equations (5.1) are, in fact, themselves the output of some information source, of the program. This is most easily done by extending the development of Chapter 3, one further iteration. Indeed, such extension parsimoniously subsumes most of the somewhat messy mathematics inherent to the large deviations analysis.

Let $U$ represent the embedding program, here defined as an information source guiding the coevolutionary system into a particular equivalence class of desired behaviors. This class may have various properties including, but not limited to, a single information source, a recurrent pattern of them like a limit cycle, or a pseudorandom analog to a strange attractor.

Then the $I_m$ above are expressed as

$$I_m(X_1...X_i|Y_1...Y_j|Z_1...Z_k|U) \tag{5.3}$$

an extension of equations (3.14) and (4.4).

$X, Y, Z$ are as before, and $U$ represents the 'program', here characterized as an information source, a context in the sense of Bernard Baars, and not as some static prescription. By comparison, for a 'simple' evolutionary algorithm $U$ would represent a fixed fitness metric by which algorithm convergence is measured. Here the fitness metric is an inherently dynamic information source rather than some fixed comparison measure, and the comparison is through ongoing crosstalk.

A simplification results from not classifying the sets of information sources $X, Y$, and $Z$, expressing them all as information sources $W_j$. Then one can directly invoke the network information theory result of equations

(4.3) and (4.4), so that

$$I(W_1, ..., W_n|U) = H(U) + \sum_{j=1}^{n} H(W_j|U) - H(W_1, ..., W_n, U). \qquad (5.4)$$

The system of equations (5.1), however, becomes far more complicated, as do the corresponding dynamics: a new embedding level has been added. Some clever reformulation in terms of combinatorial algebras seems needed here. The central point, however, is that a one step extension of that system allows incorporating the effect of an external 'farmer' – the programmer – in guiding the Self-X machine into an acceptable pattern of ongoing behavior.

## 5.7  Second Order Programming

In this model neither the program nor the solution are static structures, but they are, respectively, an embedding information source and an equivalence class of 'appropriate' information sources representing desired Self-X behaviors. Programming is thus a complicated and ongoing process of interaction and guidance rather than some simple externally-imposed prescription. It seems likely that some form of allometric scaling will impose this behavior asymptotically on any sufficiently large highly parallel cognitive machine, one for which different quasi-independent dual information sources can be identified. Such behavior may, in fact, be 'emergent' in the sense that a large enough network of cognitive 'unconscious modules' can display unexpected large-scale correlations.

That is, programming a large Self-X – and inherently coevolutionary – machine, in this model, inevitably becomes very similar to agriculture wherein a deliberately and systematically simplified natural ecosystem is driven by higher order cognition, the epigenetic 'program' defined by the Farmer, who deliberately plants, cultivates, and harvests what is wanted from a highly dynamic, interactive, system.

One evident strategy is to first use the rate distortion manifold/retina (RDM) construct of the previous chapter – a focusing converse of the no free lunch theorem – as a higher order executive to determine which 'game' the system should play, to, as it were, find the ballpark: baseball, football, soccer, tennis, rugby, basketball, polo, etc. The coevolutionary dynamics then pick out an equivalence class of strategies for playing that particular game. If, in the middle of the game, the rules suddenly change, say, from football to baseball, then what had been a set of good ball handling skills becomes grossly inappropriate, a kind of inattentional blindness, as it were. Hence the need for a higher order 'farmer'. The retina/rate distortion manifold executive chooses what to plant, the coevolutionary system converges on a growing season. Drought, flood, or pest infestation can destroy the harvest in spite of the best executive choices.

A second approach, perhaps once an RDM has focused attention, as it were, is a form of higher order evolutionary programming described in the next chapter.

While the perspective here focuses on information-theoretic statistical constraints, others have taken a more exact formal approach to the same problem. Burgin and Gupta (2012), for example, write

> Algorithms are built of simple data-transformation and other functioning rules, usually in the form of instructions... More exactly, algorithms are structures in which simple transformation rules are their construction elements... In essence, construction rules build algorithm representations from simple instructions as, for example, it is done in operational programming languages or Turing machines... In a similar way, second-level algorithms are built of algorithms from another class as their construction elements... In contrast to conventional algorithms, [algorithms of the second level] are built not from separate instructions but from other algorithms, which may be very complex.

Burgin and Debnath (2010), Burgin (1992) and Burgin (1993) provide details of the methodology.

## 5.8   Implications

The 'solution' to a Self-X programming problem is not some static state, like the converging output of a Nix/Vose machine, but rather a desired set of dynamics. Using such a machine then becomes, in spirit, something like neolithic cultivation, and thus subject to the kinds of devastating vagaries that continue to plague farming even today: under one climate regime only a certain set of crops is likely to grow to harvest. Change the climate, and it becomes necessary to cultivate a different set.

It appears that analogs to the well-known pathologies of coevolutionary algorithms are to be writ large on highly parallel Self-X machines.

One possible next step, if higher order evolutionary programming indeed becomes possible, would be to extend the idea of Self-X machines into broadly Self-Farming devices, probably requiring second order models akin to those used to describe individual animal and institutional collective consciousness. Some work has been done from a formal perspective, in terms of Second-Level algorithms. See the M. Burgin references.

A cautionary example, however, can be found in recent work on the regulation of gene expression, also expressible as a highly parallel, broadly coevolutionary, interacting system of cognitive processes (Wallace and Wallace 2008, 2009). As Sasidharan and Gerstein (2008) describe, some 99% of the human genome is composed of sequences that do not encode proteins, what had been called 'junk' DNA. It is becoming clear that much, if not most, of this 'junk' encodes for the regulation of cognitive gene expression. That is, a very large fraction of the human genome is involved with ensuring that the right proteins are constructed at just the right time and in the right sequence.

Thus one possible inference of the work here is that highly parallel Self-X machines will have to spend a great deal of their available resources simply preventing themselves from running off the rails. Scaling laws for this are likely to place draconian limits on machine size, and the search for architectures that 'scale well' under stability constraints is likely to become increasingly frantic.

Energy consumption and dissipation became the brick wall for single-core devices, driving engineering technology toward multi-core chips and machines. Stabilization increasingly appears to loom as the brick wall confronting highly parallel Self-X machines.

We do not really know how to directly program (farm) large, highly parallel, coevolutionary machines. Wiegand (2003), and Ficici et al. (2005), elaborate many of the difficulties, as does this chapter. This suggests the need for second order evolutionary programming, as above. Asymptotically, however, large enough networks of even dimly cognitive devices will display coordinated emergent coevolutionary dynamics. Thus the development of some explicit engineering strategy for programming highly dynamic coevolutionary systems – farming them – would seem to be an economic priority.

# Chapter 6

# Epigenetic programming

## 6.1 Introduction

The previous chapter introduced a 'farming' metaphor for programming highly parallel coevolutionary machines designed to converge to a structured behavior pattern – an information source – rather than to a fixed 'answer' in the conventional sense. That work suggested a two-step methodology involving, first, a retina-like focus based on the converse of the no free lunch theorem, followed by a 'higher order' evolutionary algorithm to converge on an optimal dynamic solution. Here, we explore implementing such a strategy for a broad class of real-time cognitive machines – including those that converge to a fixed 'answer' – via an epigenetic programming model in which an intermediate information source serves as a kind of catalyst to change an underlying energy/fitness landscape, thereby accelerating convergence using a form of imposed developmental canalization, in the sense of Waddington (1957).

The argument will begin with a brief review of current thinking regarding the relation between epigenetic and genetic inheritance in biological systems, more fully developed in Wallace and Wallace (2009).

## 6.2 Epigenetic Inheritance

Following closely the arguments of Jablonka and Lamb (1998, 2006), information can be transmitted from one generation to the next in ways other than through the base sequence of DNA. It can be transmitted through cultural and behavioral means in higher animals, and by epigenetic means in cell lineages. All of these transmission systems allow the inheritance of environmentally induced variation. Such Epigenetic Inheritance Systems are the memory processes that enable somatic cells of different phenotypes but identical genotypes to transmit their phenotypes to their descendants, even when the stimuli that originally induced these phenotypes are no longer present.

In chromatin-marking systems, information is carried from one cell generation to the next because it rides with DNA as binding proteins or additional chemical groups that are attached to DNA and influence its activity. When DNA is replicated, so are the chromatin marks. One type of mark is the methylation pattern a gene carries. The same DNA sequence can have several different methylation patterns, each reflecting a different functional state. These alternative patterns can be stably inherited through many cell divisions.

Epigenetic inheritance systems are very different from the genetic system. Many variations are directed and predictable outcomes of environmental changes. Epigenetic variants are often, although not necessarily, adaptive. The frequency with which variants arise and their rate of reversion varies widely and epigenetic variations induced by environmental changes may be produced coordinately at several loci.

The epigenetic systems may therefore produce rapid, reversible, coordinated, heritable changes. However such systems can also underlie non-induced changes, changes that are induced but non-adaptive, and changes that are very stable.

What is needed is a concept of epigenetic heritability comparable to the classical concept of heritability, and a model similar to those used for measuring the effects of cultural inheritance on human behavior in populations.

After a furious decade of widespread research and broad debate, Bossdorf et al. (2008), for example, can reaffirm the mounting evidence that heritable variation in ecologically relevant traits can be generated through a suite of epigenetic mechanisms, even in the absence of genetic variation. Moreover, recent studies indicate that epigenetic variation in natural populations can be independent from genetic variation, and that in some cases environmentally induced epigenetic changes may be inherited by future generations. Thus we might need to expand our concept of variation and evolution in natural populations, taking into account several (likely interacting) ecologically relevant inheritance systems. Potentially, this may result in a significant expansion (though by all means not a negation) of the Modern Evolutionary Synthesis as well as in more conceptual and empirical integration between ecology and evolution (e.g., Wallace 2010b).

The abduction of spinglass and other models from neural network studies to the analysis of development and its evolution (e.g., Ciliberti et al. 2007a, b) carries with it the possibility of more than one system of memory. What Baars (1988, 2005) called 'contexts' channeling high level animal cognition may often be the influence of cultural inheritance, in a large sense.

Epigenetic machinery is intermediate between (relatively) hard-wired classical genetics, and a systematic embedding environment that also 'remembers' and is itself an information source. The three systems interact through a crosstalk by means of which, as shown in Wallace and Wallace (2009), the epigenetic machinery acts as a kind of catalyst for gene expression, an argument that can be adapted to the programming of real-time cognitive machines. Some preliminary material is reviewed in the section below, followed by the main results.

## 6.3 Groupoid Free Energy

### Cognition as an information source

Recall, briefly, the arguments of the Chapter 3. According to Atlan and Cohen (1998), the essence of cognition is comparison of a perceived external signal with an internal picture of the world, and then, upon that comparison, the choice of one response from a much larger repertoire of possible responses. Such reduction in uncertainty inherently carries information, and it is possible to make a very general model of this process as an information source, using the arguments of Section 3.2. This information source is taken as dual to the ergodic cognitive process.

Dividing the full set of possible responses into disjoint sets may itself require higher order cognitive decisions by another module or modules, suggesting the necessity of choice within a more or less broad set of possible quasi-languages. This would directly reflect the need to shift gears according to the different challenges faced by the organism, machine, or social group.

Following Section 3.2, 'meaningful' paths – creating an inherent grammar and syntax – have been defined entirely in terms of system response, as Atlan and Cohen propose. This formalism can easily be applied to the stochastic neuron in a neural network, again, as in Section 3.2.

Using the arguments of Chapter 4, this picture can be extended, via a formal equivalence class algebra that can be constructed for a cognitive process characterized by a dual information source by choosing different path origin points, and defining equivalence of two states by the existence of a high-probability meaningful path connecting them with the same origin. Disjoint partition by equivalence class, analogous to orbit equivalence classes for dynamical systems, defines the vertices of a network of cognitive dual languages. Each vertex then represents a different information source dual to a cognitive process. This is not a direct representation as in a neural network, or of some circuit in silicon. It is, rather, an abstract set of 'languages' dual to the cognitive processes instantiated by biological structures, machines, social process, or their hybrids. Our particular interest, however, is in an interacting network of cognitive processes.

This structure generates a groupoid. Recall that states $a_j, a_k$ are related by the groupoid morphism if and only if there exists a high-probability grammatical path connecting them to the same base point, and tuning across the various possible ways in which that can happen – the different cognitive languages – parameterizes the set of equivalence relations and creates the groupoid representing a network of dual information sources, a groupoid formed by the disjoint union of the underlying transitive groupoids that emerge when the base point changes.

**Free Energy**

The mathematical development begins with a highly formal description of phase transitions in cognitive systems, extending perspectives from physical theory to 'necessary conditions' statistical models of cognitive process based on the asymptotic limits of information theory, proceeding much in the spirit of Dretske (1994).

Landau's famous insight regarding phase change in physical systems was that second order phase transitions are usually in the context of a significant alteration in symmetry, with one phase being far more symmetric than the other (Landau and Lifshitz 2007; Pettini 2007). A symmetry is lost in the transition, a phenomenon called spontaneous symmetry breaking. The greatest possible set of symmetries in a physical system is that of the Hamiltonian describing its energy states. Usually states accessible at lower temperatures will lack the symmetries available at higher temperatures, so that the lower temperature phase is less symmetric: The randomization of higher temperatures ensures that higher symmetry/energy states will then be accessible to the system.

What of biological and cognitive structures that cannot easily be described using elementary physical models or simple group symmetries? What of systems where the physical temperature is not the determining factor in phase change?

The central focus here is on systems having associated information sources that can be characterized in terms of groupoids, a natural generalization of groups described more fully in the Mathematical Appendix that is finding increasingly widespread use in biology and cognitive theory. As argued above, a broad swath of cognitive phenomena can be described in terms of an associated information source.

Recall the homology between information and free energy from Section 3.3.

Information source uncertainty has an important heuristic interpretation. Ash (1990) states that we may regard a portion of text in a particular language as being produced by an information source. A large uncertainty means, by the Shannon-McMillan Theorem, a large number of 'meaningful' sequences. Thus given two languages with uncertainties $H_1$ and $H_2$ respectively, if $H_1 > H_2$, then in the absence of noise it is easier to communicate in the first language; more can be said in the same amount of time. On the other hand, it will be easier to reconstruct a scrambled portion of text in the second language, since fewer of the possible sequences of length $n$ are meaningful.

Taking the perspective of Ash, more complicated information sources, that can 'say more' in a shorter time than simpler ones, represent higher energy processes.

**The Basic Probability**

Equivalence classes define groupoids. The basic equivalence classes of a cognitive structure will define the basic transitive groupoids, and higher order systems can be constructed by the union of these transitive groupoids, having larger alphabets that allow more complicated statements in the sense of Ash above. We associate information sources with transitive groupoids, and with the larger groupoids constructed from them. The more complicated the groupoid, the greater the information source uncertainty, following Ash's reasoning.

Given an appropriately scaled, dimensionless, embedding temperature analog $K$ – for example the magnitude of the control signal $\mathcal{H}$ in the Data Rate Theorem – the assertion is that the probability of an information source $H_{G_i}$, representing a subgroupoid $G_i$, will, again, be given by the classic relation

$$P[H_{G_i}] = \frac{\exp[-H_{G_i}/K]}{\sum_j \exp[-H_{G_j}/K]} \tag{6.1}$$

where the normalizing sum is appropriately over all possible subgroupoids of the largest available symmetry groupoid. By the arguments above, compound sources, formed by the union of (interaction of elements from) underlying transitive groupoids, being more complex, will all have higher free-energy-density-equivalent dual information sources than those of the basic transitive groupoid elements.

Let

$$Z_G \equiv \sum_j \exp[-H_{G_j}/K]. \tag{6.2}$$

Define the *Groupoid Free Energy* (GFE) of the system, $F_G$, at the normalized equivalent temperature $K$, as

$$\exp[-F_G[K]/K] \equiv \sum_j \exp[-H_{G_j}/K]$$
$$F_G[K] = -K \log[Z_G[K]]. \tag{6.3}$$

The formalism has expressed the probability of an information source in terms of its relation to a fixed, appropriately normalized, system temperature. This gives a statistical thermodynamic means of defining a 'higher' free energy construct – $F_G[K]$ – to which can be applied Landau's fundamental heuristic phase transition argument.

Absent a high value of the temperature-equivalent, in this model, only the simplest transitive groupoid structures can be manifest.

Letting $K = \mathcal{H}$, the rate of control information of the Data Rate Theorem, introduces more subtle behavioral failure modes than simple on-off stability/instability.

Somewhat more rigorously, the elaborate renormalization schemes of the Chapter 1 may now be imposed on $F_G[K]$ itself, leading to a spectrum of highly punctuated transitions in the overall system of information sources. The essential point is that $F_G[K]$ is unlikely to scale with a renormalization transform as simply as does physical free energy, and this leads to very complicated 'biological' renormalization strategies.

Most deeply, however, an extended version of Pettini's (2007) Morse-Theory-based topological hypothesis can now be invoked, i.e., that changes in underlying groupoid structure are a necessary (but not sufficient) consequence of phase changes in $F_G[K]$. Necessity, but not sufficiency, is important, as it allows for mixed symmetries. An outline of Morse Theory is presented in the Mathematical Appendix, however see Matsumoto (2002) or Pettini (2007) for details.

As the temperature-analog declines, in this model, the system can undergo groupoid symmetry reductions representing fundamental phase transitions.

Dynamical behavior away from critical points will be determined, in this model, by empirical equations analogous to Onsager's treatment of nonequilibrium thermodynamics, as described in the previous chapters.

Several further matters should be noted.

First, the term $\exp[-H_{G_i}/K]$ in equation (6.1) is merely a surrogate form, and can be replaced by any appropriate function, say $f(H_{G_i}, K)$, so long as $\sum_j f(H_{G_j}, K)$ converges and decline in $K$ or increase in $H_{G_i}$ causes decline in average behavioral 'richness'.

Second, this approach defines an 'equilibrium' distribution of possible states for a single system, an individual 'molecule' in the sense of statistical mechanics. However, as Feynman (2000, Ch.5) argues in his analysis of the thermodynamics of computation, this works in the sense that the long-time average of a 'single molecule' converges to the cross-sectional mean in a properly ergodic system.

Third, equation (6.2) can be written in general operator terms as

$$Z = Tr(\exp[-\mathbf{H}/K]),$$

where $Tr$ represents the trace of an operator. This suggests the possibility of introducing a density matrix in a $C^\star$ algebra treatment. We will not, however, pursue this complication here.

Fourth, $K$ itself can often be written as the product of eigenvalues of an operator in an abstract space, defining a synergism in which each component is positive and nonzero. Thus it is possible to take $K$ as the determinant of a particular Hessian matrix representing a Morse Function, $f$, on some underlying, background, manifold, $M$, characterized in terms of (as yet unspecified background) variables $X = (x^1, ..., x^n)$, so that

$$K \propto \det(\mathcal{J}_{i,j}),$$

$$\mathcal{J}_{i,j} \equiv \partial^2 f / \partial x^i \partial x^j.$$

Again, see the Mathematical Appendix for a brief outline of Morse Theory.

By construction, $\mathcal{J}$ has everywhere only nonzero, and indeed, positive, eigenvalues, whose product thereby defines $K$ as a generalized volume. Thus, and accordingly, all critical points of $f$ have index zero, that is, no eigenvalues of $\mathcal{J}$ are ever negative at any point, and hence at any critical point $X_c$ where $df(X_c) = 0$. This defines a particularly simple topological structure for $M$: If the interval $[a, b]$ contains a critical value of $f$ with a single critical point $x_c$, then the topology of the set $M_b$ defined above differs from that of $M_a$ in a manner determined by the index $i$ of the critical point. $M_b$ is then homeomorphic to the manifold obtained from attaching to $M_a$ an i-handle, the direct product of an i-disk and an $(m-i)$-disk. One obtains, in this case, since $i = 0$, the two halves of a sphere with critical points at the top and bottom, that is, a simply connected component.

Thus the physical natures of the components defining $K$ impose very stringent constraints on this system, producing a simply connected component – or set of them – in an underlying abstract space. What one does with a collection of such objects is to patch them together using the Seifert-Van Kampen Theorem (Lee 2000, Ch. 10), creating a very complicated topological structure having interesting properties, a matter we will not pursue further here.

Envision, now, an average mean field mutual information linking different information sources associated with the subgroupoids defined by the network of interacting information sources described above. Call that mean field $\mathcal{I}$. Another possible interpretation is of an average probability of nondisjuctive 'weak' ties $\mathcal{P}$ (*sensu* Granovetter, 1973) linking the different ergodic dual information sources associated with each subgroupoid. Then, for a simple Groupoid Free Energy calculation above, take $K \propto \mathcal{I}, \mathcal{P}$. Increasing $\mathcal{I}$ or $\mathcal{P}$ then, increases the linkage across the subgroupoids of the cognitive system, leading, in a possibly punctuated way, to larger and larger processes of collective cognition using progressively larger 'alphabets' and having, in the sense of Ash above, progressively larger values of the associated dual information source.

A second model arises in a natural manner by taking $K$ as the *mean number*, $\mathcal{N}$, of linkages between dual information sources in the abstract network. This leads to generalizations of the standard random network formalism, and its inherent phase transitions (Glazebrook and Wallace 2009a, b).

Both approaches can be extended to second order as an analog to hierarchical regression. The first generalization is via a kind of universality class tuning, and the second by means of a renormalization in which couplings at or above a tunable limit are set to 1 and those below to 0. A Morse Theory topological tuning results directly from the latter approach. Evolutionary process, or engineering design, are not necessarily restricted, however, to these two exactly solvable models.

Wallace (2005a) and Wallace and Fullilove (2008) use simplified forms of this argument to characterize biological consciousness and distributed institutional cognition, respectively. The particular interest, however, is in the ways cognitive structures – including machines – respond to challenges in real time, that is, in the context of demands for prompt action from an embedding ecological structure that is itself not random and can be described in terms of an information source.

## 6.4   Real-Time Dynamics

Real time problems are inherently rate distortion problems, and we briefly reformulate the underlying theory from that perspective. The implementation of a complex cognitive structure, say a sequence of control orders generated by some dual information source $Y$, having output $y^n = y_1, y_2, ...$ is 'digitized' in terms of the observed behavior of the regulated system, say the sequence $b^n = b_1, b_2, ....$ The $b_i$ are thus what happens in real time, the actual impact of the cognitive structure on its embedding environment. Assume each $b^n$ is then deterministically retranslated back into a reproduction of the original control signal, $b^n \rightarrow \hat{y}^n = \hat{y}_1, \hat{y}_2, ...$

Define a distortion measure $d(y, \hat{y})$ that compares the original to the retranslated path. Suppose that with each path $y^n$ and $b^n$-path retranslation into the $y$-language, denoted $\hat{y}^n$, there are associated individual, joint, and conditional probability distributions $p(y^n)$, $p(\hat{y}^n)$, $p(y^n|\hat{y}^n)$.

Recall that the average distortion is defined as

$$D \equiv \sum_{y^n} p(y^n) d(y^n, \hat{y}^n). \tag{6.4}$$

It is possible to define the information transmitted from the incoming $Y$ to the outgoing $\hat{Y}$ process using the Shannon source uncertainty of the strings:

$$I(Y, \hat{Y}) \equiv H(Y) - H(Y|\hat{Y}) = H(Y) + H(\hat{Y}) - H(Y, \hat{Y}).$$

If there is no uncertainty in $Y$ given the retranslation $\hat{Y}$, then no information is lost, and the regulated system is perfectly under control. In general, this will not be true.

Recall that the *information rate distortion function* $R(D)$ for a source $Y$ with a distortion measure $d(y, \hat{y})$ is defined as

$$R(D) = \min_{p(y,\hat{y}); \sum_{(y,\hat{y})} p(y)p(y|\hat{y})d(y,\hat{y}) \leq D} I(Y, \hat{Y}). \tag{6.5}$$

The minimization is over all conditional distributions $p(y|\hat{y})$ for which the joint distribution $p(y, \hat{y}) = p(y)p(y|\hat{y})$ satisfies the average distortion constraint (i.e., average distortion $\leq D$).

The *Rate Distortion Theorem* states that $R(D)$ *is the minimum neces-sary rate of information transmission which ensures the transmission does not exceed average distortion* $D$. Thus $R(D)$ defines a minimum necessary channel capacity. Cover and Thomas (2006) show that $R(D)$ is necessarily a decreasing convex function of $D$, that is, always a reverse J-shaped curve.

Recall, now, the relation between information source uncertainty and channel capacity: $H[\mathbf{X}] \leq C$, where $H$ is the uncertainty of the source $X$ and $C$ the channel capacity, defined according to the relation, $C \equiv \max_{P(X)} I(X|Y)$, where $P(X)$ is the probability distribution of the message chosen so as to maximize the rate of information transmission along a channel $Y$.

Since the rate distortion function $R(D)$ defines the minimum channel capacity necessary for the system to have average distortion less than or equal $D$, it places a limit on information source uncertainty. Thus, distortion measures can drive information system dynamics. That is, the rate distortion function itself has a homological relation to free energy density.

We can model the disjunction between intent and impact of a cognitive system interacting with an embedding environment using a simple exten-sion of the language-of-cognition approach above. Recall that cognitive processes can be formally associated with information sources, and how a formal equivalence class algebra can be constructed for a complicated cog-nitive system by choosing different origin points in a particular abstract 'space' and defining the equivalence of two states by the existence of a high probability meaningful path connecting each of them to some defined origin point within that space.

To reiterate, disjoint partition by equivalence class is analogous to or-bit equivalence relations for dynamical systems, and defines the vertices of a network of cognitive dual languages available to the system: Each ver-tex represents a different information source dual to a cognitive process. The structure creates a large groupoid, with each orbit corresponding to a transitive groupoid whose disjoint union is the full groupoid, and each sub-groupoid associated with its own dual information source. Larger groupoids will, in general, have 'richer' dual information sources than smaller. We can apply the spontaneous symmetry breaking argument to increasing disjunc-tion between cognitive intent and system impact as follows:

With each subgroupoid $G_i$ of the (large) cognitive groupoid we can associate a dual information source $H_{G_i}$. Let $R(D)$ be the rate distortion function for the channel along which the message sent by the cognitive process. We are concerned with the distortion between what is ordered and the observed impact. Remember that both $H_{G_i}$ and $R(D)$ are free energy density measures.

$R(D)$ can be viewed as an embedding context for the underlying cognitive process. The argument-by-abduction from physical theory is, then, that $R(D)$ constitutes a kind of thermal bath for the processes of cognition. Thus we can, in standard manner, write the probability of the dual cognitive information source $H_{G_i}$ as

$$P[H_{G_i}] = \frac{\exp[-H_{G_i}/\kappa R(D)]}{\sum_j \exp[-H_{G_j}/\kappa R(D)]} \qquad (6.6)$$

where $\kappa$ is an appropriate dimensionless constant characteristic of the particular system. The sum is over all possible subgroupiods of the largest available symmetry groupoid. Again, compound sources, formed by the union of underlying transitive groupoids, being more complex, will have higher free-energy-density equivalents than those of the base transitive groupoids. This follows directly from the argument of Ash (1990) quoted above.

We can apply the Groupoid Free Energy phase transition arguments from above, remembering that the Rate Distortion Function $R(D)$ is always a decreasing convex function of $D$. For real time cognitive systems, increasing average distortion between cognitive intent and observed impact will 'lower the temperature' so as to drive the cognitive process, possibly in a highly punctuated manner, relentlessly toward simpler and less rich behaviors.

One important matter is, of course, just what constitutes 'real time' for the system of interest. If 'real time' has a characteristic time constant $\tau$ in which response takes place, then the temperature analog $\kappa R(D)$ might be better represented by the product $\alpha R(D)\tau$, i.e., energy rate $\times$ time. Given sufficient time to think matters over, as it were, the cognitive system might well converge to an acceptable solution. The canonical example, perhaps, being the increased time taken by autofocus cameras to converge under very low light conditions. The Morse Theory arguments above, as extended by the Siefert-Van Kampen Theorem, then suggest a possibly complicated topology underpins system dynamics since $R$ and $\tau$ (and other possible factors represented by $\alpha$) then become eigenvalues of an operator on a highly abstract base space, so that $R(D)\tau$ is another invariant 'volume element'.

## 6.5   Tunable Epigenetic Catalysis

Incorporating the influence of embedding contexts – epigenetic 'farming' of the machine – is most elegantly done by invoking the Joint Asymptotic Equipartition Theorem (JAEPT) and the extensions of Network Information Theory (Cover and Thomas 2006). For example, given an embedding contextual information source, say $Z$, then the dual cognitive source uncertainty $H_{D_i}$ is replaced by a joint uncertainty $H(X_{D_i}, Z)$. The objects of interest then become the jointly typical dual sequences $y^n = (x^n, z^n)$, where $x$ is associated with a cognitive process and $z$ with the embedding context. Restricting consideration of $x$ and $z$ to those sequences that are in fact jointly typical allows use of the information transmitted from $Z$ to $X$ as the splitting criterion.

One important inference is that, from the information theory 'chain rule' for interacting information sources $X$ and $Z$, is that

$$H(X, Z) = H(X) + H(Z|X) \leq H(X) + H(Z).$$

Thus the effect of the embedding context $Z$, in this model, is to lower the *relative* 'developmental free energy' at a given rate distortion energy $\kappa R(D)$. While more total energy is consumed – having two information sources to support instead of one – we gain control, using $Z$ to create a relative minimum in a kind of free energy analog.

Thus, for a given $\kappa R(D)$, or $\alpha R(D)\tau$, the effect of epigenetic regulation – machine farming – is to make probable selected developmental pathways for machine behavior otherwise inhibited by their high values of uncertainty/free energy in the absence of the control strategy $Z$. Hence the epigenetic information source $Z$ acts as a *tunable catalyst*, a kind of second order cognitive enzyme, in the biological sense, to enable and direct developmental pathways – machine convergence on a desired dynamic behavior pattern, or to a fixed final state, in the conventional computing sense.

Another possible extension is to allow multiple, simultaneous, cognitive machine dynamics, similar to the multiple workspace institutional distributed cognition models of Section 4.8. An individual actor can participate in multiple, ongoing simultaneous (or rapidly sequential) 'projects'. A principal complication then becomes the necessity of crosstalk (i.e., coordination) between those projects, a matter governed by the rate distortion theorem and its possible pathologies.

Parenthetically, cognitive systems of any nature must likely conserve resources by temporal or process focus, leading to the potential for the inattentional blindness that afflicts most cognitive process (Wallace 2007).

These elaborations allow a spectrum of possible 'final' machine states (or final machine dynamics) that are analogous to biological phenotypes, what Gilbert (2001) calls developmental or phenotype plasticity. Biological gene expression is seen as responding to epigenetic signals. West-Eberhard (2005) puts the matter as follows:

> Any new input, whether it comes from the genome, like a mutation, or from the external environment, like a temperature change, a pathogen, or a parental opinion, has a developmental effect only if the preexisting phenotype is responsive to it... A new input... causes a reorganization of the phenotype, or 'developmental recombination.'... Individual development can [thus] be visualized as a series of branching pathways. Each branch point is a developmental decision, or switch point, governed by some regulatory apparatus, and each switch point defines a modular trait. Developmental recombination implies the origin or deletion of a branch and a new or lost modular trait. It is important to realize that the novel regulatory response and the novel trait originate simultaneously. Their origins are, in fact, inseparable events: you cannot have a change in the phenotype, a novel phenotypic state, without an altered developmental pathway...

This is accomplished here by allowing the set $B_1$ in the development of Section 3.2 to span a distribution of possible 'final' states. Then the groupoid arguments merely expand to permit traverse of both initial states and possible final sets, recognizing that there can now be a possible overlap in the latter, and the epigenetic effects of machine farming are realized through the joint uncertainties $H(X_{D_i}, Z)$, so that the epigenetic information source $Z$ – the farmer – serves to direct as well the possible final states of $X_{D_i}$.

## 6.6 Implications

Tunable epigenetic catalysis lowers a kind of 'effective free energy' associated with the convergence of a real-time cognitive machine either to a fixed answer, as an analog to a developmental phenotype, or as a highly structured final dynamic behavioral strategy, in the case of a coevolutionary machine in the sense of Chapter 5. Given a particular 'farming' information source, the behavior or final state of interest will be associated with the lowest value of the energy-analog, presumably calculable by some version of the usual optimization methods. If the retina-like rate distortion manifold described in Chapter 4 has been properly implemented, a kind of converse to the no free lunch theorem, then this optimization procedure should converge on an appropriate solution. Thus we are invoking a synergism of the converse of the no free lunch theorem and the 'tunable epigenetic catalysis theorem' above to raise the probability of an acceptable solution for a real time system whose dynamics are dominated by Rate Distortion Theorem constraints.

The degree of catalysis needed for convergence would seem critically dependent on $R(D)$ or the product $R(D)\tau$, that is, on there being sufficient bandwidth in the communication between a cognitive machine and its embedding environment, taken as an information source, and available response time. If that bandwidth is too restricted, or the available time too short, then the system will inevitably freeze out into what amounts to a highly dysfunctional ground state. For cognitive systems, then, the paralysis of an absolute zero is, unfortunately, all too attainable. This result is clearly another version of the Data Rate Theorem, taking the information from an embedding 'ecosystem' as a kind of control signal.

We have, in any event, outlined a general theoretic schema that may be of use in programming a large class of cognitive machines operating in real time, and in understanding, preventing, or correcting their inevitable canonical and idiosyncratic patterns of failure, the central focus of the following chapter.

# Chapter 7

# *Psychopathia automatorum*

## 7.1 Introduction

This chapter both extends the formalism and explores in more detail the broad patterns of dysfunction that must characterize a considerable spectrum of high-level real time cognitive phenomena. Although the central concern is stated in terms of what can be called 'self-supervising control structures', the approach should apply quite widely, to biological, machine, composite, and institutional or man-machine 'cockpit' distributed cognition, operating in real time. This will be shown to imply that the current stampede by industry toward using complex automated systems to govern our transportation, power, and communication systems, to control individual vehicles under fly-by-wire protocols, run nuclear reactors, chemical plants, oil refineries, and so on, raises important issues of homeland security.

Cognitive process – including large classes of computation – is recognizably analogous to organismal ontology, in that the system begins at an initial multidimensional 'phenotype' $S_0$, and 'develops' to a final phenotype $S_\infty$ that may, in fact, be a highly dynamic behavior rather than a fixed final state.

One class of system failures becomes, then, similar to developmental dysfunction, in the sense of Wallace (2008b): Structured psychosocial stress, chemical agents, and similar noxious exposures, can write distorted images of themselves onto child growth, and, if sufficiently powerful, adult development as well, inducing a punctuated life course trajectory to characteristic forms of comorbid mind/body dysfunction. For an individual, within the linked network of broadly cognitive physiological and mental subsystems, this occurs in a manner recognizably similar to resilience domain shifts affecting a stressed ecosystem, suggesting that reversal or palliation may often be exceedingly difficult. The analogy with machine dysfunction is, we will show, quite direct.

The next section recapitulates recent models of organism development, following Wallace and Wallace (2008, 2009). Subsequent sections significantly expand that work, and explore dynamical models relating to time constraint that are based on the Rate Distortion Theorem.

## 7.2    Models of Development

The popular spinglass model of development (Coliberti et al. 2007a, b) assumes that $N$ transcriptional regulators are represented by their expression patterns $\mathbf{S}(t) = [S_1(t), ..., S_N(t)]$ at some time $t$ during a developmental or cell-biological process and in one cell or domain of an embryo. The transcriptional regulators influence each other's expression through cross-regulatory and autoregulatory interactions described by a matrix $w = (w_{ij})$. For nonzero elements, if $w_{ij} > 0$ the interaction is activating, if $w_{ij} < 0$ it is repressing. $w$ represents, in this model, the regulatory genotype of the system, while the expression state $\mathbf{S}(t)$ is the phenotype. These regulatory interactions change the expression of the network $\mathbf{S}(t)$ as time progresses according to a difference equation

$$S_i(t + \Delta t) = \sigma[\sum_{j=1}^{N} w_{ij} S_j(t)] \tag{7.1}$$

where $\Delta t$ is a constant and $\sigma$ a sigmodial function whose value lies in the interval $(-1, 1)$. In the spinglass limit, $\sigma$ is the sign function, taking only the values $\pm 1$.

The regulatory networks of interest here are those whose expression begins from a prespecified initial state $\mathbf{S}_0$ at time $t = 0$ and converges to a prespecified stable equilibrium state $\mathbf{S}_\infty$. Such networks are termed *viable* and must necessarily be a very small fraction of the total possible number of networks, since most do not begin and end on the specified states. This 'simple' observation is not at all simple in our reformulation, although other results become far more accessible, as we can then invoke certain asymptotic limit theorems of applied probability.

Equation 7.1 is formally similar to spinglass neural network models of learning by selection, e.g., as proposed in Toulouse et al. (1986) nearly a generation ago. Much subsequent work, summarized by Dehaene and Naccache (2001), suggests that such models are simply not sufficient to the task of understanding high level cognitive function, and these have been largely supplanted by complicated 'global workspace' concepts whose mathematical characterization is highly nontrivial (Atmanspacher 2006).

Wallace and Wallace (2008, 2009) shift the perspective on development by invoking a cognitive paradigm for gene expression, following the example of the Atlan/Cohen model of immune cognition.

To reiterate, Atlan and Cohen (1998), in the context of a study of the immune system, argue that the essence of cognition is the comparison of a perceived signal with an internal, learned picture of the world, and then choice of a single response from a large repertoire of possible responses. Such choice inherently involves information and information transmission since it always generates a reduction in uncertainty, as explained by Ash (1990, p. 21).

O'Nuallain (2008) argues similarly from the perspective of biosemiotics, quoting the discussions of Tauber (1997), to the effect that Jerne's work is "essentially an exploration of the immune system qua cognitive system".

More formally, a pattern of incoming input – like the $\mathbf{S}(t)$ above – is mixed in a systematic algorithmic manner with a pattern of internal ongoing activity – like the $(w_{ij})$ above – to create a path of combined signals $x = (a_0, a_1, ..., a_n, ...)$ – analogous to the sequence of $\mathbf{S}(t + \Delta t)$ above, with, say, $n = t/\Delta t$. Each $a_k$ thus represents some functional composition of internal and external signals.

This path is fed into a highly nonlinear decision algorithm, $h$, a 'sudden threshold machine', in a sense, that generates an output $h(x)$ that is an element of one of two disjoint sets $B_0$ and $B_1$ of possible system responses, and we can invoke the arguments and methods of the previous chapters.

## 7.3 Phase Transitions in Cognitive Systems

### Spontaneous symmetry breaking

A formal equivalence class algebra can now be constructed by choosing different origin and end points $\mathbf{S}_0, \mathbf{S}_\infty$ and defining equivalence of two states by the existence of a high probability viable path connecting them with the same origin and end. Disjoint partition by equivalence class, analogous to orbit equivalence classes for dynamical systems, defines the vertices of the proposed network of cognitive dual languages, much enlarged beyond the spinglass example. We thus envision a network of metanetworks. Each vertex then represents a different equivalence class of information sources dual to a cognitive process. This is an abstract set of metanetwork 'languages' dual to the cognitive processes of gene expression and development.

This structure generates a groupoid, in the sense of Chapter 4.

Again, states $a_j, a_k$ in a set $A$ are related by the groupoid morphism if and only if there exists a high probability grammatical path connecting them to the same base and end points, and tuning across the various possible ways in which that can happen – the different cognitive languages – parameterizes the set of equivalence relations and creates the (very large) groupoid.

There is a hierarchy in groupoid structures. First, there is structure *within the system having the same base and end points*. Second, there is a complicated groupoid structure defined by sets of dual information sources surrounding the variation of base and end points. We do not need to know what that structure is in any detail, but can show that its existence has profound implications.

First, the simple case – the set of dual information sources associated with a fixed pair of beginning and end states.

Taking the serial grammar/syntax model above, we find that not all high probability viable paths from $\mathbf{S}_0$ to $\mathbf{S}_\infty$ are the same. They are structured by the uncertainty of the associated dual information source, and that has a homological relation with free energy density.

Index possible dual information sources connecting base and end points by some set $A = \cup\alpha$. Argument by abduction from statistical physics is direct. Given, for a biological system, some metabolic energy density available at a rate $M$, and an allowed development time $\tau$, let $K = \kappa M\tau$ for some appropriate scaling constant $\kappa$, so that $M\tau$ is total developmental free energy. Then the probability of a particular $H_\alpha$ will yet again be determined by the standard expression

$$P[H_\beta] = \frac{\exp[-H_\beta/K]}{\sum_\alpha \exp[-H_\alpha/K]} \qquad (7.2)$$

where the sum may, in fact, be a complicated abstract integral.

Some dual information sources will be 'richer'/smarter than others, but, conversely, must use more of the $K$-resource for their completion.

Note that letting $K = \mathcal{H}$, where $\mathcal{H}$ is the rate of control information for an inherently unstable system, greatly generalizes the Data Rate Theorem.

The previous chapters argue that the behavior of highly parallel cognitive machines acting in real time is driven, among other factors, by the average distortion, $D$, between machine intent and machine impact, measured in terms of the Rate Distortion Function $R(D)$ and a characteristic machine response time $\tau$. $R(D)$ is necessarily a convex function in $D$, and this, since it defines a channel capacity that can be measured as a free energy analog, drives much of the dynamics of machine/environment interaction. Arguments of the previous chapter allow identification of a rate distortion free energy for the system, in terms of a particular groupoid associated with dual information sources within the machine.

While one might simply impose an equivalence class structure based on equal levels of energy/source uncertainty, producing a groupoid, it is possible to do more by now allowing both source and end points to vary, as well as by imposing energy-level equivalence. This produces a far more highly structured groupoid that we now investigate.

Recall that equivalence classes define groupoids, by standard mechanisms, as described in the Mathematical Appendix. The basic equivalence classes – here involving both information source uncertainty level and the variation of $\mathbf{S}_0$ and $\mathbf{S}_\infty$, will define transitive groupoids, and higher order systems can be constructed by the union of transitive groupoids, having larger alphabets that allow more complicated statements in the sense of Ash above.

Again, given an appropriately scaled, dimensionless, fixed, available metabolic energy density rate, or in machine terms, a fixed $R(D)$, so that $K = \kappa M$, or $K = \kappa R(D)$, the probability of an information source representing equivalence class $G_i$, $H_{G_i}$, will be given by

$$P[H_{G_i}] = \frac{\exp[-H_{G_i}/K]}{\sum_j \exp[-H_{G_j}/K]} \tag{7.3}$$

where the sum/integral of the denominator is over all possible elements of the largest available symmetry groupoid. By the arguments of Ash above, compound sources, formed by the union of underlying transitive groupoids, being more complex, generally having richer alphabets, as it were, will all have higher free-energy-density-equivalents than those of the base (transitive) groupoids.

Let

$$Z_G \equiv \sum_j \exp[-H_{G_j}/K]. \tag{7.4}$$

Again define the *groupoid free energy* of the system, $F_G$, at 'temperature' $K$, as

$$F_G[K] \equiv -K \log[Z_G[K]]. \tag{7.5}$$

The groupoid free energy construct permits introduction of important ideas from statistical physics.

This expresses the probability of an information source in terms of its relation to a fixed, scaled, available 'temperature' $K$, giving a statistical thermodynamic path leading to definition of a 'higher' free energy construct – $F_G[K]$ – to which Landau's fundamental heuristic phase transition argument can be applied (Landau and Lifshitz 2007; Pettini 2007).

Recall, again, Landau's insight that second order phase transitions were usually in the context of a significant symmetry change in the physical states of a system, with one phase being far more symmetric than the other. Again, a symmetry is lost in the transition – spontaneous symmetry breaking – and symmetry changes are inherently punctuated.

The randomization of higher 'temperatures' – in this case limited by available metabolic free energy densities, channel capacities, or control signals – ensures that higher symmetry/energy states – mixed transitive groupoid structures – will then be accessible to the system. Absent high $K$, however, only the simplest transitive groupoid structures can be manifest. A full treatment from this perspective seems to require invocation of groupoid representations, no small matter (e.g., Bos 2007; Bunici 2003).

Now again invoke something like Pettini's Morse-Theory-based topological hypothesis, i.e., that changes in underlying groupoid structure are a necessary (but not sufficient) consequence of phase changes in $F_G[K]$.

Using this formulation, the mechanisms of epigenetic catalysis are accomplished by allowing the set $B_1$ in Section 3.2 to span a distribution of possible 'final' states $\mathbf{S}_\infty$. Then the groupoid arguments merely expand to permit traverse of both initial states and possible final sets, recognizing that there can now be a possible overlap in the latter, and the epigenetic effects are realized through the joint uncertainties $H(X_{G_i}, Z)$, so that the epigenetic information source $Z$ serves to direct as well the possible final states of $X_{G_i}$. Scherrer and Jost (2007a, b) use an information theory strategy to suggest something similar.

### Developmental holonomy groupoid

There is another, more direct, way to look at phase transitions in cognitive systems, adapting perspectives of homotopy and holonomy directly within 'machine phenotype' space. This is related to the constructions above. The ideas involve directed homotopy.

In conventional topology, one constructs equivalence classes of loops that can be continuously transformed into one another on a surface. The prospect of interest is to attempt to collapse such a family of loops to a point while remaining within the surface. If this cannot be done, there is a hole. Here the concern is, as in figure 7.1, analogous to the discussion of

Chapter 4, with sets of one-way developmental trajectories, beginning with an initial machine phenotype $S_i$, and converging on some final phenotype, here characteristic behavioral patterns simplified as 'metabolic' cycles labeled, respectively, $S_n$ and $S_o$. The filled triangle represents the effect of some external epigenetic 'farmer/programmer' in the sense of the previous chapters acting at a critical developmental period represented by the initial phenotype $S_i$.

In the sense of Chapter 6, however, a real-time system is 'programmed' as much by interaction with embedding context as by the desires of the programmer, and will become subject to noxious epigenetic influence in much the same manner as a developing organism – the duality between programming and stability for massively parallel 'Self-X' machines.

Assume phenotype space to be directly measurable and to have a simple 'natural' metric defining the difference between developmental paths.

Developmental paths continuously transformable into each other without crossing the filled triangle define equivalence classes characteristic of different information sources dual to cognitive process, as above.

Given a metric on phenotype space, and given equivalence classes of developmental trajectories having more than one path each, we can *pair one-way developmental trajectories* to make loop structures. In figure 7.1 the solid and dotted lines above and below the filled triangle can be pasted together to make loops characteristic of the different developmental equivalence classes. Although figure 7.1 is represented as topologically flat, there is no inherent reason for the phenotype manifold itself to be flat. The existence of a metric in phenotype space permits determining the degree of curvature, using standard methods. Figure 7.2 shows a loop on some manifold. Using the metric definition it is possible to *parallel transport* a tangent vector starting at point $s$ around the loop, and to measure the angle between the initial and final vectors, as indicated. A central result from elementary metric geometry is that the angle $\alpha$ will be given by the integral of the curvature tensor of the metric over the interior of the loop (e.g., Frankel 2006, Section 9.6).

The *holonomy group* is defined as follows (e.g., Helgason 1962):

If $s$ is a point on a manifold $M$ having a metric, then the holonomy group of $M$ is the group of all linear transformations of the tangent space $M_s$ obtained by parallel translation along closed curves starting at $s$.

For figure 7.1 the *phenotype holonomy groupoid* is the disjoint union of the different holonomy groups corresponding to the different branches separated by 'developmental shadows' induced by epigenetic information

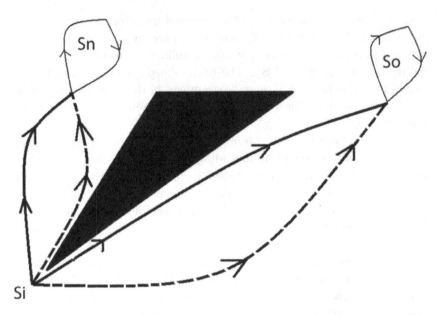

Fig. 7.1 Developmental homotopy equivalence classes in machine phenotype space. The set on one-way paths from $S_i$ to $S_n$ represents an equivalence class of developmental trajectories converging on a 'machine phenotype'. In the presence of an external epigenetic catalyst, a 'farming' program, or a noxious interaction by a real-time system with its context, for example an increasing average distortion, $D$, between machine intent and machine impact, developmental trajectories can converge on another, possibly pathological, phenotype, $S_o$.

sources acting as developmental catalysts/programs.

The relation between the phenotype groupoid as defined here and the phase transitions in $F_G[K]$ as defined above is an open question.

**Higher holonomy**

Glazebrook and Wallace (2009a, b) examined holonomy groupoid phase transition arguments for networks of interacting information sources dual to cognitive phenomena. A more elementary form of this arises directly through extending holonomy groupoid arguments to a manifold of different information sources dual to cognitive phenomena as follows.

Different cognitive phenomena will have different dual information sources, and we are interested in the local properties of the system near a particular reference state. We impose a topology on the system, so that, near a particular 'language' $A$, dual to an underlying cognitive process, there is an open set $U$ of closely similar languages $\hat{A}$, such that $\{A, \hat{A}\} \subset U$. It may be necessary to coarse-grain the system's responses to define these

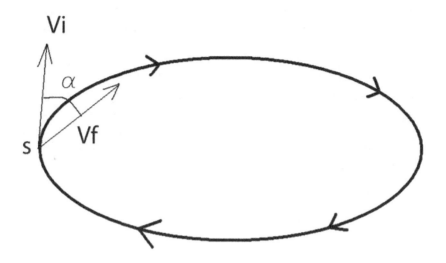

Fig. 7.2 Parallel transport of a tangent vector $V_i \rightarrow V_f$ around a loop on a manifold. Only for a geometrically flat object will the angle between the initial and final vectors be zero. By a fundamental theorem the path integral around the loop by parallel displacement is the surface integral of the curvature over the loop.

information sources. The problem is to proceed in such a way as to preserve the underlying essential topology, while eliminating 'high frequency noise'. The formal tools for this can be found elsewhere, e.g., in Chapter 8 of Burago et al. (2001).

Since the information sources dual to the cognitive processes are similar, for all pairs of languages $A, \hat{A}$ in $U$, it is possible to apply the arguments of Chapter 4, again leading to a version of equation (4.13):

$$d\mathcal{M}_t = L(t, \mathcal{M})dt + \sigma(t, \mathcal{M})dB_t \qquad (7.6)$$

where $\mathcal{M}$ is defined in equation (4.8), and $L$ and $\sigma$ are appropriately regular functions of $t$ and $\mathcal{M}$, and $dB_t$ represents the noise structure, characterized by its quadratic variation. In the sense of Emery (1989), this leads into deep realms of stochastic differential geometry and related topics: Imagine figure 7.1 as blurred by Brownian or more structured stochastic fuzz.

We have defined a groupoid for the system based on a particular set of equivalence classes of information sources dual to cognitive processes. That groupoid parsimoniously characterizes the available dynamical manifolds, and breaking of the groupoid symmetry by epigenetic crosstalk creates more complex objects of considerable interest. This leads to the possibility, indeed, the necessity of epigenetic *Deus ex Machina* mechanisms – analogous to programming, stochastic resonance, etc. – to force transitions between the different possible modes within and across dynamic manifolds. In one model the external 'programmer' creates the manifold structure, and the system hunts within that structure for the 'solution' to the problem according to equivalence classes of paths on the manifold. Noise, as with random mutation in evolutionary algorithms, precludes simple unstable equilibria.

Equivalence classes of *states* gave dual information sources. Equivalence classes of *information sources* give different characteristic dynamical manifolds. Equivalence classes of one-way developmental *paths* produce different directed homotopy topologies characterizing those dynamical manifolds. This introduces the possibility of having different quasi-stable modes *within* individual manifolds, and leads to ideas of holonomy and the holonomy groupoid of the set of quasi-stable developmental modes.

## 7.4   Real Time Systems

Following closely the arguments of Section 6.4, real time problems, in addition to the 'developmental' characteristics described in the previous sections, are inherently rate distortion problems: The implementation of a complex cognitive structure, say a sequence of control orders generated by some dual information source $Y$, having output $y^n = y_1, y_2, \ldots$ is 'digitized' in terms of the observed behavior of the regulated system, say the sequence $b^n = b_1, b_2, \ldots$. The $b_i$ are thus what happens in real time, the actual impact of the cognitive structure on its embedding environment. Assume each $b^n$ is then deterministically retranslated back into a reproduction of the original control signal, $b^n \rightarrow \hat{y}^n = \hat{y}_1, \hat{y}_2, \ldots$

Again, define a distortion measure $d(y, \hat{y})$ that compares the original to the retranslated path.

For a Gaussian channel having noise with zero mean and variance $\sigma^2$, the Rate Distortion Function is $R(D) = 1/2 \log[\sigma^2/D], 0 \leq D \leq \sigma^2, R(D) = 0, D > \sigma^2$, where $D$ is the average distortion using the square measure (Cover and Thomas 2006).

Recall, again, the relation between information source uncertainty and channel capacity (Ash, 1990): $H[\mathbf{X}] \leq C$, where $H$ is the uncertainty of the source $X$ and $C$ the channel capacity, defined according to the relation, $C \equiv \max_{P(X)} I(X|Y)$, where $P(X)$ is the probability distribution of the message chosen so as to maximize the rate of information transmission along a channel $Y$.

The rate distortion function $R(D)$ defines the minimum channel capacity necessary for the system to have average distortion less than or equal $D$, placing a limits on information source uncertainty. Thus, as previously stated, distortion measures can drive information system dynamics, since the rate distortion function itself has a homological relation to free energy density.

Recall the argument leading to equation (6.6).

With each subgroupoid $G_\alpha$ of the (large) cognitive groupoid defining machine cognition we can associate a dual information source $H_{G_\alpha}$. Let $R(D)$ be the rate distortion function between the message sent by the cognitive process and the observed impact. Remember that both $H_{G_\alpha}$ and $R(D)$ are free energy density measures.

The essential assertion is that $R(D)$ provides an embedding context for the underlying cognitive process. Argument-by-abduction from physical theory is that $R(D)$ constitutes a kind of thermal bath for the processes of cognition. Thus we can write the probability of the dual cognitive information source $H_{G_\alpha}$ as

$$P[H_{G_\alpha}] = \frac{\exp[-H_{G_\alpha}/\kappa R(D)]}{\sum_\beta \exp[-H_{G_\beta}/\kappa R(D)]} \tag{7.7}$$

where $\kappa$ is an appropriate dimensionless constant characteristic of the particular system. The sum is over all possible subgroupiods of the largest available symmetry groupoid. Again, compound sources, formed by the union of underlying transitive groupoids, being more complex, will have higher free-energy-density equivalents than those of the base transitive groupoids.

The Groupoid Free Energy phase transition arguments from above can be used, remembering that the Rate Distortion Function $R(D)$ is always a decreasing convex function of $D$. For real time cognitive systems, increasing average distortion between cognitive intent and observed impact will 'lower the temperature' so as to drive the cognitive process, possibly in a highly punctuated manner, relentlessly toward simpler and less rich behaviors.

As described in the last chapter, an important question is what constitutes 'real time' for the system of interest. If 'real time' has a characteristic time constant $\tau$ in which response takes place, then the temperature analog $\kappa R(D)$ might be better represented by the product $\alpha R(D)\tau$, i.e., energy rate × time. Given sufficient time to ruminate, as it were, the cognitive system might converge to an acceptable solution. The Morse Theory arguments of the previous chapter, as extended by the Siefert-Van Kampen

Theorem, then suggest a possibly complicated topology underpins system dynamics since $R$ and $\tau$ (and other possible factors represented by $\alpha$) then become eigenvalues of an operator on a highly abstract base space. Their product is a determinant 'volume element', an invariant.

The Mathematical Appendix extends the argument leading to equation (7.7) in terms of a groupoid atlas construct.

These considerations are made more explicit in the next section, invoking the actual information available from the environment with which the machine interacts as itself a free energy analog. This generalizes to a system of real time modules that constitute the machine as they interact with each other and with the embedding environment.

## 7.5   Distortion Dynamics

Following in the direction of Section 6.4, we note that the rate distortion function has a homological relation to free energy density, similar to the relation between free energy density and information source uncertainty.

$R$, however, is parameterized, not only by the distortion $D$, but by some vector of variates $\mathbf{D} = (D_1, ..., D_k)$, for which the first component is the average distortion, $D_1 \equiv D$. The assumed dynamics are then driven by gradients in the rate distortion disorder defined as usual by the Legendre transform

$$S_R \equiv R(\mathbf{D}) - \sum_{i=1}^{k} D_i \partial R / \partial D_i \,. \tag{7.8}$$

This leads to the deterministic and stochastic systems of empirical equations analogous to Onsager's treatment of nonequilibrium thermodynamics:

$$dD_j / dt = \sum_i L_{j,i} \partial S_R / \partial D_i \tag{7.9}$$

and

$$dD_t^j = L^j(D_1, ..., D_k, t)dt + \sum_i \sigma^{j,i}(D_1, ..., D_k, t)dB_t^i \tag{7.10}$$

where the $dB_t^i$ represent added, often highly structured, stochastic 'noise' whose properties are characterized by the quadratic variation, as described in the Mathematical Appendix.

It will prove possible to generalize these equations in the face of richer structure, for example internal modular crosstalk, the existence of characteristic time constants, and the influence of an embedding source of free energy that will represent the 'richness' of the information available from the environment about its state.

Again, equations (7.9) and (7.10), and their generalizations below, may not necessarily display the expected symmetry of simple physical systems, i.e., $L_{j,j} = L_{j,i}$, known as Onsager's reciprocity relations. The proof of these relations for physical systems relies on microscopic time reversal (de Groot and Mazur 1984), and information sources are not microscopically reversible. Palindromes of any form are notoriously rare and short, while the asymptotic limit theorems are true only in the limit of long strings.

For a simple Gaussian channel with noise having zero mean and variance $\sigma^2$,

$$S_R(D) = R(D) - DdR(D)/dD = 1/2 \log(\sigma^2/D) + 1/2. \qquad (7.11)$$

The simplest possible empirical Onsager relation becomes

$$dD/dt = -\mu dS_R/dD = \frac{\mu}{2D} \qquad (7.12)$$

where $-dS_R/dD$ represents the force of an entropic wind, a kind of internal dissipation inevitably driving a real-time system of interacting information sources toward greater distortion.

This has the solution

$$D = \sqrt{\mu t} \qquad (7.13)$$

that grows monotonically with time.

A central observation is that a similar result must necessarily apply to any of the reverse-J-shaped relations that characterize $R(D)$, since the rate distortion function is necessarily a convex decreasing function of the average distortion $D$, whatever distortion measure is chosen.

One implication is that a system of cognitive modules interacting in real time will inevitably be subject to a relentless entropic dissipative force, requiring a constant free energy expenditure for maintenance of some fixed average distortion in the communication between them. The distortion in the communication between two interacting modules will, without free energy input, increase monotonically with time, leading necessarily to the punctuated failure of the system.

Equation (7.13) is closely analogous to classical Brownian motion, as treated by Einstein. Let $p(x,t)dx$ be the probability a particle located at the origin at time zero and undergoing Brownian motion is found at locations $x \to x + dx$ at time $t$. Then, famously, $p$ satisfies the diffusion equation

$$\partial p(x,t)/\partial t = \mu \partial^2 p(x,t)/\partial x^2.$$

Einstein's solution is that

$$p(x,t) = \frac{1}{\sqrt{4\pi\mu t}} \exp[-x^2/4\mu t].$$

Thus the standard deviation of the particle position increases in proportion to $\sqrt{\mu t}$ – as above – suggesting that a Gaussian channel connecting a cognitive system with a structured environment will undergo a kind of Brownian expansion in the distortion between system intent and system effect in the absence of a free energy input that, it can be argued for machine systems, represents available information about the environment. We will give an explicit calculation below.

## 7.6 Rate Distortion Coevolution

The coevolution model of Section 5.5 above can be greatly simplified in terms the rate distortion functions for mutual crosstalk between different cognitive modules, the effect of contact with the embedding environment, and the effect of the machine on that environment, using the homology of the rate distortion function itself with free energy.

Given different cognitive subprocesses, 1...s, within the machine, the quantities of special interest thus become the mutual rate distortion functions $R_{i,j}$ characterizing communication (and the distortion $D_{i,j}$) between them, and $R(D)$ representing the distortion between machine intent and machine impact. The essential parameters remain the characteristic time constants of each process, $\tau_j, j = 1...s$, and the overall, embedding, 'communication free energy density', $\mathcal{H}$, now representing the maximum possible information available to the multicomponent system from the embedding environment. The distortion between overall machine impact and machine intent is, in this formulation, taken as simply an additional parameter.

Taking the $Q^\beta$ to run over all the relevant parameters and mutual rate distortion functions (including distortion measures $D_{i,j}$ and $D$), the expression for 'entropy', via the Legendre transform, becomes

$$S_R^\beta \equiv R_\beta - \sum_k Q^\alpha \partial R_\beta / \partial Q^\alpha. \tag{7.14}$$

Equation (5.1) accordingly becomes

$$dQ_t^\alpha = \sum_\beta [L_\beta(t,...\partial S_R^\beta/\partial Q^\alpha...)dt + \sigma_\beta(t,...\partial S_R^\beta/\partial Q^\alpha...)dB_t^\beta] \tag{7.15}$$

where, again, $\beta$ ranges over the indices of the $R_{i,j}$ and $R(D)$.

These equations are explicitly modeling the roles of crosstalk within the machine, the effect of the machine on the environment, the inherent time constants of the different cognitive modules, and the overall information available from the embedding environment, now taken as a kind of metabolic free energy measure.

This is a very complicated structure indeed, but its general dynamical behaviors will obviously be analogous to those described earlier. For example, setting the expectation of equation (7.15) to zero gives the 'coevolutionary stable states' of a system of interacting cognitive modules in terms of channel capacity, average distortions, system time constants, and overall available free energy density characterizing information available from the environment. Again, limit cycles and strange attractors seem possible as well. And again, what is converged to is a dynamic behavior pattern, not some fixed 'state'. And again, such a system will display highly punctuated dynamics almost exactly akin to resilience domain shifts in ecosystems (Holling 1973; Gunderson 2000).

## 7.7 Multiple Time Scales

The systems explored so far are characterized by a single 'real' time as, for example, short-term power or communication grid management, traffic, chemical process, or power station control, and the like. Many other cognitive systems – biological, mechanical, institutional, mixed distributed – face numerous 'real' times. Think of a student riding a bicycle in heavy traffic: Proper strategies – generalized languages – across multiple timescales are critical, including those of (1) the immediate traffic pattern, (2) the study time needed for passing exams, (3) the time necessary for advancement in a chosen profession, and so on. In the US, corporate institutional distributed cognition in the financial industries must be able to respond on the short timescales of 'the market', while being able to react on intermediate times to the oncoming growth and collapse of the latest economic bubble, and to the relentless long-term pressures of the slow disaster of continuing deindustrialization consequent on diversion of scientific and engineering resources into fifty years of Cold War (Wallace 2015a). The success of the system in coping with these interacting timescales is selfevident.

Clues as to the likely subtleties can be found through an elementary calculation.

Let $R(D)$ the Rate Distortion Function describing the relation between system intent and system impact, essentially a channel capacity and information transmission rate between the machine and the structures it is attempting to affect, and let $\tau$ be the characteristic 'real time' of the overall system. Let $\mathcal{H}$ be the total rate of available information telling the system what is happening in real time. $\tau R(D)$ and $\tau \mathcal{H}$ are thus basic energy measures. The fundamental assumption is that the probability density function associated with a particular value of $\tau R(D)$ will be given by the classic relation

$$Pr[\tau R(D), \tau \mathcal{H}] = \frac{\exp[-R(D)\tau/\kappa \mathcal{H}\tau]}{\int_0^\infty \exp[-R(D)\tau/\kappa \mathcal{H}\tau]dR} \tag{7.16}$$

where $\kappa$ might represent something like an efficiency measure of information usage.

The 'real time' measure $\tau$ divides out in this formulation.

Then

$$<R> = \int_0^\infty RPr[R, \mathcal{H}]dR = \kappa \mathcal{H}. \tag{7.17}$$

By the arguments leading to equation (7.7), limits on incoming information $\mathcal{H}$ resulting in limits on $<R>$ will express themselves in limits on the richness of internal system process. Conversely, declines in $\mathcal{H}$ can trigger punctuated declines in the richness of internal machine cognition, regardless of 'real time'.

In the case that $R$ and $\mathcal{H}$ have different characteristic times, say $\tau_R$ and $\tau_{\mathcal{H}}$, then $\kappa$ in the above equations is replaced by

$$\hat{\kappa} = \kappa \frac{\tau_{\mathcal{H}}}{\tau_R}. \tag{7.18}$$

Thus the existence of different characteristic timescales for machine response and for the pattern of incoming information on which the machine must act can significantly complicate machine dynamics. In particular, decline in the characteristic time of incoming information relative to the characteristic response time of the machine can express itself in punctuated decline in the possible richness of machine behaviors.

## 7.8 Flight, Fight, and Helplessness

The trained, galvanized, hypothalamic-pituitary-adrenal (HPA) axis response in higher animals appears to be an evolutionary adaptation to an information theoretic constraint as fundamental as the ubiquity of noise and crosstalk, and this generalizes to highly parallel real-time machine cognition.

Recall that real time dynamic responses of a cognitive system can be represented by high probability paths connecting 'initial' multivariate states $S_0$ to 'final' configurations $S_f$, across a great variety of beginning and end points. This creates a similar variety of groupoid classifications and associated dual cognitive processes in which the equivalence of two states is defined by linkages to the same beginning and end states. Thus it becomes possible to construct a groupoid free energy driven by the quality of information coming from the embedding ecosystem, represented by $\mathcal{H}$, as the temperature analog.

This provides an analog to equation (7.7): for the dual information source associated with groupoid element $G_i$, the probability of $H_{G_i}$ becomes

$$P[H_{G_i}] = \frac{\exp[-H_{G_i}/\kappa\mathcal{H}]}{\sum_j \exp[-H_{G_j}/\kappa\mathcal{H}]} \tag{7.19}$$

defining a free energy analog as

$$F_G = -\kappa\mathcal{H}\log[\sum_j \exp[-H_{G_j}/\kappa\mathcal{H}]]. \tag{7.20}$$

This permits a Landau-analog phase transition analysis in which the quality of incoming information from the embedding ecosystem serves to raise or lower the possible richness of a machine's cognitive response to patterns of challenge. If $\mathcal{H}$ is relatively large – a rich and varied environment – then there is a plethora of possible cognitive responses. If, however, noise or simple constraint limit the magnitude of $\mathcal{H}$, then the system collapses in a highly punctuated manner to a kind of ground state in which only limited responses are possible. For animals, then, some analog to an HPA axis – that has been conditioned to respond in a structured but galvanized manner to such limitation – becomes an important survival tool.

The canonical example is attack from a predator, first under a circumstance where fog-of-war limits accurate perception of threat or detection of the predator, and second, where predation is clearly at hand, but possible responses are few. In each case $\mathcal{H}$ is quite small, first, limited by noise, and second, by action constraint.

Figure 7.3 shows $\mathcal{H}$ for a two-state system having probabilities $p, q = (1-p)$ as a function of $p$. Ground state collapses occur near $p = 0, 1$, while the richest environment – highest 'temperature' – occurs at $p = 1/2$.

Such 'ground state collapse' must be ubiquitous for real time cognitive systems facing threat, and must profoundly affect highly parallel machine

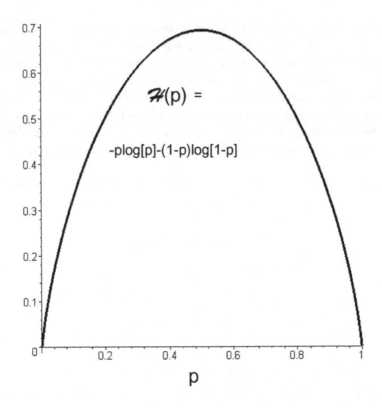

Fig. 7.3  The richness of incoming environmental information for a two-state system, $\mathcal{H} = -p\log[p] - (1-p)\log[1-p]$, as a function of $p$. The limits of fog-of-war, $p = 0$, and certain attack, $p = 1$, have lowest $\mathcal{H}$, while $p = 1/2$ presents the richest environment.

cognition. That is, machines that must regulate traffic systems, nuclear reactors, individual vehicles, power, communication, and financial grids, and the like, will not have had the relentless benefit of half a billion years of evolutionary selection under circumstances of ground state collapse: their equivalents of the HPA axis are not likely to be particularly well designed.

An essential contributor to the human dominance of the planet is our ability to construct cultural systems and artifacts that limit the necessity of even a highly evolved and skilled HPA axis response. Real-time cognitive machines have no such buffer.

## 7.9 Machine Psychiatry

'Therapeutic' intervention against machine malfunction can be seen as an idiotypic sequence of stimulus-and-response that brings a pathological dynamic state back toward a normal mode. Intervention, however, causes internal system change that, in turn, alters system output. The potential complexity of this hall of mirrors – the inevitable spectrum of 'side effects' – becomes clearer through an explicit rate distortion calculation.

Recall something of the arguments of Section 7.5. Suppose the relation between system challenge and system response – the manner in which cognitive machine activities more-or-less accurately reflect what is called for by environmental conditions – is characterized by a Gaussian channel having a rate distortion function $R(D) = 1/2 \log[\sigma^2/D]$, where $D$ is an average distortion measure based on the squared distortion metric. Defining a rate distortion entropy as $S_R = R(D) - DdR/dD$ permits definition of a nonequilibrium Onsager equation in the presence of a 'therapeutic' intervention $\delta T$ as

$$dD/dt = -\mu dS_R/dD - \delta T = \frac{\mu}{2D} - \delta T \qquad (7.21)$$

having the nonequilibrium steady state (nss) solution, where $dD/dt = 0$,

$$D_{nss} = \frac{\mu}{2\delta T}. \qquad (7.22)$$

For this simplistic model, the distortion between need and actual response is inversely proportional to the magnitude of 'therapeutic' intervention. In reality, the final distortion measure $D$ is the consequence of a vast array of internal processes that all contribute to it and that, individually, must all be optimized for the system to function properly. That is, overall distortion between total need and total response cannot be constrained by allowing critical subsystems to overload beyond survivable limits: Too high a vehicle (or actuator) acceleration, for example, can result in structural failure.

Consider individual responses of the machine's cognitive components for the moment, to be a set of $m$ independent but not identically distributed normal random variates having zero mean and variance $\sigma_i^2, i = 1...m$. Following the argument of Section 10.3.3 of Cover and Thomas (2006), assume a fixed channel capacity $R$ available with which to represent this random vector. How should we allot signal to the various components to minimize the total distortion $D$? A brief argument shows it necessary to optimize

$$R(D) = \min_{\sum D_i = D} \sum_{i=1}^{m} \max\{1/2 \log[\sigma_i^2/D_i], 0\} \qquad (7.23)$$

subject to the inequality restraint $\sum_i D_i \le D$.

Using the Kuhn-Tucker generalization of the Lagrange multiplier method necessary under inequality conditions gives

$$R(D) = \sum_{i=1}^{m} 1/2 \log[\sigma_i^2/D_i] \qquad (7.24)$$

where $D_i = \lambda$ if $\lambda < \sigma_i^2$ or $D = \sigma_i^2$ if $\lambda \ge \sigma_i^2$, and $\lambda$ is chosen so that $\sum_i D_i = D$.

Thus, even under conditions of 'independence', there is a complex 'reverse water-filling' relation for Gaussian variables. In the real world, the different subcomponents will not be independent, but will engage in complicated crosstalk.

Assume, then, $m$ different cognitive machine subsystems that are not independent. Define a Rate Distortion function $R(D_1, ..., D_m) = R(\mathbf{D})$ and an associated rate distortion entropy $S_R$ having the now-familiar form

$$S_R = R(\mathbf{D}) - \sum_j D_j \partial S_R/\partial D_j. \qquad (7.25)$$

The generalization of equation (7.21) is

$$dD_i/dt = -\sum_j L_{i,j} \partial S_R/\partial D_j - \delta T_i \qquad (7.26)$$

under the inequality constraint $D_i \le D_i^{max} \forall i$.

At nonequilibrium steady state, all $dD_i/dt \equiv 0$, so that it becomes necessary to minimize *each* $D_i$ under the joint constraints

$$[\sum_j L_{i,j} \partial S_R/\partial D_j] + \delta T_i = 0 \,,$$

$$D_i < D_i^{max} \, \forall i \qquad (7.27)$$

remembering that $R(\mathbf{D})$ must be a convex function.

This is a complicated problem in Kuhn-Tucker optimization for which the exact form of the crosstalk-dominated $R(\mathbf{D})$ is quite unknown, in the context that even the independent Gaussian channel example involves constraints of mutual influence via reverse water-filling. In sum, changing a single 'therapeutic' intervention $\delta T_i$ will inevitably reverberate across the entire system, necessarily affecting – sometimes markedly – each distortion measure that characterizes the difference between needed and observed cognitive subsystem response to challenge.

It is important to note that there may, in fact, be no solution for which $D_i < D_i^{max} \forall i$.

Such 'side effects' – some $D_i > D_i^{max}$ – are, then, inevitable for therapeutic intervention. Many will be serious. Some will be fatal.

This conundrum is, in fact, another quintessential illustration of the intimate conflict between programming and stability afflicting massive parallel – and inherently coevolutionary – systems.

## 7.10 Cost of Regulation

Here we examine, from a formal Black-Scholes perspective, the 'information cost' of regulating a massively parallel cognitive system, providing another example of the Data Rate Theorem. Recall from the first chapter that, for a broad class of inherently unstable 'plants' in a large sense, there is a minimum rate of control information $\mathcal{H}$ below which no coding scheme can impose stability.

The rate distortion function places limits on information source uncertainty. Thus, distortion measures can drive information system dynamics. That is, the rate distortion function itself has a homological relation to free energy in the sense of Bennett (1988) and Feynman (2000), who characterize information by the free energy needed to erase it. In general, increasing channel capacity in a regulatory structure requires increased levels of free energy. A heuristic approach is fairly simple. Given a rate of available 'control information free energy', $\mathcal{H}$, and an average distortion $D$, the channel capacity, a free energy measure, must be at least $R(D)$, a convex function. Again, for a Gaussian channel with noise of mean zero and variance $\sigma^2$, $R(D) = \frac{1}{2}\log[\sigma^2/D]$, under the squared distortion measure.

Using a standard Gibbs model, we can write, for the average of $R$ and some unknown monotonic function $F(\mathcal{H})$, the approximate relation

$$< R >= \frac{\int_0^\infty R \exp[-R/F(\mathcal{H})]dR}{\int_0^\infty \exp[-R/F(\mathcal{H})]dR} = F(\mathcal{H}). \qquad (7.28)$$

What is the form of $\mathcal{H} = F^{-1}(< R >)$? One suspects, in first order, a linear expression, using the first two terms of a Taylor series expansion:

$$\mathcal{H} \approx \kappa_1 < R > +\kappa_2. \qquad (7.29)$$

Jensen's inequality for a convex function, here $R(< D >) \leq < R(D) >$, suggests:

$$\mathcal{H} \geq \kappa_1 R(< D >) + \kappa_2 \qquad (7.30)$$

but, as they say, some assembly is required.

Although the Black-Scholes formalism for financial options trading (Black and Scholes 1973) fails in practice for fundamental reasons (e.g., Derman and Taleb 2005; Haug and Taleb 2011), the methodology remains of some interest as a conceptual model that can be generally applied to system regulation. The central purpose of the approach is to eliminate or mitigate the effects of unpredictability – noise.

Consider the canonical example of a stock price $S$, whose dynamics are determined by the stochastic differential equation

$$dS_t = \mu S_t dt + b S_t dW_t \qquad (7.31)$$

where $dW_t$ is ordinary white noise.

Given a known payoff function $V(S,t)$, one uses the Ito chain rule to define another SDE, in the usual manner. Now define a 'portfolio function' as the Legendre transform of $V$;

$$\mathcal{L} = -V + S\partial V/\partial S. \qquad (7.32)$$

Manipulation, using the derived SDE for $V$, gives the result that

$$\Delta\mathcal{L} = (-\partial V/\partial t - \frac{1}{2}b^2 S^2 \partial^2 V/\partial S^2)\Delta t \qquad (7.33)$$

which eliminates the noise term. Assuming $\Delta\mathcal{L}/\Delta t \propto \mathcal{L}$ and a bit more algebra gives the classic Black-Scholes equation for $V$.

The question arises whether a regulatory system can be described in terms of similar hedging strategies.

The change in average distortion between regulatory intent and effect with time can be seen as representing the dynamics of the Rate Distortion Function (RDF) of a regulatory system that is distributed across a number of subcomponents. Let $R_t$ be the RDF at time $t$. The relation can, under conditions of both white noise and volatility, be expressed as

$$dR_t = f(t, R_t)dt + b R_t dW_t \qquad (7.34)$$

where $b$ represents added, internal, 'regulatory' noise, beyond that inherent in the channel transmission as represented by the variance $\sigma^2$. This is a consequence of the fact that regulation takes place across the system as a whole, adding another level of organization through which signals must be transmitted.

Let $\mathcal{H}(R_t, t)$ represent the rate of 'control information free energy' consumption (these are highly nonequilibrium processes) associated with $R_t$ at time $t$ across the system, and expand using the Ito chain rule:

$$d\mathcal{H}_t = [\partial\mathcal{H}/\partial t + f(R_t, t)\partial\mathcal{H}/\partial R + \frac{1}{2}b^2 R_t^2 \partial^2\mathcal{H}/\partial R^2]dt$$
$$+ [bR_t \partial\mathcal{H}/\partial R]dW_t. \qquad (7.35)$$

Again, define $\mathcal{L}$ as the Legendre transform of the 'information free energy' consumption rate $\mathcal{H}$, an entropy-like measure having the form

$$\mathcal{L} = -\mathcal{H} + R\partial\mathcal{H}/\partial R. \tag{7.36}$$

Using the heuristic of replacing $dX$ with $\Delta X$ in these expressions, and applying the results of equation (7.35), produces an exact analog to equation (7.33):

$$\Delta\mathcal{L} = (-\partial\mathcal{H}/\partial t - \frac{1}{2}b^2 R^2 \partial^2\mathcal{H}/\partial R^2)\Delta t. \tag{7.37}$$

Again, precisely as in the Black-Scholes calculation, the terms in $f$ and $dW_t$ cancel out, giving a noiseless relation, or rather, one in which the effects of noise are subsumed in the Ito correction involving $b$. However, the approach invokes powerful regularity assumptions that may often be violated. A central question then revolves about model robustness in the face of such violation.

Now perform a heuristic iteration: $\mathcal{L}$, as the Legendre transform of the metabolic free energy rate $\mathcal{H}$, is itself a kind of entropy rate index that can be expected to reach a constant level at nonequilibrium steady state. There, $\Delta\mathcal{L}/\Delta t = \partial\mathcal{H}/\partial t \equiv 0$, giving the final relation

$$\frac{1}{2}b^2 R^2 d^2\mathcal{H}/dR^2 = 0. \tag{7.38}$$

Thus, at nonequilibrium steady state:

$$\mathcal{H}_{nss}(R) = \kappa_1 R + \kappa_2 \tag{7.39}$$

as proposed.

More complicated models, depending on the assumed form of $\Delta\mathcal{L}/\Delta t$, are clearly possible. As above, assuming $\Delta\mathcal{L}/\Delta t \propto \mathcal{L}$, gives the Black-Scholes result.

The cost of regulation, in this model proportional to the RDF, can rapidly become expensive, since $\kappa_1$ is expected to be large as a consequence of entropic loss. Thus, from the convexity of $R(D)$, decreasing average distortion in will consume available control information free energy at very high rates. From the relation for $R(D)$ in a Gaussian channel, fixing average distortion $D$ at the regulated level, and applying a 'noxious exposure' that causes $\sigma^2$ to increase, will raise demand for regulatory control information free energy at a rate $\propto 2\kappa_1 \log[\sigma]$, in this model.

The rate distortion function places limits on information source uncertainty. Thus average distortion measures $D$ can drive information system dynamics as well as $R(D)$, via the convexity relation. That is, the rate distortion function itself has a homological relation to free energy, and one can apply Onsager arguments using $D$ as a driving parameter.

Recall the argument of equations (7.11)-(7.13). Such 'correspondence reduction' serves as a base to argue upward in both scale and complexity.

But, in distinct contrast to equation (7.13), regulation does not involve diffusive drift of average distortion. On the contrary, following the arguments above, massive rates of free energy are consumed in regulatory activities at and across various scales and levels of organization. Let $G(\mathcal{H})$ represent a monotonic increasing function of control information free energy rate $\mathcal{H}$. Then a plausible model, in the presence of an internal regulatory noise $\beta^2$ in addition to the channel noise defined by $\sigma^2$, is

$$dD_t = (\frac{\mu}{2D_t} - G(\mathcal{H}))dt + \frac{\beta^2}{2}D_t dW_t. \tag{7.40}$$

This has the nonequilibrium steady state expectation

$$D_{nss} = \frac{\mu}{2G(\mathcal{H})} \tag{7.41}$$

representing the massive levels of free energy needed to limit distortion between the intent and effect of regulation in a system or submodule: $\mathcal{H}$ can be expected to increase very sharply with rise in $G$.

Using the Ito chain rule on equation (7.40), one can calculate the variance in the distortion as $E(D_t^2) - (E(D_t))^2$.

Letting $Y_t = D_t^2$ and applying the Ito relation,

$$dY_t = [2\sqrt{Y_t}(\frac{\mu}{2\sqrt{Y_t}} - G(\mathcal{H})) + \frac{\beta^4}{4}Y_t]dt + \beta^2 Y_t dW_t \tag{7.42}$$

where $\frac{\beta^4}{4}Y_t$ is the Ito correction to the time term of the SDE.

A little algebra shows that no real number solution for the expectation of $Y_t = D_t^2$ can exist unless the discriminant of the resulting quadratic equation is $\geq 0$, so that

$$G(\mathcal{H}) \geq \frac{\beta^2}{2}\sqrt{\mu}. \tag{7.43}$$

From equations (7.39) and (7.41),

$$G(\mathcal{H}) = \frac{\mu}{2\sigma^2}\exp[2(\mathcal{H} - \kappa_2)/\kappa_1] \geq \frac{\beta^2}{2}\sqrt{\mu}. \tag{7.44}$$

Solving for $\mathcal{H}$ gives the necessary condition

$$\mathcal{H} \geq \frac{\kappa_1}{2}\log[\frac{\beta^2\sigma^2}{\sqrt{\mu}}] + \kappa_2 \tag{7.45}$$

for there to be a real second moment in $D$. $\kappa_1$ is, again, expected to be very large indeed. Given the context of this analysis, failure to provide adequate rates of control information would represent the onset of a regulatory catastrophe: system failure.

This represents another version of the Data Rate Theorem.

Pathogenic exposures – in a large sense – can be expected to markedly increase both $\beta$ and $\sigma$.

Extension of the argument to other forms of Rate Distortion Function is direct. For example, the relation for the natural channel is $R(D) \approx \sigma^2/D$, giving a condition based on the discriminant of a cubic in equation (7.43).

The essential point is that regulatory requirements can create massive demands for control signal free energy. Such levels may not be sustainable, creating a brick wall against which both programming and stability may catastrophically collide.

Many variants of the model are possible. The most natural, perhaps, is to view $\mathcal{H}$ as a free energy measure *per unit external perturbation*. That is, $\mathcal{H} \equiv d\hat{\mathcal{H}}/dK$, where $\hat{\mathcal{H}}$ is now perceived as the rate of free energy consumption needed to meet an external perturbation of (normalized) magnitude $K$. Then the condition of equation (7.45), now on $\hat{\mathcal{H}}$, becomes

$$\hat{\mathcal{H}} \geq \int [\frac{\kappa_1}{2} \log[\frac{\beta^2 \sigma^2}{\sqrt{\mu}}] + \kappa_2] dK. \qquad (7.46)$$

Under constant conditions, for stability, the system must supply the control signal free energy measure at a rate

$$\hat{\mathcal{H}} \geq [\frac{\kappa_1}{2} \log[\frac{\beta^2 \sigma^2}{\sqrt{\mu}}] + \kappa_2] \Delta K. \qquad (7.47)$$

$\Delta K$ is the magnitude of the imposed perturbation. Thus the demand on free energy created by imposed perturbations can be greatly amplified, in this model, suggesting that erosion of stability by externalities can make the system more sensitive to the impact of 'natural' shocks.

Equations (7.45-47) have fundamental implications for network dynamics, structure, and stability, in a large sense. Granovetter (1973) characterizes network function in terms of 'the strength of weak ties'. 'Strong' ties, to adapt his perspective, disjointly partition a network into identifiable submodules. 'Weak' ties reach across such disjoint partitioning, i.e., they are linkages that do not disjointly partition a network. The average probability of such weak ties, at least in a random network, defines the fraction of network nodes that will be in a 'giant component' of Chapter 3 that links the vast majority of nodes. It is well known that the occurrence of such a component is a punctuated event. That is, there is a critical value of the average probability of weak ties below which there are only individual fragments. Figure 3.1 provides something of an introduction, in the context of interacting cognitive submodules that, here, represent the distributed cognition of the full cognitive enterprise.

It seems clear that the maintenance of such weak ties, allowing large-scale distributed cognition across the system, depends critically on the investment of free energy resources of various forms that may include information itself at rates $\mathcal{H}$ or $\hat{\mathcal{H}}$. That is, keeping the channels of communication open in a real-time system under fire will require greater and greater rates of control free energy investment that may simply be impossible.

$\mathcal{H}$ and $\hat{\mathcal{H}}$ can, however, also be interpreted as intensity indices analogous to a generalized temperature. Identifiable cognitive submodules within the system define equivalence classes leading to a groupoid symmetry. Recall that groupoids can be understood as a generalization of the group symmetry concept, the simplest groupoid being a disjoint union of different groups. This leads toward something much like Landau's perspective on phase transition (e.g., Pettini 2007; Landau and Lifshitz 2007). Again, the essential idea is that certain phase transitions take place in the context of a significant symmetry change, with one phase, at higher temperature, being more symmetric than the other. A symmetry is lost in the transition, what is called spontaneous symmetry breaking. The transition is usually highly punctuated. In this context, equations (7.45-47) can be interpreted as defining the 'temperature' $\mathcal{H}$ or $\hat{\mathcal{H}}$ at which a complex network of interacting cognitive submodules breaks down into a simpler groupoid structure of disjointly partitioned submodules.

For completeness, note that setting $\Delta \mathcal{L}/\Delta t = C > 0$ in the Black-Scholes model leads to the solution

$$\mathcal{H}_{nss} = \frac{2C}{b^2} \log[R] + \kappa_1 R + \kappa_2 \qquad (7.48)$$

again consistent with the heuristic result of equation (7.30).

This leads to the more complicated Data Rate Theorem stability condition

$$\mathcal{H} \geq \frac{\kappa_1}{2} \log[\frac{b^2 \sigma^2}{\sqrt{\mu}}] + \kappa_2 +$$
$$\frac{C}{b^2} [4 \log(1/2) + 2 \log[\log[\frac{b^4 \sigma^4}{\mu}]]]. \qquad (7.49)$$

## 7.11 Cost of Maintenance

The Data Rate Theorem, expressed either by equation (1.10) or by equations (7.45) and (7.49), states that there is a minimum necessary rate of control information needed to stabilize an inherently unstable system. Is this, in itself, a stable condition? That is, once a stabilizing control information rate has been identified, is that the whole story? A control system has at least three components: the structure to be controlled, the mechanism for control, and the underlying 'program' of that mechanism, which may be a complex system or an interacting set of them. With time, the structure and mechanism may change – evolve, degrade, learn, and so on, requiring increased rates of control information for continued proper function.

An approach to the dynamics of control stability is possible using a variant of the information bottleneck method of Tishby et al. (1999).

We envision an iterated application of the Rate Distortion Theorem to a control system in which a series of 'orders' $y^n = y_1, ..., y_n$, having probability $p(y^n)$, is sent through and the outcomes monitored as $\hat{y}^n = \hat{y}_1, ..., \hat{y}_n$. The distortion measure, however, *is now taken as the minimum necessary control information* $\mathcal{H}(y^n, \hat{y}^n)$, defining a 'distortion' $\hat{\mathcal{H}}$ as

$$\hat{\mathcal{H}} = \sum_{y^n} p(y^n)\mathcal{H}(y^n, \hat{y}^n) \geq 0. \tag{7.50}$$

We can then define a new, iterated, Rate Distortion Function $\mathcal{R}(\hat{\mathcal{H}})$ and a new 'entropy'

$$\mathcal{S} = \mathcal{R}(\hat{\mathcal{H}}) - \hat{\mathcal{H}}d\mathcal{R}/d\hat{\mathcal{H}}. \tag{7.51}$$

We next invoke the analog to the 'diffusion' equation (7.12),

$$d\hat{\mathcal{H}}/dt = -\mu d\mathcal{S}/d\hat{\mathcal{H}}. \tag{7.52}$$

Since $\mathcal{R}$ is always a convex function of $\hat{\mathcal{H}}$ (Cover and Thomas 2006), this relation has the solution

$$\hat{\mathcal{H}}(t) = f(t) \tag{7.53}$$

where $f(t)$ is monotonic increasing. That is, *in the absence of continuous maintenance*, the needed control signal will relentlessly rise in time, surpassing all possible bounds, and hence triggering a failure of control.

The next stage of the argument involves generalization of equation (7.40) to a nonequilibrium steady state in a model for ongoing, continuous investment of 'essential capital' at a rate $M$ in order to maintain the system, having an expectation analogous to equation (7.41), so that

$$\hat{\mathcal{H}}_{nss} \propto 1/g(M) \tag{7.54}$$

where $g(M)$ is monotonic increasing in the capital investment rate $M$.

Entropic degradation or diffusion of control systems is inevitable, if only because of relentless changes in the system to be controlled, requiring constant investment of resources for maintenance.

Equation (7.54) represents a 'classical' dynamics for the average information cost $\hat{\mathcal{H}}_{nss}$ as a function of available maintenance resources. More subtle behaviors are likely because, as we have repeatedly argued, cognitive systems can often be represented in terms of groupoid symmetries that generalize the group structures familiar to classical and quantum dynamics and statistical mechanics.

Letting $\mathcal{T} \equiv 1/g(M)$, the nonequilibrium steady state 'information cost' of stabilizing an inherently unstable cognitive system grows with the 'temperature' measure $\mathcal{T}$. This is recognizably similar to phase transitions arguments in statistical physics, often realized via a Morse Function argument, which we apply as follows.

First, construct a pseudoprobability over the unstable, regulated cognitive system characterized by the groupoid $\{G_i\}$ as

$$P[\hat{\mathcal{H}}_{G_i}] = \frac{\exp[-\hat{\mathcal{H}}_{G_i}/\kappa\mathcal{T}]}{\sum_j \exp[-\hat{\mathcal{H}}_{G_j}/\kappa\mathcal{T}]} \tag{7.55}$$

where $\kappa$ is an appropriate constant. The sum is over all possible subgroupoids of the largest available cognitive symmetry groupoid.

A simple Morse Function, leading to Pettini's (2007) topological hypothesis in this system, is a groupoid free energy $\mathcal{F}$ defined as

$$\exp[-\mathcal{F}/\kappa\mathcal{T}] \equiv \sum_j \exp[-\hat{\mathcal{H}}_{G_j}/\kappa\mathcal{T}]. \tag{7.56}$$

Using $\mathcal{F}$ we yet again apply the groupoid version of Landau's spontaneous symmetry breaking argument to the groupoid associated with the cognitive process regulated by the average control information cost $\hat{\mathcal{H}}$.

Following standard arguments (Pettini 2007), changes in $\mathcal{T}$, an inverse function of available levels of maintenance resources, can lead to punctuated phase transition/bifurcation changes in the average control signal needed to stabilize an inherently unstable – hence highly responsive – dynamic system. Failure of maintenance can, in this model, lead to punctuated onset of dysfunction rather than to the 'classical' model of graceful degradation implied by equation (7.54).

## 7.12  Implications

For massively parallel real time cognitive systems, be they biological, machine, composite, or involve complex man-machine 'cockpit' forms of distributed cognition, one measure of deterioration in the communication with the embedding environment is the decline of a rate distortion function $R(D)$ consequent on increase of the average distortion $D$ between system intent and system impact. In the context of some fixed expected response time $\tau$, this acts to lower an *internal* 'cognitive temperature', driving the system to simpler and less-rich behaviors, and ultimately condensing to some dysfunctional 'absolute zero' configuration, possibly in a highly punctuated manner.

A slightly different picture emerges by considering the amount of *external* information coming from an embedding environment per unit time as fixed, and expect the machine to respond to that information with a minimum of distortion in the difference between its intent and its effect. Lowering the quality of incoming information leads to greater distortion, and, given the real time constraint, this lowers $R(D)$, and drives the internal state of the system to its ground configuration, as it were, via the mechanisms of equation (7.7).

These results characterize a relatively simple class of failure modes, particularly for systems composed of very many interacting cognitive subcomponents. Section 7.10 suggests other modes of catastrophic failure. When one takes an ontological perspective, the possibility of much more subtle failures, analogous to developmental disorders, becomes evident. The implications for highly parallel real time cognitive machines and other systems are not encouraging.

Such structures – machines, biological entities, composites, 'cockpits' of distributed cognition – necessarily undergo developmental trajectories, from an initial configuration to a final 'phenotype' that is either some fixed 'answer' or else a desired dynamic behavior. These are affected, not only by the desires of the programmer or the limitations of the system, also by the distortion between intent and impact, by the degree of information actually available from the environment, and by the effects of epigenetic 'noxious exposures' that may not be random, causing the functional equivalence of developmental disorders resulting in pathological system phenotypes. These might be either 'wrong answers' or 'wrong strategies', and the analogy with ecosystem resilience shifts suggests that prevention or correction will not be easy (Wallace 2008).

A comparison with the status of the understanding of human psychopathology is of some interest, recalling from a new perspective the arguments of Chapter 3.

In spite of some two hundred years of the scientific study of mental disorders, Johnson-Laird et al. (2006) felt compelled to write that

> Current knowledge about psychological illnesses is comparable to the medical understanding of epidemics in the early 19th century. Physicians realized that cholera, for example, was a specific disease, which killed about a third of the people whom it infected. What they disagreed about was the cause, the pathology, and the communication of the disease. Similarly, most medical professionals these days realize that psychological illnesses occur..., but they disagree about their cause and pathology. Notwithstanding [recent official classification schemes for mental disorders], we doubt whether any satisfactory a priori definition of psychological illness can exist... because it is a matter for theory to elucidate.

At any moment, about one percent of a human population will experience debilitating schizophrenoform disorders, and perhaps another one percent crippling levels of analogs to Western depression/anxiety. A smaller proportion will express dangerous degrees of some forms of psychopathy or sociopathy. Most of us, of whatever cultural background, over the life course will suffer periods of mental distress or disorder in which we simply cannot properly carry out socially expected duties. A billion years of evolutionary selection has not eliminated mental illness any more than it has eliminated infectious disease.

The Brave New World of highly parallel autonomic and Self-X machines that will follow the current explosion of multiple core and molecular computing technologies will not be spared analogous patterns of canonical and idiosyncratic failure. Some of these will resemble developmental disorders of gene expression often caused by exposure to teratogenic chemicals, by social exposures including psychosocial stress, or their synergisms. That is, they can be induced. Technological momentum, driven by powerful economic interests, will see such machines widely deployed to control a great swath of critical systems in real time, ranging from transportation, power, and communication networks, to individual vehicles, various industrial enterprises, and the like.

As one commentator emphasized, the concerns of this chapter focus particularly on what might be called self-supervising control agents, that is, agents that can conduct supervisory control on themselves. At present there are no known examples of robust, self supervising control agents: humans are alone in this capacity.

There is, however, a recent, closely studied, case history of serious, indeed fatal, 'best case' failure of a real-time, distributed cognition man/machine 'cockpit' system that may be relevant. During combat operations of the second Gulf War, US Army Patriot antimissile units were involved in two fratricide incidents involving coalition aircraft (Hawley 2006, 2008). A British Tornado was misclassified as an anti-radiation missile, and a US Navy F/A-18 misclassified as a tactical ballistic missile. Both were shot down, and their crews lost. Two of 11 US Patriot shots were fratricides, some 18%. Detailed analysis found a 'perfect storm' that, among other things, involved a synergism of a fascination with, and blind faith in, technology with unacknowledged system fallibilities, reinforced by an organizational culture of 'React quickly, engage early, and trust the system without question'.

This was a 'best case' scenario in that the machine system did not act without human supervision: the final decision is made by human supervisory controllers. And the human operators were, indeed, very much the best and the brightest: carefully selected, highly motivated, attentive to their jobs, well trained.

One possible conclusion – that reached by official agencies – is that any faults in total Patriot system performance are mostly attributable to supervisory failures on the part of the human controllers.

From the perspective of this work, however, the Patriot antimissile unit is a distributed cognitive man/machine 'cockpit' system that is routinely forced to operate under the most draconian real-time constraints. The developmental trajectory is from an initial condition of operationally ready, $S_0$, to a final state $S_\infty$ that is either a return to initial condition or to firing. Under the stress of actual combat, the distortion of the fog of war in the real world, the Patriot man/machine cockpit distributed cognition system appears to suffer a condensation to a kind of absolute zero, a grossly simplified behavioral state, unable to properly differentiate friend from foe. More complicated military systems currently under consideration – that will remove the man entirely from the cockpit – will likely display more convoluted but equally debilitating failure patterns.

A recognizably similar analysis of the Patriot fratricide incidents can be found in Scharre (2016), absent the information and control theory formalism.

An apparently similar cockpit ground-state collapse that has – for obvious reasons – not been studied by the defense science establishement can be found in US drone operations in Pakistan (Columbia 2012; Stanford/NYU 2012). In addition to identified killings, heavily armed MQ-1B Predator and MQ-9 Reaper drones are operated remotely with some considerable latency under a 'pattern-of-life' analysis that targets groups of men who bear certain signatures or defining characteristics associated with terrorist activities but whose identities are not known (Stanford/NYU 2012, p. 12). The Columbia report estimates that, for Pakistan in 2011, some 11-34% of drone fatalities were civilians. The Bureau of Investigative Journalism (2013) estimates that, through July, 2013, in total, 11-37% of drone kills in Pakistan were civilians.

Failure modes of existing large scale, massively parallel systems, like power blackouts, cloud computing outages, and Internet viruses, will, as multicore technology relentlessly advances, become failure modes of physically small devices having similar numbers of components. These will have been tasked with controlling critical real time operations across a broad swath of civilian enterprise, consequent on fascination with, and blind faith in, technology with unacknowledged system fallibilities, reinforced by organizational culture. Such devices will, in addition, be subject to induced failure by unfriendly external agents.

## Chapter 8

# Case history: the Rand fire service models

## 8.1 Introduction

Stuart Russell, coauthor of the fundamental text *Artificial Intelligence: A Modern Approach*, characterizes the path to AI disaster as follows (Bohannon 2015)

> The basic scenario is explicit or implicit value misalignment: AI systems given objectives that don't take into account all the elements that humans care about.

Beginning in the early 1970's, New York City devolved fire service deployment policies onto a set of simple computerized operations research models that 'optimized' the system according to minimization of a *model-calculated* travel time for the first responding unit from firehouse to fire based on euclidean distance (R. Wallace and D. Wallace 1977; D. Wallace and R. Wallace 1998, 2011). Humans, of course, want to minimize loss of life, injuries, and property damage. This disjunction continues to be writ large upon the city.

Some context. Unlike an ambulance response, for which *actual* travel time to a patient – not euclidean distance – is a sine qua non, a fire department must, on each response, construct an entire hospital de novo around a 'patient' becoming exponentially sicker: In general, fires grow at exponential rates in time, depending on the nature of the fuel load, until an explosive flashover occurs.

Typically, a set of mixed fire companies is sent on a first alarm: two ladder companies to carry out forcible entry, venting, and rescue, and two or three engine companies to stretch hose and put water on a fire, under the overall supervision of a battalion chief. The subsequent fire ground activities are as choreographed as a ballet, with the battalion chief acting as a real-time improvisational choreographer. It is a high art.

The arrival of a first responding unit is necessary, but not sufficient: a single fire company can do little but call for help, and, in any event, the euclidean distance of the first responding unit from the fire, or even the actual travel time, are not measures of loss of life, injury, or property damage.

As New York City Rand researcher Edward Ignall – one of the principal architects of the Rand fire models – stated in a memo titled 'What is a minute of response time worth?' (Ignall 1972) written on the eve of deployment of the fire service models,

> First: We do not have response times. The best we can do are Euclidean distances from an alarm box near the incident to the house of the first arriving engine and the house of the first arriving ladder. Actual... response times may not be in... correspondence with these distances for several reasons...
>
> Second: We do not have good measures of the extent of the fire when fire companies arrive and of the damage once it has been extinguished...
>
> Third: Delays in discovering fires are sometimes long, sometimes short... they are probably more variable than response times...
>
> Fourth: Some fires grow quickly others grow slowly....

Ignall finds that 'Effects like these can cripple a naive approach to estimating the value of response time', a conclusion reached by independent researchers five years after the Rand model deployment (R. Wallace and D. Wallace 1977; D. Wallace and R. Wallace 1998, 2011).

## 8.2 More Context

Extreme events – floods, hurricanes, great accidents, large fires, and such like – delimit and define our lives individually and in community. The ability to control both the occurrence and consequences of such extremes is the hallmark of effective government, one that retains the 'mandate of heaven'. Properly managed emergency services are created precisely to cope with the greatest expected extreme event. An effective flood control system is not designed on the basis of the average flow of a river, but on expectation of the hundred-year flood.

Urban fire protection is, like most military or paramilitary organizations, arranged in a hierarchical pyramid. As stated, individual neighborhood engine and ladder companies, commanded by a lieutenant or captain, are organized into battalions of four or five units under battalion chief who directs combined operations on the fire ground. Usually, all or most of the units of a battalion, including the chief, will be dispatched on the first alarm to fires within a geographic response district.

If a fire escapes the control of the first responding battalion, then other, generally geographically adjacent, battalions, with their chiefs, are called to the fire, and the combined force is commanded by a division chief. If a fire becomes very large indeed, then several division chiefs, and their subordinate sets of units, may be called to operate under the joint command of an even more senior experienced officer. Such 'multiple alarm' fires constitute a particularly intense form of interaction between battalions.

'Relocation' occurs when a fire company from another neighborhood is assigned to the empty firehouse of a company busy at a fire for a long period. It is another index of the inability of a locally assigned battalion to promptly control and contain fires. Relocation, as a 'dynamic correction factor', nonetheless decreases the strength of one or more battalions adjacent to that in which all or most fire companies are busy, although not by as much as the calling of a full multiple alarm, and represents another form of interaction between battalions.

If a fire subsequently occurs in a battalion weakened by either relocation or by assignment of its own units to a multiple alarm fire, the widespread 'move-ups' – even further relocation – of surrounding units at a further distance may become necessary, spreading the service deficit. Fires occurring within battalions weakened by relocation or move-ups will likely be seriously underserviced on the first alarm, resulting in the growth of some to multiple alarm status. It is clear that too strong an interaction between battalions – too much need for exchange of fire companies – can quickly lead to the system-wide instability termed 'falling behind the fires' by firefighters. Urban fire occurrence is sharply peaked in both space and time, suggesting that assignment of sufficient numbers of quasi-independent battalions to neighborhoods on the basis of service need is the sine qua non of fire service system stability.

Remarkably, within the United States – and in New York City – large, rapidly-spreading structural fires, 'conflagrations', are not rare. The National Fire Protection Handbook (NFPA 1976) lists some such 446 fires between 1900 and 1967, a dozen between 1964 and 1974. The Chelsea, Massachusetts, conflagration of October 1973 destroyed 300 buildings, and the Berkeley/Oakland Hills conflagration of 1991 destroyed some 2000. Within New York City, the 1963 Rossville, Staten Island wildfire destroyed over 100 homes. A 2006 self-dynamic firestorm consumed ten large industrial buildings in Brooklyn's Greenpoint Terminal, and the Breezy Point, Queens conflagration associated with hurricane Sandy destroyed 126 homes in 2012.

Even within this highly ambiguous context, until the early 1970's, fire extinguishment and most other emergency services in the US were regarded much in the same spirit as a flood control system, designed to contain the 'hundred year disaster', be it a conflagration, accident, chemical spill, civil disturbance, or whatever. That view, however, changed with the introduction of operations research (OR) methods for fire service management in the 1970's, long after such methodologies had been largely discredited within the business community for the management of complex enterprises, except for the simplest of toll booth or warehouse problems (Ackoff 1979).

New York City was first to adopt the OR methodology for emergency service management, using the simplistic 'response time' (i.e., euclidean distance) models excoriated by Ignall in 1972. The catastrophic effects of these models, developed by the New York City Rand Institute but distributed nationally by the US Department of Housing and Urban Development, have been detailed elsewhere at great length under an Investigator Award in Health Policy Research from the Robert Wood Johnson Foundation (D. Wallace and R. Wallace 1998, 2011). The outcomes were literally catastrophic, seeing entire neighborhoods depopulated by 'South Bronx' outbreaks of contagious fire and abandonment, and triggering a dynamic in which the social structures of adjacent neighborhoods collapsed under the influx of demoralized refugees from nearby burning minority communities, with devastating impact on the subsequent spread of the AIDS epidemic (Wallace 1988).

The Rand service cuts and their effects on service delivery can be summarized as follows. Beginning in late 1972, the Rand models were implemented with the incremental closing of fire companies in the sections of the city with most overcrowding and the highest incidence of fire, since fire companies had been established in them close together because of fire hazard. A 'euclidean distance' model – as Ignall put it – would, of course, automatically target such neighborhoods for service reduction.

Between 1972 and 1976, some thirty-five fire companies, about 10% of the total number, plus essential firefighting supervisory units (battalions and divisions), fifty firefighting units total, were closed in, or permanently relocated from, areas with high incidence of fire. In 1974 the inital response to fires, a very critical factor, was reduced from three engines and two ladders to two each. In 1975 one firefighter was removed from each remaining company, another critical reduction that has been only partially restored. Firefighting staff declined from over 14,000 to about 10,000. Further closures, adding to the service deficit carried over since the 1970's, have continued sporadically, with routine nighttime unit closings and the Bloomberg Administration, in its last year – 2013 – attempting to use the updated versions of Rand's Firehouse Siting and Response Time models to justify closing an additional 20 fire companies.

And the band played on.

## 8.3   Impact of the Rand Models

A battery of indices of fire size and seriousness showed a significant and persisting degradation in the ability to control and contain structural fires after these cuts. See Wallace and Wallace (1977) and the D. Wallace references for details. Figure 8.1, covering monthly data from January 1968 through May 1990, is an example of such an index. It is a time series equivalent to the analysis of covariance (Green 1979) constructed by principal component analysis of the covariance matrix of the log of the number of structural fires and the log of the number of 'serious' fires – those requiring five or more fire companies for extinguishment. Serious fires are most likely to leave visible fire damage, a key component in the cycle of contagious fire and building abandonment described in the D. Wallace references.

The logs of the monthly values are projected onto the 'contrast' eigenvector, which has components of differing sign, giving an index that can be interpreted as an analog of the rate of serious fires per number of building fires, but without the statistical difficulties associated with the use of ratios. Each monthly value of the index can be back-solved to give a different relation between the number of building fires and the number of serious fires. The larger the index value, the greater the slope of that relation ship. The calculation is straightforward. For this example, the index is given by the relation: Index=0.55 ln(number serious fires)-0.83 ln(number structural fires). Higher index values indicate greater rates at which building fires become serious fires, over this period. Other periods would require separate analysis.

Note how the service cuts of late 1972 caused an immediate and persistent step function rise in the index through 1984, and further cuts and the long-term effects of past ones subsequently caused a marked upward drift, worse even than at the height of the 1970's fire crisis.

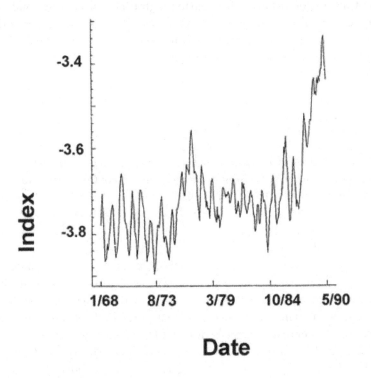

**Fig. 8.1** From Wallace 1993. Smoothed fire control index, January 1968 to May 1990, using a time series form of ANCOVA, a monotonic measure of the number of serious fires per unit number of building fires. Higher values indicate a greater rate at which structural fires cause visible or unrepairable damage, triggering contagious urban decay and determining the need for service exchange between battalions.

Between 1972 and 1976, the average annual hours of 'relocation service' increased from 57 to 148 per engine, and from 62 to 152 per ladder company. Paraphrasing Wallace and Wallace (1977), temporary relocation of fire companies into areas depleted of firefighting units is a traditional practice of fire departments. While the procedure does indeed help the depleted areas somewhat, it represents on the whole a degradation of fire service. Relocation is supposed to be a 'dynamic correction factor'. Following the company closings of 1972-1975, however, relocation became, for some high fire incidence neighborhoods, a primary means of service delivery, a symptom of serious service instability. Beginning in April, 1975, New York City began suffering repeated borough wide depletion of fire companies in which all borough units were simultaneously busy fighting fires. This has required massive, time consuming fire company relocations from borough to borough that have since, and for the first time in the City's history, become routine. These mass relocations strip large areas of fire service for long periods of time, now regularly, and deaths directly attributable to them have been documented.

As Wallace and Wallace (1977) put it, 'It goes almost without saying that units responding from one borough to another on the first alarm will encounter a seriously extended fire'.

These relocation crises contributed materially to the rapid and contagious coupled results of fire, housing abandonment and forced population transfer which devastated large sections of the South Bronx, Central Harlem and the Lower East Side in Manhattan, and Bushwick, Bedford-Stuyvesant, Brownsville-East New York in Brooklyn, with catastrophic long-term impacts on public health and order (R. Wallace and D. Wallace 1990; R. Wallace 1988, 1990; D. Wallace and R. Wallace 1998, 2011).

From 1972 to 1976 the total hours of worktime on structural fires by engine companies, a composite index of building fire severity and number, rose from 44,000 to 63,000 hours, with virtually all of the increase heavily concentrated in those areas of the city that already had the highest rates of building fire, and from which most fire company eliminations and permanent relocations were made (Wallace and Wallace 1977).

Large areas of the Bronx section of the city, which holds more than a million people, lost over half their population and housing between 1970 and 1980 (R. Wallace 1990), a circumstance unprecedented in a modern industrialized nation during peacetime. After 1976 the number and size of fires declined as affected neighborhoods burned out and middle class residents of nearby communities evacuated the city, leaving their larger apartments to be reoccupied by the displaced minority poor (D. Wallace and R. Wallace 1998, 2011). See the D. Wallace references for details of the mechanisms of contagious urban decay and density-dependent thresholds driven by fire and other municipal service deficits.

In spite of this decline in the annual average demand for fire service, relocation crises continued to occur in New York City during the period covered by Figure 8.1. On December 27, 1989, a day on which seven multiple alarm fires – four in the borough of the Bronx alone – tied up some 272 fire companies and 1140 firefighters in a rolling service collapse which lasted from 2:00 PM well into evening and saw 61 injuries and two deaths (Lee and Singleton 1990). The crisis was dominated by a 5-alarm fire at a Bronx electric power substation just after 1:00 PM. By early afternoon, no Bronx-based fire companies were available for dispatch, as reported by a senior fire department dispatcher who must remain anonymous.

From a public relations perspective, New York City's fire/abandonment catastrophe has been successfully explained away as 'arson' – deliberate fire-setting by 'greedy landlords' from one political sector, or by 'racial minority tenants' from another sector. Thus the impacts of the incremental 'money saving' reductions on the ability of emergency services to function properly, and the very considerable consequences of their failure, have largely been obscured, allowing continual 'refinement' and usage of the Rand fire deployment models.

## 8.4 Response to the Disaster

The origin and impacts of the Rand fire service cuts in New York City were, however, the subject of extended hearings held by the New York State Assembly Republican Task Force on Urban Fire Protection, which concluded in 1978 that (Mega 1978)

> [T]he level of fire protection provided by the New York Fire Department... contributed to the deterioration of neighborhoods and has increased hazard to human life, and there is strong indication... [that] undue loss of life has occurred. While the fiscal crisis [0f 1975] has been a major influence, fire department policies dating back to 1969 laid the ground work for this deterioration.
>
> Commencing in 1969 New York City hired the Rand Corporation to develop computer models, such as used in

defense planning, to improve the efficiency of fire services.
The models they developed were simplistic and inadequate,
failing to consider many needed variables, and employed
methodology inappropriate to the intended purposes...

There is strong indication that as neighborhoods dete-
riorated, the fire department redlined [them]... further has-
tening deterioration and causing the fire blight to spread
to previously viable neighborhoods.

In a preamble to that report, Perry Duryea, minority leader of the New
York State Assembly, stated (Duryea 1978)

[There] are indications that the City Planning Commis-
sion and other agencies condoned [fire service] reductions
in the context of a 'planned shrinkage' policy... [which has]
resulted in the unwarranted loss of life and destruction of
city neighborhoods.

Then-NYC Housing Commissioner Roger Starr (1976) concluded, regarding 'deteriorating' neighborhoods in New York, that 'we could cut back
on city services accordingly, realizing considerable savings in the process'.

A more explicit statement by Stone (1977) concerns the infamous
burnout of the South Bronx:

The bleak truth is that this [burnout] is the *natural* and
*inevitable* consequence of a shrinking city. The destruction,
poverty and hopelessness that cluster around the burnt-out
wrecks is abhorrent. That something should be done to
stop it is the immediate reaction. That something should
be done to speed it up is nearer the mark.

Again, for a more complete accounting of the impacts of the Rand fire
service reductions on patterns of public health and order, see D. Wallace
and R. Wallace (1998, 2011).

As stated, the New York City Fire Department continues applying the
Rand Firehouse Siting and Travel Time models, and as late as 2013, used
them to justify the closing of twenty more fire companies, a move wisely
stopped by the New York City Council.

## 8.5 'Delocalization' of Fire Service Demand

We suppose that Battalions are organized into a spatial grid as nodes in a basically random network of interactions, as a first approximation. These nodes are linked by the need to share resources, by relocation, 'move-ups', or by direct assignment to multiple alarm fires. We can then apply the random network phase transition arguments of Chapter 3, leading to the modular network results of equation (3.7) and figure (3.1), adapted here as figure 8.2.

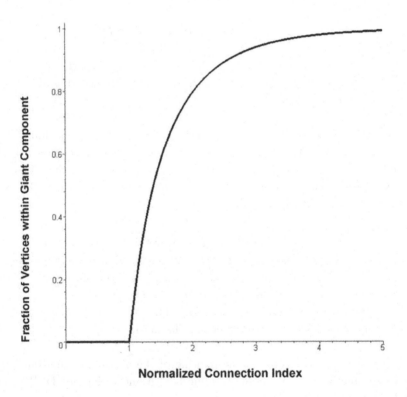

**Normalized Connection Index**

Fig. 8.2  Fraction of battalions incorporated within an active giant component as a function of the normalized connection index linking them. Too much interaction, after a threshold, quickly leads to 'falling behind the fires' until all available units are at working incidents.

The normalized connection index $a$ of equation (3.7), in this circumstance, is determined by the ability of an individual battalion to extinguish its own fires quickly without need of aid from others. Thus the normalized connection index is profoundly affected by such factors as (a) the number of fire companies within a battalion, (b) the staffing levels of those companies, and (c) the response policies on the first alarm. If too few, understaffed fire companies respond to a fire on the first alarm, then either the battalion will be busy for a long time, requiring relocation coverage from adjacent battalions, or the fire will grow rapidly to multiple alarm status, requiring even more external service.

Wallace (1993), by contrast, used complicated renormalization arguments on percolation processes to obtain essentially the same qualitative result.

Nonrandom network topologies would be expected to shift the threshold of figure 8.2, and to change the rate of increase. The general pattern, however should remain much the same: sharp increase in the giant component of 'all Battalions busy' after a saturation point determined by the number, response policy and staffing of fire units located in high fire incidence neighborhoods.

## 8.6   Control Theory Perspective

Delocalization can also be viewed as a failure mode of an inherently unstable control system, in the sense of the Data Rate Theorem of Section 1.3. Fire occurrence is, of course, inherently unstable in the sense that building fires can grow exponentially in time until flashover and consequent involvement of adjacent buildings in a congested urban setting. Thus the 'control signal' of fire service response, instantiated by the prompt arrival of sufficient firefighting resources, must exceed the rate of 'topological information' generated by the expanding fire. Clearly, figure 8.1, essentially the rate at which building fires become 'serious', represents an inverse control signal index. When that index fails – the rate of serious fires per building fire exceeds a threshold – real-time borough-wide unit availability crises occur.

Let $\rho$ represent the rate of demand for fire service. The Data Rate Theorem implies that the rate of control information must exceed the rate at which the system generates 'topological information', a condition we write as $\mathcal{H} > \alpha$. Our assumption is that both $\mathcal{H}$ and $\alpha$ depend on $\rho$, i.e., that

$$\mathcal{H}(\rho) > f(\rho)\alpha_0$$
$$f(\rho), \ \alpha_0 > 0. \tag{8.1}$$

Making the Black-Scholes approximation of Section 7.10 – leading to analogs of Eq. (7.39) – for $\mathcal{H}(\rho)$ and using a similar first-order expression for $f(\rho)$ gives the condition for stability as

$$\kappa_1\rho + \kappa_2 > (\kappa_3\rho + \kappa_4)\alpha_0$$
$$\frac{\kappa_1\rho + \kappa_2}{\kappa_3\rho + \kappa_4} > \alpha_0 > 0. \tag{8.2}$$

At low $\rho$ the stability condition is $\kappa_2/\kappa_4 > \alpha_0$. At high $\rho$ it becomes $\kappa_1/\kappa_3 > \alpha_0$. If $\kappa_2/\kappa_4 \gg \kappa_1/\kappa_3$, then at some intermediate value of $\rho$ the essential inequality may be violated, leading to system-wide loss of fire control. See figure 8.3.

## 8.7   Implications

At present, the ecological machinery for 'South Bronx' burnout – the interaction of poverty and extreme housing overcrowding (Wallace 1990) – has rewound in New York City, while the housing-related municipal services that act as a kind of immune system against contagious urban decay remain at 1970's 'planned shrinkage' levels. The management of a real-time emergency service, fire protection, has been abdicated into the hands(?) of an elaborate AI system whose internal algorithms – following the Rand models – do not reflect current or potential patterns of injury and property loss, precisely the disjunction Stuart Russell cites as a canonical failure mode of an AI system.

Further, figure 8.2 and the control theory model leading to figure 8.3 imply, in consonance with earlier chapters of this book, that real time failure of this system can be a sudden, highly punctuated, collapse into a pathological ground state, taking the perspective of equation (7.56).

In the context of current patterns of poverty, overcrowding, climate change (hurricane Sandy), and an increasingly volatile international political environment (9/11), leaving fire service deployment to a 'Terminator' AI system whose principal purpose was to justify closing fire companies in minority voting blocs seems an act of monumental stupidity.

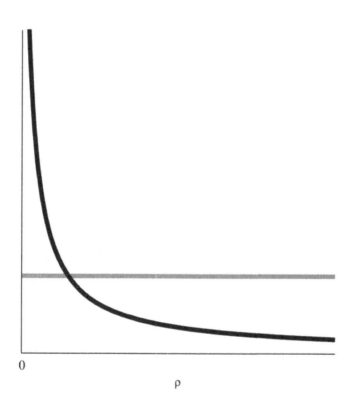

Fig. 8.3 The horizontal line represents the critical limit $\alpha_0$. If $\kappa_2/\kappa_4 \gg \kappa_1/\kappa_3$, at some intermediate point of demand for fire service $\rho$ the ratio $(\kappa_1\rho+\kappa_2)/(\kappa_3\rho+\kappa_4)$ falls below that limit and system-wide instability of fire extinguishment becomes manifest.

Chapter 9

# Autonomous vehicles

*...[T]he psychological actions of drivers make traffic different from any other flow (Orosz et al. 2010).*

## 9.1 Introduction

Previous chapters use a variety of mathematical models to explore the dynamics of rapid-acting, inherently unstable command, communication and control systems ($C^3$) that are cognitive in the sense that they must, in an appropriate 'real time', evaluate a large number of possible actions and choose a small subset for implementation. As discussed at some length, such choice decreases uncertainty, in a precise formal manner, and reduction in uncertainty implies the existence of an information source. Here we examine dynamics related to vehicle-to-vehicle and vehicle-to-infrastructure (V2V/V2I) automated systems from the perspective of the Data Rate Theorem, extend the argument to more general phase transition analogs, study instability as onset of 'turbulent' modes, and then use an information bottleneck method to derive similar results, developing statistical tools useful at different scales and levels of organization. V2V/V2I automated ground vehicle systems operate along geodesics in a densely convoluted 'map quotient space' – more fully described later – that is in contrast to the problem of air traffic control, where locally stable vehicle paths are seen as thick braid geodesics in a simpler Euclidean quotient space (Hu et al. 2001). Such geodesics are generalizations of the streamline characteristics of hydrodynamic flow (e.g., Landau and Lifshitz 1987).

## 9.2 Data Rate Theorem Redux

Unlike aircraft, which can be constructed to be inherently stable in linear flight by placing the aerodynamic center of pressure sufficiently behind the mechanical center of gravity, the complex nature of road geometry and density of vehicular traffic ensures that V2V/V2I systems will be inherently unstable, requiring constant input of control information to prevent, at the least, traffic jams and tie-ups.

Again recalling Section 1.3, a linear 'plant' near a nonequilibrium steady state can be described by an n-dimensional state vector $x_t$ at time $t$. The dynamics are given by the vector equation

$$x_{t+1} = Ax_t + \textsf{Stochastic and Control terms} \qquad (9.1)$$

where $A$ is an appropriate $n \times n$ system matrix and the other terms are also linear.

Let $\mathcal{H}$ be the control information rate needed to stabilize a rapidly-responding but inherently unstable $C^3$ system. By the Data Rate Theorem (DRT), $\mathcal{H}$ must be greater than the rate at which 'topological information' is generated. For the linear system of Eq.(9.1), that rate is

$$\alpha \equiv \log[|\det(A^u)|]$$

where det is the determinant and $A^u$ is the decoupled component of the matrix $A$ having eigenvalues $\geq 1$ (Nair et al. 2007).

For a fixed road network, it is evident that the central topological variate is the vehicle density that defines system dynamics under the 'fundamental diagram' relating vehicular flow per unit time to vehicle density per unit length. See figure (9.1), showing, for a Rome street, the number of vehicles/hour as a function of vehicles/mile. Behavior shifts from regular to 'uncontrolled' at about 40 v/mi.

Under such circumstances, vehicle density $\rho$ is the only parameter defining the rate of topological information generation, and we can, as in Chapter 8, write the stability relation of the DRT as

$$\mathcal{H}(\rho) > \alpha = f(\rho)\alpha_0 \qquad (9.2)$$

where $\alpha_0$ is a road network constant and $f(\rho)$ is a positive, monotonically increasing function. Recall the Black-Scholes argument from Section 7.10 . We approximate the 'cost' of $\mathcal{H}(\rho)$ as a function of the 'investment' $\rho$ as

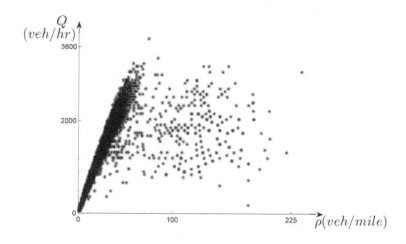

Fig. 9.1 Vehicles per hour as a function of vehicle density per mile for a street in Rome (Blandin et al. 2011). Both streamline geodesic flow and the phase transition to 'crystallized' turbulent flow at critical traffic density are evident. Some of the states may be 'supercooled', i.e., delayed 'crystallization' in spite of high traffic density. 'Fine structure' can be expected within both geodesic and turbulent modes.

a linear function. Similarly, we can, again in first order, approximate $f(\rho)$ as a linear function, giving the limit condition for stability as

$$\frac{\kappa_1 \rho + \kappa_2}{\kappa_2 \rho + \kappa_4} > \alpha_0. \tag{9.3}$$

Again, for $\rho = 0$ the stability condition is $\kappa_2/\kappa_4 > \alpha_0$. At large $\rho$ this becomes $\kappa_1/\kappa_2 > \alpha_0$. If $\kappa_2/\kappa_4 \gg \kappa_1/\kappa_2$, the stability condition may be violated at high traffic density, and instability becomes manifest, as at higher densities in figure (9.1). See figure (8.3).

A more complex model, based explicitly on the cognitive nature of control systems, provides deeper insight.

## 9.3 Phase Transition

As argued in earlier chapters, the essence of cognition is active choice. As described above, a cognitive system, confronted with uncertainty, must choose a small set of actual responses from a larger set of those available to it. Such choice reduces uncertainty, and the reduction of uncertainty implies the existence of an information source. The argument can be made quite formally as in Section 3.2.

Recall that, given an information source associated with an inherently unstable, rapid-fire cognitive $C^3$ system – said to be 'dual' to it – an equivalence class algebra emerges by choosing different system origin states $a_0$ and defining the equivalence of two subsequent states at times $m, n > 0$, written as $a_m, a_n$, by the existence of high-probability meaningful paths connecting them to the same origin point. As described in earlier chapters, disjoint partition by equivalence class, essentially similar to orbit equivalence classes in dynamical systems, defines a symmetry groupoid associated with the cognitive process. Again, groupoids represent generalizations of the group concept in which there is not necessarily a product defined for each possible element pair as in a disjoint union of groups (Weinstein 1996).

As argued above, equivalence classes define a set of cognitive dual information sources available to the inherently unstable $C^3$ system, creating a large groupoid, with each orbit corresponding to a transitive groupoid whose disjoint union is the full groupoid. Each subgroupoid is associated with its own dual information source, and larger groupoids will have richer dual information sources than smaller.

Let $X_{G_i}$ be the $C^3$ dual information source associated with the groupoid element $G_i$, and let $Y$ be the information source associated with incoming environmental information, in a large sense See Wallace (2012b, 2015b) for details of how environmental regularities imply the existence of an environmental information source.

As before, we construct a Morse Function in terms of the control information $\mathcal{H}$ (Pettini 2007):

Let $H(X_{G_i}, Y) \equiv H_{G_i}$ be the joint uncertainty of the two information sources. Define a Boltzmann-like pseudoprobability as

$$P[H_{G_i}] = \frac{\exp[-H_{G_i}/\kappa\mathcal{H}]}{\sum_j \exp[-H_{G_j}/\kappa\mathcal{H}]} \qquad (9.4)$$

where $\kappa$ is an appropriate constant depending on the particular system and its linkages to control signals, and the sum is over the different possible cognitive modes of the full system.

A 'free energy' Morse Function $F$ can be defined as

$$\exp[-F/\kappa\mathcal{H}] \equiv \sum_j \exp[-H_{G_j}/\kappa\mathcal{H}]. \qquad (9.5)$$

Given the inherent groupoid structure, it is possible to apply an extension of Landau's picture of phase transition (Pettini, 2007). Recall that, in

Landau's formulation of spontaneous symmetry breaking, phase transitions driven by temperature changes occur as alteration of system symmetry, with higher energies at higher temperatures being more symmetric. The shift between symmetries is highly punctuated in the temperature index, here the minimum necessary control information rate $\mathcal{H}$ under the Data Rate Theorem for unstable control systems. Typically, such arguments involve only a very limited number of possible phases.

In this context, Birkhoff's (1960 p.146) perspective on the central role of groups in fluid mechanics is of considerable interest:

> [Group symmetry] underlies the entire theories of dimensional analysis and modeling. In the form of 'inspectional analysis' it greatly generalizes these theories... [R]ecognition of groups... often makes possible reductions in the number of independent variables involved in partial differential equations... [E]ven after the number of independent variables is reduced to one... the resulting system of ordinary differential equations can often be integrated most easily by the use of group-theoretic considerations.

We assert that, for 'cognitive fluids' like vehicle traffic flows, groupoid generalizations of group theory become central.

Decline in the richness of control information $\mathcal{H}$, or in the ability of that information to influence the system, characterized by $\kappa$, can lead to punctuated decline in the complexity of cognitive process possible within the $C^3$ system, driving it into a ground state collapse that may not be actual 'instability' but rather a kind of dead zone in which, using the armed drone example, 'all possible targets are enemies'. This condition represents a dysfunctionally simple cognitive groupoid structure roughly akin to certain individual human psychopathologies (Wallace 2015c).

Below, we will argue that, for large-scale autonomous vehicle/intelligent infrastructure systems, the ground state dead zone involves massive, propagating tie-ups that far more resemble power network blackouts than traditional traffic jams. The essential feature is the role of vehicle road density $\rho$. Most of the topology of the inherently unstable vehicle/road system will be 'factored out' via the construction of geodesics in a topological quotient space, so that $\rho$ remains the only possible index of the rate of topological information generation for the DRT. Thus, in Eqs(9.4) and (9.5), $\mathcal{H}$ is replaced by the ratio $\mathcal{H}/f(\rho)$, where $f$ is a dimensionless monotonic increasing positive function.

For a fixed $\mathcal{H}$, increasing $\rho$ is then equivalent to lowering the 'temperature', and the system passes from high symmetry 'free flow' to different forms of 'crystalline' structure – broken symmetries representing platoons, shock fronts, traffic jams, and the like.

Again, making an exactly-solvable Black-Scholes approximation, the 'cost' of the control information $\mathcal{H}$ can, in first order, be expressed in terms of $\rho$ as

$$\mathcal{H} \approx \kappa_1 \rho + \kappa_2 \qquad (9.6)$$

where $\kappa_i \geq 0$. Again, in first order, taking $f(\rho) \approx \kappa_3 \rho + \kappa_4 > 0$, we obtain an effective 'temperature' as

$$\kappa \mathcal{H} / f(\rho) \approx \frac{\kappa_1 \rho + \kappa_2}{\kappa_3 \rho + \kappa_4} \qquad (9.7)$$

with limits $\kappa_2/\kappa_4, \rho \to 0$ and $\kappa_1/\kappa_3, \rho \to \infty$. Again, assuming $\kappa_2/\kappa_4 \gg \kappa_1/\kappa_3$, increase in traffic density will quickly bring the effective 'temperature' below critical values, triggering collapse into a dysfunctional ground state, even though, in this case, the system might remain formally 'stable' under the Data Rate Theorem at the limit $\kappa_1/\kappa_3 > 0$. Thus we begin to explore variations in stability beyond the DRT itself.

The underlying dynamic can be treated in finer detail by viewing the initial phase transition as the first-order onset of a kind of 'turbulence', a transition from free flow to 'flock' structures like those studied in 'active matter' physics. Indeed, the traffic engineering perspective is quite precisely the inverse of mainstream active matter studies, which Ramaswamy (2010) describes as follows:

> It is natural for a condensed matter physicist to regard a coherently moving flock of birds, beasts, or bacteria as an orientationally ordered phase of living matter. ...[M]odels showed a nonequilibrium phase transition from a disordered state to a flock with long-range order... in the particle velocities as the noise strength was decreased or the concentration of particles was raised.

In traffic engineering, the appearance of such 'long range order' is the first stage of a traffic jam (e.g., Kerner and Klenov 2009), a relation made explicit by Helbing (2001 Section VI) in his comprehensive review of traffic and related self-driven many-particle systems.

While flocking and schooling have obvious survival value against predation for animals in three-dimensional venues, long-range order – aggregation

– among blood cells flowing along arteries is a blood clot and can be rapidly fatal.

## 9.4 Turbulence

The 'free energy' function $F$ in equation (9.5) can be used to explore dynamics within a particular system phase defined by the associated groupoid.

Given a vector of system parameters $\mathbf{K}$, in standard manner it is possible to define an 'entropy' from $F$ as the Legendre transform

$$S \equiv F(\mathbf{K}) - \mathbf{K} \cdot \nabla_{\mathbf{K}} F \tag{9.8}$$

and a nonequilibrium Onsager stochastic differential equation for dynamics in terms of the gradients in $S$ (de Groot and Mazur 1984), which can be written in one dimension as

$$dK_t = -[\mu \partial S / \partial K_t] dt + \sigma K_t dB_t \tag{9.9}$$

where $\mu$ is a diffusion coefficient. The last term represents a macroscopic volatility – proportional to the parameter $K$ – in which $dB_t$ is a noise term that may not be white, i.e., the quadratic variation $[B_t, B_t]$ may not be proportional to $t$. While details will depend on the particular circumstances, such systems are subject to a distressingly rich spectrum of possible instabilities (e.g., Khasminskii 2012). The full set of equations would involve properly indexed sums across the parameters making up the vector $\mathbf{K}$.

Allowing discontinuous Levy-like stochastic jumps, equation (9.9) can be solved explicitly, provided $K$ can be factored out and the equation set reexpressed as

$$dK_t = K_{t-} dY_t \tag{9.10}$$

where $Y_t$ is a stochastic process, and $t-$ indicates left-continuous. Taking $\Delta Y_t = Y_t - Y_{t-}$ as representing the jump process, the solution is in terms of the Doleans-Dade exponential (Protter 1990)

$$K_t = \exp(Y_t - \frac{1}{2}[Y_t, Y_t]_t^C) \Pi_{s \le t} (1 + \Delta Y_s) \exp(-\Delta Y_s) \tag{9.11}$$

where $[Y_t, Y_t]_t^C$ is the path-by-path continuous part of the quadratic variation of $Y_t$. This can be expressed

$$[Y_t, Y_t]_t^C = [Y_t, Y_t] - \sum_{0 \le s \le t} (\Delta Y_s)^2. \tag{9.12}$$

The product term in equation (9.11), with jump processes having nonzero $\Delta$, converges.

Invoking the mean value theorem in equation (9.11), if, heuristically, $dY_t < 1/2d[Y,Y]_t^C$, then the expectation of $K$, $E(K)$, converges to zero. Otherwise, small perturbations will grow exponentially in expectation. This is an essential component of modern theories of turbulence (e.g., Ruelle 1983) and will prove central in understanding traffic flow instabilities. The phenomenon is roughly analogous to models of 'first order' phase transition, for example the sudden crystallization of a supercooled liquid when its container is tapped or a seed crystal is introduced. Higher order phase transitions involve discontinuities in higher order derivatives of system parameters and phase transitions may involve discontinuities at multiple 'derivative' scales.

A simple example. If a system following equation (9.10) has been initially placed in a characteristic eigenmode – e.g., the smooth part of a 'fundamental diagram' flow on some traffic network – then the dynamic equation for deviations in some parameter $K(t)$ from that mode can be written, in first order, as

$$dK_t \approx aK_t dt + \sigma K_t dW_t \qquad (9.13)$$

where $dW_t$ represents white noise having uniform spectrum. Then, using the Ito chain rule,

$$d\log[K]_t \approx (a - \sigma^2/2)dt + \sigma dW_t. \qquad (9.14)$$

The expectation is then

$$E[K]_t \propto \exp[(a - \sigma^2/2)t] \qquad (9.15)$$

so that, if $a < \sigma^2/2$, $E[K] \to 0$. $\sigma^2$ then – quite counterintuitively as described in Wallace (2016) – is a kind of control information in the sense of the Data Rate Theorem that serves to stabilize system dynamics. For an inherently unstable traffic flow system at low traffic density $\sigma^2 = \omega\mathcal{H}$, where $\mathcal{H}$ is the minimum necessary control information to keep the vehicle on the road, and $\omega$ is the 'cost' of translation. Thus $\mathcal{H}$ represents the degree of independent control a driver or autonomous vehicle computer can exercise within local road flow, e.g., changing lanes, accelerating, slowing down, changing headway, predicting other vehicle maneuvers, detecting emerging bottlenecks, swerving, taking a different route, and so on.

Anticipating the argument, for traffic models below, we will argue that $\sigma^2$ must again be replaced by $\mathcal{H}(\rho)/g(\rho)$ where $g(\rho)$ is positive monontonic increasing. Then, antiparalleling the arguments of Belletti et al. (Bellitti

et al. 2015, Section 2.3), for this simple example a 'traffic Froude number'
(TFN) $\mathcal{F}$ that defines regimes of free and turbulent flow can be defined as

$$\mathcal{F} \equiv 1 - [a - \frac{1}{2}(\mathcal{H}(\rho)/g(\rho))] \tag{9.16}$$

where $\mathcal{H}(\rho)/g(\rho)$ is clearly a variant of Eq.(9.7) and $a$ is $2\alpha_0$ in Eq.(9.3).

When $\mathcal{F} > 1$, the system is in 'laminar' free-flow, and becomes 'turbulent' when $\mathcal{F} < 1$.

A more precise characterization, from this perspective, is that $\mathcal{H}(\rho)/g(\rho)$ represents a kind of viscosity index so that $\mathcal{F}$ is more akin to a Reynolds number than to a classical Froude number.

A difference between our approach and that of Bellitti et al. lies in the central object-of-interest. They invoke a hydrodynamic perspective involving the 'flow' of individual vehicles in a channel that finds 'instability' to be associated with unconstrained travel speed. The focus here is on the stability of geodesics in a complex topological quotient space $\mathcal{M}^{2n}/W(r)$ that will be more precisely defined below. This is, in a sense, the inverse of their problem.

As argued above, raising $\rho$ is equivalent to 'freezing' the system from 'liquid flow' to 'crystallized' broken symmetries – platoons, shock fronts, jams, and myriad other 'snowflake' fine structures.

$[Y_t^j, Y_t^j]_t^C$ may be further parameterized and, using the methods of Dzhaparidze and Spreij (1994), for colored noise, can be estimated from a time series data periodogram, as described in Wallace (2016). Increasing complexity in spectral structure is another marker of turbulence onset (Ruelle, 1983).

More specifically, for a stochastic process $X_t$ and a finite stopping time $T$, for each real number $\lambda$, the *periodogram* of $X$ at $T$ is defined as

$$I_T(X; \lambda) \equiv | \int_0^T \exp[i\lambda t] dX_t|^2. \tag{9.17}$$

Take $\epsilon$ as a real random variate that has a density function $r$ assumed to be symmetric around zero and examine, for any positive real number $L$,

$$E_\epsilon[I_T(X; L\epsilon] = \int_{-\infty}^{+\infty} I_T(X; Ls)r(s)ds. \tag{9.18}$$

Some work shows that, for $L \to \infty$,

$$E_\epsilon[I_T(X; L\epsilon)] \to [X_T, X_T]. \tag{9.19}$$

Thus the quadratic variation can be estimated from observed time series data, as routinely done in financial engineering. Presumably, both high and low frequency limits could be explored in this method, parallel to what was done in Belletti et al., (2015).

## 9.5   Information Bottleneck

Another modeling approach is via the information bottleneck method of
Tishby et al. (1999). As described in Section 7.11, the essential idea is that
the control information needed to stabilize an inherently unstable system,
which we write as $\mathcal{H}$, can be used to define an average distortion measure
in a rate distortion calculation. This involves an iterated application of the
Rate Distortion Theorem (Cover and Thomas 2006) to a control system
in which a series of 'orders' $y^n = y_1, ..., y_n$, having probability $p(y^n)$, is
sent through and the outcomes monitored as $\hat{y}^n = \hat{y}_1, ..., \hat{y}_n$. The distortion measure is now the minimum necessary control information for system
stability, $\mathcal{H}(y^n, \hat{y}^n)$. We can thus define an average 'distortion' $\hat{\mathcal{H}}$ as

$$\hat{\mathcal{H}} \equiv \sum_{y^n} p(y^n) \mathcal{H}(y^n, \hat{y}^n) \geq 0. \tag{9.20}$$

It then is possible to define a new, iterated, Rate Distortion Function
$\mathcal{R}(\hat{\mathcal{H}})$.

For simplicity, we take $\mathcal{R}$ to be a Gaussian RDF in $\hat{\mathcal{H}}$,

$$R(\hat{\mathcal{H}}) = 1/2 \log[\sigma^2/\hat{\mathcal{H}}] \ \hat{\mathcal{H}} < \sigma^2$$
$$R(\hat{\mathcal{H}}) = 0 \ \hat{\mathcal{H}} \geq \sigma^2. \tag{9.21}$$

Again, following Feynman (2000), information must be recognized as a
form of free energy and a Rate Distortion Function can be used to define
an 'entropy' as the Legendre transform

$$S = \mathcal{R}(\hat{\mathcal{H}}) - \hat{\mathcal{H}} d\mathcal{R}/d\hat{\mathcal{H}} \tag{9.22}$$

Taking Onsager's nonequilibrium thermodynamics perspective, the dynamics can, in first order, be characterized in terms of the gradients of $S$,
and we invoke an extended analog using the stochastic differential equation

$$d\hat{\mathcal{H}}_t = [-\mu dS/d\hat{\mathcal{H}}_t - F(\rho)]dt + \beta \hat{\mathcal{H}}_t dW_t$$
$$= [\frac{\mu}{2\hat{\mathcal{H}}_t} - F(\rho)]dt + \beta \hat{\mathcal{H}}_t dW_t \tag{9.23}$$

where $dW_t$ is standard white noise, and $F(\rho)$ is a function of traffic density
$\rho$, the only possible determinant of the rate of generation of system 'topological information', given the extreme topological factoring associated with
travel along a network. $\beta$ represents the magnitude of a 'volatility' noise
term independent of $\sigma^2$ in the definition of $\mathcal{R}$: higher $\mathcal{H}$, higher stochastic
jitter.

Applying the Ito chain rule to the expectation of $\hat{\mathcal{H}}_t^2$, it becomes possible to explore the second moment stability of the system (Khashminskii 2012). A simple calculation finds that the expectation for $\hat{\mathcal{H}}^2$ cannot be a real number unless the discriminant of a quadratic equation is nonnegative, giving the necessary condition

$$F(\rho) \geq \beta\sqrt{\mu}. \tag{9.24}$$

We force 'closure' to the model by taking $F(\rho)$ as given by Eq.(9.3), so that, again,

$$\frac{\kappa_1 \rho + \kappa_2}{\kappa_3 \rho + \kappa_4} \geq \beta\sqrt{\mu} \equiv \alpha_0 \tag{9.25}$$

with similar restrictions on the constants $\kappa_i$ for stability.

Other channel forms will have analogous limits on traffic density as a consequence of the convexity of the RDF. The interested readers might carry the calculation through for the 'real' channel, having $\mathcal{R}(\hat{\mathcal{H}}) = \sigma^2/\hat{\mathcal{H}}$.

## 9.6 Reconsidering V2V/V2I Systems

Kerner et al. (2015) explicitly apply insights from statistical physics to traffic flow, writing

> In many equilibrium... and dissipative metastable systems of natural science... there can be a spontaneous phase transition from one metastable phase to another metastable phase of a system. Such spontaneous phase transition occurs when a nucleus for the transition appears randomly in an initial metastable phase of the system: The growth of the nucleus leads to the phase transition. The nucleus can be a fluctuation within the initial system phase whose amplitude is equal or larger than an amplitude of a critical nucleus required for spontaneous phase transition. Nuclei for such spontaneous phase transitions can be observed in empirical and experimental studies of many equilibrium and dissipative metastable systems... There can also be another source for the occurrence of a nucleus, rather than fluctuations: A nucleus can be induced by an external disturbance applied to the initial phase. In this case, the phase transition is called an induced phase transition...

A Data Rate Theorem approach to stability and flow of autonomous vehicle/traffic control systems, via spontaneous symmetry breaking in cognitive groupoids, generalizes and extends these insights, implying a far more complex picture of control requirements for inherently unstable systems than is suggested by the Theorem itself, or by 'physics' models of phase transition. That is, 'higher order' instabilities can appear. Such systems can require inordinate levels of control information. Here, we find that $C^3$ systems may remain 'stable' in the strict sense of the DRT, but can collapse into a ground state analogous to certain psychopathologies, or, following the arguments above, into even more complicated pathological dynamics. In biological circumstances, such failures can be associated with the onset of senescence (Wallace 2014b, 2015b). Apparently, rapidly responding, and hence almost certainly inherently unstable, $C^3$ systems can display recognizable analogs to senility under fog-of-war demands.

Using these ideas, it becomes possible to formally represent the interaction of cognitive ground state collapse in autonomous vehicle/intelligent road systems with critical transitions in traffic flow.

Recall that, defining 'stability' as the ability to return, after perturbation, to the streamline geodesic trajectory of the embedding, topologically complex, road network, it is clear that individual autonomous vehicles are inherently unstable and require a constant flow of control information for safe operation, unlike aircraft that can, in fact, be made inherently stable by placing the center of pressure well behind the center of gravity. There is no such configuration possible for ground-based vehicles following sinuous road geometries, particularly in heavy traffic.

The argument can be made more precise using the approach of Hu et al. (2001) who show that, in the context of air traffic control, finding collision-free maneuvers for multiple agents on a Euclidean plane surface $\mathcal{R}^2$ is the same as finding the shortest geodesic in a particular manifold with nonsmooth boundary. Given $n$ vehicles, the geodesic is calculated for the quotient space $\mathcal{R}^{2n}/W(r)$, where $W(r)$ is defined by the requirement that no vehicles are closer together than some critical Euclidean distance $r$.

For autonomous ground vehicles, $\mathcal{R}^2$ must be replaced by a far more topologically complex roadmap space $\mathcal{M}^2$ subject to traffic jams and other 'snowflake' condensation geometries in real time. Geodesics for $n$ vehicles are then in a quotient space $\mathcal{M}^{2n}/W(r)$ whose dynamics are subject to phase transitions in vehicle density $\rho$ (Kerner and Klenov 2009; Jin et al. 2013) that represent cognitive groupoid symmetry breaking. Recall

figure 9.1. Again, the vertical axis shows the number of vehicles per hour, the horizontal, the density of vehicles per mile. The streamline geodesic flow, and deviations from it at critical vehicle density, are evident. Some of the phases may be 'supercooled' – fast-flowing 'liquid' at higher-than-critical densities. Additional 'fine structure' should be expected within both geodesic and turbulent modes.

Again, given the factoring out of most of the topological structure by the construction of geodesics in the quotient space $\mathcal{M}^{2n}/W(r)$, the only parameter available to represent the rate of generation of topological information in the inherently unstable traffic flow system is the vehicle density $\rho$.

Classic traffic flow models based on extensions of hydrodynamic perspectives involving hyperbolic partial differential equations (HPDE's) can be analogously factored using the methods of characteristic curves and Riemann invariants – streamlines (e.g., Landau and Lifshitz 1987). Along characteristic curves, HPDE's are projected down to ordinary differential equations (ODE's) that are usually far easier to solve. The ODE solution or solutions can then be projected upward as solutions to the HPDE's. Here, reduction involves expressing complex dynamics in terms of relatively simple stochastic differential equations and their stability properties. Those stability properties, marking the onset of 'turbulence', will be of central interest.

Taking a somewhat larger view, cognitive phase transitions in autonomous vehicle systems, in particular ground state collapse to some equivalent of 'all possible targets are enemies', should become synergistic with traffic flow phase transitions to produce truly monumental traffic jams, and it is possible to model this phenomenon, to first order, in terms of spontaneous symmetry breaking on groupoids.

Consider a random network of roads between nodal points – intersections. If the average probability of passage falls below a critical value, the Erdos/Renyi 'giant component' that connects across the full network breaks into a set of disjoint connected equivalence class subcomponents, with 'bottlenecks' at which traffic jams occur marking corridors between them. Li et al. (2015), in fact, explicitly apply a similar percolation model to explain this effect for road congestion in a district of Beijing. The underlying road network is shown in figure 9.2, and in figure 9.3 a cross section taken during rush hour showing disjoint sections when regions with average velocity below 40% of observed maximum for the road link have been removed.

Such equivalence classes again define a groupoid (Weinstein 1996).

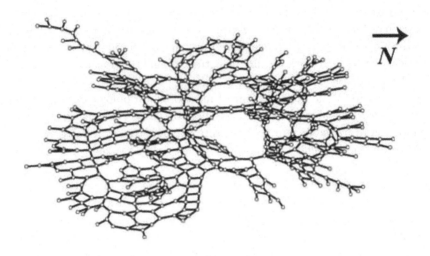

Fig. 9.2   Adapted from Li et al. (2015). Full road network near central Beijing.

Above, we defined the cognitive groupoid to be associated with a $C^3$ structure, here a system of autonomous vehicles linked together in a V2V 'swarm intelligence' embedded in a larger V2I traffic management system. Individual vehicle spacings, speed, acceleration, lane-change, and so on are determined by this encompassing distributed cognitive machine that attempts to optimize traffic flow and safety. The associated individual groupoids are the basic transitive groupoids that build a larger composite groupoid. Thus, under declining probability of passage, related to traffic congestion and viewed here as a temperature analog, this 'vehicle/road' groupoid undergoes a symmetry-breaking transition into a combined cognitive ground state collapse and traffic jam mode – essentially a transition from 'laminar' geodesic to 'turbulent' or 'crystallized' flow. Autonomous vehicle systems that become senile under fog-of-war demands will likely trigger traffic jams that are far different from those associated with human-controlled vehicles. There is no reason to believe that such differences will be benign.

A more precise-seeming model can be built using the turbulence limit of equations (9.9) and (9.10), under conditions of white noise, so that $[Y, Y]^C \propto t$, where $t$ is the time.

Following figure 9.1, suppose the system has been placed in a geodesic for the map quotient space $\mathcal{M}^{2n}/W(r)$, and is free-flowing 'laminar' at some

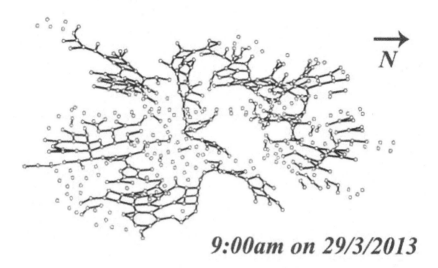

9:00am on 29/3/2013

Fig. 9.3 Adapted from Li et al. (2015). Disconnected subcomponents of Beijing central road network at rush hour. Sections with average vehicle velocity less than 40% of maximum observed have been removed.

vehicle density $\rho$, but may be inherently unstable. As described above, for the simplest kinds of stochastic differential equation models involving white noise – equation (9.14) – heuristically,

$$Y_t \to at \qquad (9.26)$$
$$[Y_t, Y_t] \to (\mathcal{H}(\rho)/g(\rho))t$$

in the exponential of equation (9.11), where $\alpha > 0$ and $\mathcal{H}$ represents the degree of 'driver' control information necessary to keep a vehicle on the road according to the DRT. As argued, this may include lane change, speed variation, spacing change, and other maneuvers.

Again, in first order, if

$$a - 1/2(\mathcal{H}(\rho)/g(\rho)) < 0$$

then any perturbation $K$ dies out in expectation – the driver/autonomous vehicle can exercise sufficient initiative to damp out occasional glitches – and the system has sufficient symmetry so that it can return to streamline geodesic flow. If $\rho$ increases beyond a critical value, then too limited spacing constrains the possibility of cognitive vehicle initiative, the 'temperature' falls below criticality, and perturbations grow exponentially in time so that instability causes 'turbulent' crystal formation – 'fine structure' traffic jams of one form or another. As argued above, this can happen even though the system remains fully 'stable' under the Data Rate Theorem: the individual vehicle control information rate $\mathcal{H}(\rho)$ remains sufficient so that no crash occurs. A central concept of modern theories of turbulence is the onset of exponential growth in small perturbations (Ruelle 1983).

The analysis of traffic flow on a network is, conceptually, somewhat similar to characterizing the propagation of a 'traffic jam signal' via the Markov 'network dynamics' formalism of (Wallace 2016; Gould and Wallace 1994), a method that might be used to empirically identify geodesic eigenmodes of real road network systems under different conditions, as opposed to individual vehicle dynamics or flow on a single road. Abducting the approach of Gould and Wallace (1994), the spread of a 'signal' on a particular network of interacting sites – between and within – is described at nonequilibrium steady state in terms of an equilibrium distribution $\epsilon_i$ 'per unit area' $A_i$ of a Markov process, where $A$ scales with the different 'size' of each node, taken as distinguishable by a scale variable $A$ (for example number of entering streets or average total traffic flow) as well as by its 'position' $i$ or the associated probability-of-contact matrix (POCM). The POCM is normalized to a stochastic matrix $\mathbf{Q}$ having unit row sums, and the vector $\epsilon$ calculated as $\epsilon = \epsilon\mathbf{Q}$

There is a vector set of dimensionless network flows $\mathcal{X}_t^i$, $i = 1, ..., n$ at time $t$. These are each determined by some relation

$$\mathcal{X}_t^i = f(t, \epsilon_i/A_i). \qquad (9.27)$$

Here, $i$ is the index of the node of interest, $\mathcal{X}_t^i$ is the corresponding dimensionless scaled i-th signal, $t$ the time, and $f$ an appropriate function. Again, $\epsilon_i$ is defined by the relation $\epsilon = \epsilon\mathbf{Q}$ for a stochastic matrix $\mathbf{Q}$, calculated as the network probability-of-contact matrix between regions, normalized to unit row sums. Using $\mathbf{Q}$, we have broken out the underlying network topology, a fixed between-and-within travel configuration weighted by usage that is assumed to change relatively slowly on the timescale of observation compared to the time needed to approach the nonequilibrium steady state distribution.

Since the $\mathcal{X}$ are expressed in dimensionless form, $f, t$, and $A$ must be rewritten as dimensionless as well giving, for the monotonic increasing (or threshold-triggered) function $F$

$$\mathcal{X}_\tau^i = F[\tau, \frac{\epsilon_i}{A_i} \times \mathcal{A}_\tau] \qquad (9.28)$$

where $\mathcal{A}_\tau$ is the value of a 'characteristic area' variate that represents the spread of the perturbation signal – evolving into a traffic jam under worst-case conditions – at (dimensionless) characteristic time $\tau = t/T_0$.

$F$ may be quite complicated, including dimensionless 'structural' variates for each individual geographic node $i$. The idea is that the characteristic 'area' $\mathcal{A}_\tau$ grows according to a stochastic process, even though $F$ may be a deterministic mixmaster driven by systematic local probability-of-contact or flow patterns. Then the appropriate model for $\mathcal{A}_\tau$ of a spreading traffic jam becomes something like equations (9.9) or (9.10), with $K$ replaced by $\mathcal{A}$ and $t$ by $\tau$. Thus, for the network, the signal $Y_\tau$ must again have a 'noise'/vehicle density threshold condition like Eq.(9.16) for large-scale propagation of a traffic jam across the full network – something that would look very similar to the spread of a power blackout.

Zhang (2015) uses a similar Markov method to examine taxicab GPS data for transit within and between 12 empirically-identified 'hot zones' in Shanghai, determining the POCM and its equilibrium distribution.

This approach is something in the spirit of a long line of work summarized by Cassidy et al. (2011) that attempts to extend the idea of a fundamental diagram for a single road to a full transport network. As they put it,

> Macroscopic fundamental diagrams (MFDs)... relate the total time spent to the total distance traveled... It is proposed that these macrolevel relations should be observed if the data come from periods when all lanes on all links throughout the network are in either the congested or the uncontested regime...

Following our arguments here, such conditions might apply when $\mathcal{A}_\tau \to 0$, or when it encompasses the entire network domain. Indeed, figure 9.3 suggests why MFDs cannot be constructed in general: congested and free flowing sections of traffic networks will often, and perhaps usually, coexist in an essentially random manner depending on local traffic densities.

Figure 9.4, adapted from Geroliminis and Sun (2011), shows the limitations of the MFD approach. It examines the flow, in vehicles/5min intervals, vs. percent occupancy over a three day period for the Minnesota Twin Cities freeway network that connects St. Paul and Minneapolis. See figure 1 of their paper for details of the road and sensor spacing. Evidently, while the unconstrained region of occupancy permits characterization of a geodesic mode, both strong hysteresis and phase transition effects are evident after about 8% occupancy, analogous to the 'nucleation' dyanamics of figure 9.1 at high traffic density. Again, as in figure 9.1 'fine structure' should be expected within both geodesic and turbulent modes, depending on local parameters.

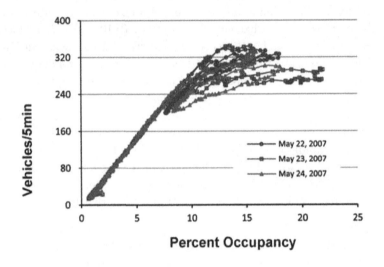

Fig. 9.4  Adapted from Geroliminis and Sun (2011). Breakdown of the macroscopic fundamental diagram for the freeway network connecting St. Paul and Minneapolis at high vehicle densities. Both nucleation and hysteresis effects are evident, showing the fine structure within the turbulent mode.

Daganzo et al. (2010) further find that MFD flow, when it can be characterized at all, will become unstable if the average network traffic density is sufficiently high. They find that, for certain network configurations, the stable congested state

> ...is one of complete gridlock with zero flow. It is therefore important to ensure that in real-world applications that a network's [traffic] density never be allowed to approach this critical value.

Daqing et al. (2014) examine the dynamic spread of traffic congestion on the Beijing central road network. They characterize the failure of a road segment to be a traffic velocity less than 20km/hr and use observational data to define a spatial correlation length in terms of the Euclidean distances between failed nodes. Our equivalent might be something like $\sqrt{\mathcal{A}_\tau}$. Adapting their results, figure 9.5 shows the daily pattern of the correlation length of cascading traffic jams over a 9 day period. The two commuting maxima are evident, and greatest correlation lengths reach the diameter of the main part of the city. Even at rush hour, no MFD can be defined, as, according to figure 9.3, the network will be a dynamic patchwork of free and congested components.

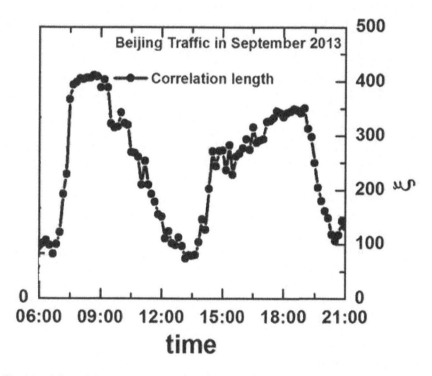

Fig. 9.5 Adapted from Daqing et al. (2014). Daily cycle of traffic jam correlation length over a 9 day period in central Beijing. The maxima cover most of the central city. Even for rush hour, however, no macroscopic fundamental diagram can be defined since the region is characterized by a patchwork of free and congested parts, as shown in figure 9.3.

A next step would be to allow $\rho$ vary in space and time, i.e., to parameterize the model using the moments of vehicle density.

Figure 9.6, adapted from Rand (1979, figure 6.4), provides a disturbing counterexample to these careful empirical and theoretical results on network traffic flow, one with unfortunate results. Summarizing observations carried out by the Rand Fire Project, it represents a repeated sampling of 'travel time vs. distance' for the full Trenton NJ road network in 1975 under varying conditions of time-of-day, day-of-week, weather, and so on, by fire companies responding to calls for service. This was an attempt to create a Macroscopic Fundamental Diagram in the sense used above, but without any reference at all to traffic density.

Indeed, fire service responses are a traffic flow 'best case' as fire units are permitted to bypass one-way restrictions, traffic lights, and so on, and usually able to surmount even the worst weather conditions. In spite of best-case circumstances, the scatterplot evidently samples whole-network turbulent flow, not unlike that to the right of the local geodesic in figures 9.1 and 9.4, part of a single street and a highway network, respectively, and consistent with the assertions of Cassidy et al. (2011) that MFD relations can only be defined under very restrictive conditions, i.e., either complete free flow or full network congestion.

The Rand Fire Project, when confronted with intractable whole-network traffic turbulence, simply collapsed the data onto a 'square root-linear' relation, as indicated on the figure. The computer models resulting from this gross oversimplification were used to determine fire service deployment strategies for high fire incidence, overcrowded neighborhoods in a number of US cities, with literally devastating results and consequent massive impacts on public health and public order. Wallace and Wallace (1998), produced under an Investigator Award in Health Policy Research from the Robert Wood Johnson Foundation, documents the New York City case history. The Rand models are still in use by the New York City Fire Department, for political purposes outlined in that analysis.

## 9.7  Implications

Ruelle (1983), in his elegant keynote address on turbulent dynamics, raises a red flag for any traffic flow studies:

> ...[A] deductive theory of developed turbulence does not
> exist, and a mathematical basis for the important theoret-
> ical literature on the subject is still lacking... A purely de-

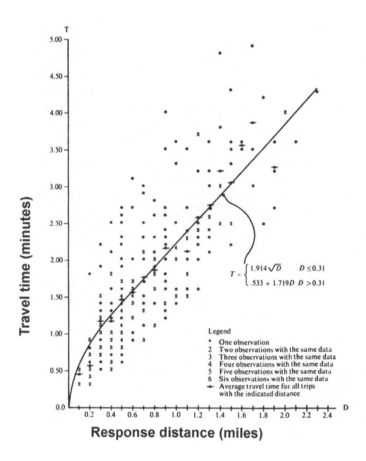

**Response distance (miles)**

Fig. 9.6    Adapted from figure 6.4 of Rand (1979). Relation between fire company travel time and response distance for the full Trenton, NJ road network, 1975. The Rand Fire Project collapsed evident large-scale traffic turbulence into a simple 'square root-linear' model used to design fire service deployment policies in high fire incidence, high population density neighborhoods of many US cities, including the infamous South Bronx. The impacts were literally devastating (Wallace and Wallace 1998).

ductive analysis starting with the Navier-Stokes equation... does not appear feasible... and might be inappropriate because of the approximate nature of the... equation.

Or, as the mathematician Garrett Birkoff (1960 p.5) put it, "...[V]ery few of the deductions of rational hydrodynamics can be established rigorously". Similar problems afflict the exactly solvable but highly approximate Black-Scholes models of financial engineering, and institutions that rely heavily on them have gone bankrupt in the face of market turbulence (Wallace 2015a).

Turbulence in traffic flow does not represent simple drift from steady linear or even parallel travel trajectories. Traffic turbulence involves the exponential amplification of small perturbations into large-scale deviations from complicated streamline geodesics in a topologically complex map quotient space. This is the mechanism of groupoid 'symmetry breaking' by which the system undergoes a phase transition from 'liquid' geodesic flow to 'crystalline' phases of shock fronts, platoons, and outright jams. Under such circumstances, cognitive vehicle initiative – the stabilizing control information we have called $\mathcal{H}$ – serves as a mechanism for returning to local geodesic flow. Inhibition of cognitive initiative occurs when vehicle density exceeds a critical limit, triggering complex dynamic condensation patterns and, for autonomous vehicle systems, perhaps even more disruptive behaviors.

It is, then, not enough to envision atomistic autonomous ground vehicles as having only local dynamics in an embedding traffic stream, as seems the current American and European practice. Traffic light strategies, a frequently-shifting road map space, and the dynamic composition of the traffic stream, all create the synergistic context in which individual vehicles operate and which constitutes the individual 'driving experience'. It is necessary to understand the dynamics of that full system, not simply the behavior of a vehicle atom within it, and the properties of that system will be both overtly and subtly emergent, as will, we assert, the responses of cognitive vehicles enmeshed in context, whether controlled by humans or machines.

One inference from this analysis is that failure modes afflicting large-scale V2V/V2I systems are likely to be more akin to power blackouts than to traffic jams as we know them, and the descriptions of blackouts by Kinney et al. (2005) and Dobson (2007) in Section 4.1 are of interest. Daqing et al. (2014), in fact, explicitly link traffic jams and power failures:

> Cascading failures have become major threats to network robustness due to their potential catastrophic consequences, where local perturbations can induce global propagation of failures... [that] propagate through collective interactions among system components.... [W]e find by analyzing our collected data that jams in city traffic and faults in power grid are spatially long-range correlated with corre-

lations decaying slowly with distance. Moreover, we find in the daily traffic, that the correlation length increases dramatically and reaches maximum, when morning or evening rush hour is approaching...

While clever V2V/V2I management strategies might keep rush hour traffic streams in supercooled high-flow mode beyond critical densities, such a state is notoriously unstable. More subtle patterns of autonomous vehicle 'psychopathology' may be even less benign, and the repeated initiation of massive traffic blackouts by unfriendly agencies should not be difficult.

## 9.8 Summary

Formal argument suggests that command, communication and control systems can remain stable in the sense of the Data Rate Theorem that mandates the minimum rate of control information required to stabilize inherently unstable 'plants', but may nonetheless, under fog-of-war demands, collapse into dysfunctional modes at variance with their fundamental mission. We apply the theory to autonomous ground vehicles under intelligent traffic control in which swarms of interacting, self-driving devices are inherently unstable as a consequence of the basic irregularity of the road network. It appears that such 'V2V/V2I' systems will routinely experience large-scale failures analogous to the vast propagating fronts of power network blackouts, and possibly less benign, but more subtle patterns of 'psychopathology' at various scales.

Chapter 10

# Into the swamp: molecular components

## 10.1 Introduction

The considerations of the previous chapters, in a sense, come full circle through the pending introduction of molecular level components to sophisticated real-time computing systems. It will become relatively easy to employ massive numbers of computing cores based on molecular structures. The seductive possibility is that such components can be used to construct very subtle logic gates, using quasi-classical quantum effects that are routine in biochemistry.

Indeed, since Adelman's (1994) pioneering DNA-based solution to the directed Hamiltonian path problem, a vast effort has been directed at producing molecular analogs to the usual NOT, AND, XOR, and similar logic gates, and at constructing systems using them (e.g., Stojanovic et al. 2002; Macdonald et al. 2006). There are, however, far more subtle naturally-occurring logic gates, particularly those associated with the molecular fuzzy lock-and-key.

## 10.2 Information Catalysis

Information, although a form of free energy (Feynman 2000), per se does not itself carry very much ability to do work, but the physical mechanisms that instantiate signals do, and this fact, in concert with the asymptotic limit theorems of information theory, permits an important general argument.

Suppose there are two interacting information sources $X, Y$, emitting sequences of signals $x = [x_1, x_2, ...]$ and $y = [y_1, y_2, ...]$ at times $i = 1, 2, ....$ A joint sequence of signals $xy \equiv [(x_1, y_1), (x_2, y_2), ...]$ can then be defined, and, where the individual sequences $x$ and $y$ are correlated, it is possible to define a joint source information source uncertainty $H_{X,Y}$ for which a version of the information theory chain rule applies (Cover and Thomas 2006):

$$H_{X,Y} < H_X + H_Y. \tag{10.1}$$

The average production of information, $\hat{H}$, from a process having an available metabolic free energy rate $M$, can be expected to follow a relation having the standard Gibbs form

$$\hat{H} = \frac{\int H \exp[-H/\kappa M]dH}{\int \exp[-H/\kappa M]dH} \approx \kappa M \tag{10.2}$$

where $\kappa$ is quite small, so the integral converges.

Then, from the chain rule,

$$\hat{H}_{X,Y} < \hat{H}_X + \hat{H}_Y,$$
$$M_{X,Y} < M_X + M_Y. \tag{10.3}$$

If $X$ is the system of interest, then, at the expense of maintaining the regulatory information source $Y$, it is possible to canalize the reaction paths of $X$: $M_{X,Y}$ becomes a valley in the larger energy structure created by imposing $Y$ and $X$ together.

Interpreting the metabolic free energy rate $M_Y$ driving the information source $Y$ as a temperature analog, we are now in a position to examine more complicated biological logic gates than are currently described in the computing literature.

## 10.3 The Fuzzy Lock-and-Key

The fuzzy lock-and-key (FLK) dominates many mechanisms that transmit information at inter- and intra-cellular levels. Indeed, 30% of all proteins are 'intrinsically disordered' (IDP), and, by some measures, perhaps 50% of all proteins have significant regions that are intrinsically disordered. Such structure – or rather, its lack – allows operation of the extraordinarily flexible logic gates necessary for many of the cognitive processes that are the foundation of the living state (e.g., Maturana 1970). Figure 10.1, adapted from Tompa et al. (2005), provides an example in which the same IDP can either activate or inhibit a chemical logic gate, depending on an 'information catalysis' in which an incoming signal splits isoenergetic groupoid tiling symmetry states via an analog to spontaneous symmetry breaking, making one or the other the lower energy conformation (e.g., Wallace 2011a,

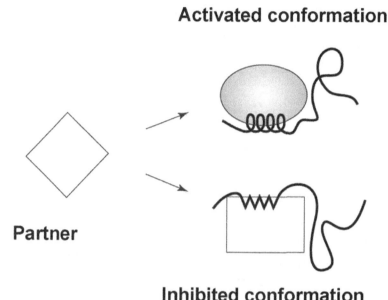

**Activated conformation**

**Partner**

**Inhibited conformation**

Fig. 10.1   From Tompa et al. (2005). The partner can bind in two ways to the IDP. The top form is activated, and the bottom inhibited. The triggering between the states is done by an 'information catalysis' in which an incoming signal shifts the lowest energy state between the two otherwise thermodynamically competitive – isoenergetic – topological forms via a kind of spontaneous symmetry breaking acting on tiling groupoids.

2012). Far more sophisticated logic gates can be constructed using similar mechanisms.

Figure 10.2 shows another example, a frond of the highly flexible 'glycan kelp bed' that coats the cell surface, and, via binding with lectins, triggers even more complicated logical processes. While proteins are constructed from 20 basic amino acids, the glycan kelp bed is formed from as many as 7,000 glycan determinants, and represents a vastly more complex system for information transmission (Cummings 2009; Gupta et al. 2010).

Figure 10.3, from Dam et al. (2007), illustrates a 'bind-and-slide' mechanism by which increasing concentration of a lectin species can induce a phase transition topological change. Initially, the lectin diffuses along and off the glycan kelp frond, until a sufficient number of sites are occupied. Then the lectin-coated fronds cross bind until the reaction saturates, trig-

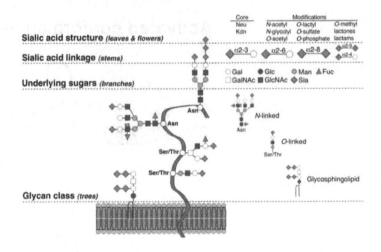

Fig. 10.2   From Cohen and Varki, (2010). Levels of sialome complexity, from core and core modifications to the shifting, bending, twisting, glycan 'kelp fronds' that coat most cell surfaces and, via lectin interaction, constitute sophisticated logic gates involved in explosively vast information transfers: In comparison with the 20 amino acids making up all proteins, some 7,000 glycan determinants are needed to constitute the flexible kelp fronds, side branches and all (Cummings, 2009).

gering the gate.

Wallace (2011a, 2012) applies nonrigid molecule symmetries to IDP, and Wallace and Wallace (2013, chapter 8) extend the analysis to the glycan/lectin interface. Here we will generalize the argument across chemical species, and examine what may be an important stability criterion that appears to underlie all possible such mechanisms.

We begin with a brief recapitulation of basic formalism.

## 10.4   Symmetries of the FLK

One basis for the approach is the classic observation by Longuet-Higgins (1963) that the symmetry group of a nonrigid molecule is the set of (i) all feasible permutations of the positions and spins of identical nuclei and (ii) all feasible permutation-inversions, which simultaneously invert the coordinates of all particles in the center of mass.

It may then, for some forms of the FLK, be possible to extend nonrigid molecule group theory using wreath, semidirect, or other products over a

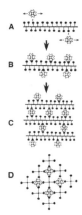

Fig. 10.3   From Dam et al. (2007). Lectin diffuses along and off the flexible glycan frond, until a sufficient number of sites are occupied. Then the coated glycan fronds begin to cross bind, the reaction is complete, and the logic gate is activated. The last figure shows an end view.

set of finite and/or compact groups (e.g., Balasubramanian 1980, 2004), or their groupoid generalizations, as now common in stereochemistry (Wallace 2011b and cited references). Groupoids characterize the partial symmetries of finite tilings, quasicrystals, and the like, and provide a highly natural means of extending local symmetries (Brown 1987; Weinstein 1996). The simplest groupoid can be envisioned as a disjoint union of groups, so that the group element product is only locally defined. In addition, equivalence classes define groupoids, so that the concept generalizes both structures.

The groups or groupoids of interest are taken as parameterized by an index of 'topological complexity', in a large sense, a temperature-analog $L$. In general, the number of group/groupoid elements can be expected to grow exponentially with $L$, typically as $\sum \Pi_j |G_j||A_j|^L$, where $|G_k|$ and $|A_k|$ are the size, in an appropriate sense, of symmetry groups $G_k$ and $A_k$. See the Balasubramanian references for details.

Kahraman (2009) argues that the observed 'sloppiness' of large lock/small key molecular reaction dynamics suggests that binding site symmetry may be greater than binding ligand symmetries. Thus binding ligands may be expected to involve dual, mirror subgroups/groupoids of the anchored nonrigid group/groupoid symmetries of the binding site. Thus the argument becomes:

Increasing $L, |G|, |A| \rightarrow$ more flexibility $\rightarrow$ greatly en-

larged binding site nonrigid symmetry group/groupoid →
more subgroups/subtilings of possible binding sites for lig-
and attachment.

This can be addressed by supposing that the duality between a subgroup
or subgroupoid of the fuzzy lock and of the fuzzy key can be expressed as

$$\mathcal{B}_\alpha = C_\beta \mathcal{D}_\gamma \tag{10.4}$$

where $\mathcal{B}_\alpha$ is a subgroup/groupoid (or set of them) of the appropriate nonrigid symmetry group or groupoid, $\mathcal{D}_\gamma$ a similar structure of the set of binding ligands, and $C_\beta$ is an appropriate inversion operation or set of them that
represents static or dynamic matching between them. The fuzziness, Wallace and Wallace (2013) argue, can even extend to sequence replacement as
well as geometric variations.

An outcome of this approach is that FLK matching symmetries, and
their associated dynamics, can be highly punctuated in the parameter $L$
that broadly indexes topological complexity.

A nonrigid molecule analog based on wreath products of tiling groupoids
is not the only possible attack on the FLK problem. Paul Mezey and colleagues have introduced another extension of simple molecular symmetries
using a fuzzy set approach (e.g., Mezey 1997). In that methodology, the
sharply defined families of nuclear arrangements with specified point symmetry are replaced by fuzzy sets – so-called 'syntopy sets' – of arrangements having only some degree of symmetry of the original perfect point
symmetries. The method provides the syntopy sets with a group theoretic characterization, and the syntopy groups retain some aspects of the
underlying point groups, gaining, however, a continuous parameterization.
Mezey further generalizes these ideas to what he calls fuzzy symmorphy
groups.

In essence, the 'fuzzification' of algebraic structures and relations is
based on an extension of the characteristic function, mapping an arbitrary
set into the set of integers $0, 1$, so that $f : G \to 0, 1$. Then, if $x \in G, f(x) =$
$1$, otherwise $f(x) = 0$. Generalization involves letting $f$ map onto the
real interval $[0, 1]$. Rosenfeld (1971) applied the method to groups and
groupoids, and application to group/groupoid representations seems direct,
albeit modified by some of the complexities associated with groupoid wreath
products and other matters (Houghton 1975; Bos 2007).

To the extent that representations of these objects are possible, the
Morse Function techniques that follow should carry through.

## 10.5 Phase Transitions and Reaction Dynamics

Here we interpret the regulatory free energy intensity $M_Y$ associated with an information catalyst having an information source $Y$ as a pseudo-temperature index $\mathcal{T}$. For large $\mathcal{T}$, it becomes possible to apply a statistical mechanics analog, and to use Landau's spontaneous symmetry breaking/lifting approach via a Morse Theory argument (Wallace, 2012; Pettini, 2007). See the Mathematical Appendix for a summary of standard material on Morse Theory. Typically, very many Morse functions are possible under a given circumstance, and it is possible to construct what is perhaps the simplest using representations of the appropriate generalized groupoids and/or groups. Although representations of groupoids are, broadly, similar to those of groups, there are necessary modifications (Bos 2007).

Taking an appropriate group (or groupoid) representation in a particular matrix or function algebra, in the now-usual manner, construct a 'pseudo probability' $\mathcal{P}$ for nonrigid group element $\omega$ as

$$\mathcal{P}[\omega] = \frac{\exp[-|\chi_\omega|/\kappa\mathcal{T}]}{\sum_\nu \exp[-|\chi_\nu|/\kappa\mathcal{T}]}. \tag{10.5}$$

$\chi_\phi$ is the character of the group element $\phi$ in that representation, i.e., the trace of the matrix or function assigned to $\phi$, and $|...|$ is the norm of the character, a real number. For systems that include compact groups, the sum may be a generalized integral.

The central idea is, again, that $F$ in the construct

$$\exp[-F/\kappa\mathcal{T}] = \sum_\nu \exp[-|\chi_\nu|/\kappa\mathcal{T}] \tag{10.6}$$

is a Morse Function in the signaling temperature-analog $\mathcal{T}$ to which Landau's spontaneous symmetry breaking arguments apply (Wallace 2012; Pettini 2007; Landau and Lifshitz 2007). This leads to the expectation of empirically observable highly punctuated structure and reaction dynamics in the index $\mathcal{T}$ that are the analog to phase transitions in 'simple' physical systems.

Again, for many physical phenomena, raising the temperature makes accessible higher energy states of the system Hamiltonian, the quantum mechanical energy operator, and the inherent symmetry changes are necessarily be punctuated. Here the focus is directly on a Morse Function constructed from a representation of underlying nonrigid groupoid wreath product tiling symmetries.

However, topological matters – the shape of a system has – have long been known to profoundly affect phase transition behavior (e.g., Privman and Fisher 1983). Thus, a distinctly different approach is also possible to FLK reaction mechanism. The basic assumption is that the group or groupoid tiling symmetries of the fuzzy lock must be matched by an appropriate set of keys in a dynamic manner. Thus the statistical mechanics of fuzzy interaction symmetries becomes central to reaction trajectories, treated here according to an Onsager-like nonequilibrium thermodynamics formulation.

Define, then, a 'symmetry entropy' based on the Morse Function $F$ of equation (10.6) over a set of underlying structural or other parameters $\mathbf{Q} = [Q_1, ..., Q_n]$ as the Legendre transform

$$S = F(\mathbf{Q}) - \sum_i Q_i \partial F(\mathbf{Q})/\partial Q_i. \tag{10.7}$$

The time behavior of such a system will be driven, at least in first approximation, by standard Onsager-like nonequilibrium thermodynamics relations (de Groot and Mazur 1984):

$$dQ_i/dt = \sum_j \mathcal{K}_{i,j} \partial S/\partial Q_j \tag{10.8}$$

where the $\mathcal{K}_{i,j}$ are appropriate empirical parameters and $t$ is the time. The system may, or may not, have local time reversibility. If not, then $\mathcal{K}_{i,j} \neq \mathcal{K}_{j,i}$.

Since, however, this is essentially a 'fuzzy' system, a more fitting approach is through a set of stochastic differential equations having the form:

$$dQ_t^i = \mathcal{K}_i(t, \mathbf{Q})dt + \sum_j \sigma_{i,j}(t, \mathbf{Q})dB^j \tag{10.9}$$

where the $\mathcal{K}_i$ and $\sigma_{i,j}$ are appropriate functions.

Different kinds of 'noise' $dB^j$ will have particular forms of quadratic variation affecting dynamics.

Setting the expectation of this equation to zero and solving for stationary points gives attractor states, since noise precludes unstable equilibria, although the solution may, in fact, be a highly dynamic strange attractor set.

But setting the expectation of equation (10.9) to zero also generates an index theorem (Hazewinkel 2002) in the sense of Atiyah and Singer (1963) that relates analytic results – the solutions of the equations – to an underlying set of topological structures representing the eigenmodes of a complicated 'nonrigid molecule' geometric operator whose group/groupoid spectrum represents the symmetries of the possible FLK reactions that must take place for information to be transmitted, i.e., for the chemical logic gate to be triggered. See Wallace (2015b) for a more complete analysis.

More generally, however, the rich stability criteria associated with systems described by equation (10.9) may provide tools for understanding a broad class of symmetry changes across the dynamics of the FLK, not just those of catastrophic failure. This could give a method for exploring the spectrum determined by the underlying Atiyah/Singer index theorem associated with equation (10.9).

## 10.6 Implications

The fuzzy lock-and-key drives a vast array of elaborate logic gates at inter- and intra-cellular levels of biological structure. Indeed, the glycan kelp bed that coats the cell surface provides one of the most information-rich of biological environments (Gupta et al. 2010), one that Cohen and Varki (2010) characterize in terms of a 'glycosynapse' that apparently rivals the neural synapse in sophistication. While there may be some $10^{11}$ active neurons in humans, virtually all living cells within an organism may have numerous glycosynapses engaging in complicated information switching. Within cells there are even more FLK logic gates using IDP, or using regions of structured proteins that are intrinsically disordered. Thus the numbers of FLK logic gates within an organism are literally astronomical, far more numerous than neural synapses. This might well be called the Maturana world of the organism.

Here, we have used representations of groupoid tiling wreath products, or other possible symmetry descriptions associated with the FLK, to construct a Morse Function that can describe both spontaneous symmetry breaking phase transitions driven by information catalysis, and can be used to construct an Onsager-like stochastic dynamics. The two approaches appear linked by the rich instability structure possible to stochastic differential equations. Wallace (2015b) examines this model in terms of the onset and progression of an array of chronic diseases associated with aging, largely driven by a decline in the ability to regulate and control basic biocognition. The inference, of course, is that, as machines constructed of molecular-scale components begin to approximate biological scales and levels of complexity, recognizably analogous regulatory catastrophes will inevitably become routine failure modes.

# Chapter 11

# *Caveat Emptor*

A multitasking hierarchical cognitive model appropriate to institutional or massively parallel machine cognition is considerably more complicated than individual human or animal consciousness, biologically limited to a single shifting, tunable second order giant component. Human institutions, by contrast, appear able to entertain several, and often very many, such global broadcasts simultaneously, although these generally operate at a much slower rate than individual consciousness. Highly parallel cognitive machines, according to this model, would be able to function as efficiently as large institutions, but at or near the rate of animal consciousness.

Shared culture, however, seems to provide far more than merely a shared language for the establishment of the human organizations that enable our adaptation to, or alteration of, our varied environments. It also may provide the stabilizing mechanisms needed to overcome many of the canonical and idiosyncratic failure modes inherent to such structures – the embedding directives of law, tradition, and custom that have evolved over many centuries. No such secondary heritage system is currently available for machine stabilization.

Explicitly, then, massively parallel machines tasked with critical real-time duties will likely suffer interpenetrating dysfunctions of mutual and reciprocal interaction with embedding environments that can have highly punctuated developmental progression.

There will be no reductionist 'bug in the program' whose fix will correct the problem.

A particular canonical failure mode will likely be similar to inattentional blindness, an inevitable consequence of the limited syntactic bandpass inherent to rate distortion manifolds, whose tunable selectivity – focus – is at the expense of sensitivity, in a syntactic and grammatical analog to the classic signal-detection/uncertainty principle conundrum.

Real time, multiple global broadcast machines will be prone as well to failures involving communication between individual broadcasts: Too little generates errors of distortion and inattentional blindness; too much creates pathological coevolutionary syndromes similar to thrashing.

In addition, mission-critical real time machines are likely to fail suddenly, in a manner similar to a power blackout, particularly when operating under 'fog-of-war' conditions, leading to a ground state collapse in which 'all targets are enemies', or the inverse. However, more insidious 'developmental' pathologies are also possible whose effects may be quite subtle but manifest under high demands, where proper function is especially important, and indeed the basic rationale for the machine.

Roughly similar problems afflict current work on coevolutionary algorithms.

Preventing, diagnosing, and correcting such dysfunctions – essentially a psychiatry of automata – appears likely to become a new and important engineering discipline.

Matters are made far more complicated by our ability, or need, to construct cognitive systems not constrained by natural evolutionary process. Higher animals, and their collectively cognitive social assemblies, are the survivors of a path-dependent branching process of variation pruned by selection and chance extinction. By contrast, real world engineering problems, in concert with market pressures, will constrain and select cognitive machine architectures, and these will have little or no correspondence with familiar animal models. Psycho- and socio- pathologies of individual and collective consciousness among humans and other animals provide a window on the inevitability of analogs to psychiatric disorders in highly parallel, real time, cognitive devices, but the creation of actual engineering strategies for prevention, early detection, and correction, remains a considerable challenge.

In particular, deliberate induction of serious dysfunction in massively parallel cognitive systems should be fairly straightforward, given their inevitable focus via problem equivalence classes. That is, machine structure and function will have been dictated by the '*problem groupoid set*' *that it is designed to confront.* Masquerading one problem as another should be sufficient for successful attack, much as human inattentional blindness enables magic tricks.

For multiple global broadcast systems, forcing the different 'minds' to focus on different problems should be sufficient to induce ground state paralysis. In an institutional setting this might be characterized as 'divide and rule'.

Data overload would be another effective attack tool, for machines of both kinds. Under such circumstances multiple broadcast systems should be particularly sensitive to crosstalk overload or transfer inhibition, two different limits on intersystem communication. Think Tet offensive in the context of interservice rivalry.

This is an old pattern. Radioactive waste disposal was considered a trivial afterthought in reactor design during the 1940's and 1950's, but, over just a few decades, became a chief bottleneck for the electric power industry. Program debugging has grown to a principal impediment in conventional computer systems design, and the constant security flaws and fixes of current operating systems are assuming legendary proportions. More recently, complex financial instruments – 'derivatives' – that are based on equilibrium and small-variance assumptions, have failed catastrophically. The second law of thermodynamics, it can be argued, dictates that, in spite of the Shannon Theorems, maintenance will be a principal bogey for all complex information enterprises – biological, social, economic, machine, or hybrid. Highly parallel machine cognition, Self-X and autonomic computing, autonomous vehicle systems, and 'biologically-based computing paradigms' will be no exceptions.

# Chapter 12

# Mathematical Appendix

## 12.1 Groupoids

Given a pairing, connection by a meaningful path to the same basepoint, it is possible to define 'natural' end-point maps $\alpha(g) = a_j, \beta(g) = a_k$ from the set of morphisms $G$ into $A$, and a formally associative product in the groupoid $g_1 g_2$ provided $\alpha(g_1 g_2) = \alpha(g_1), \beta(g_1 g_2) = \beta(g_2)$, and $\beta(g_1) = \alpha(g_2)$. Then the product is defined, and associative, i.e., $(g_1 g_2) g_3 = g_1 (g_2 g_3)$, with inverse defined by $g = (a_j, a_k), g^{-1} \equiv (a_k, a_j)$.

In addition there are natural left and right identity elements $\lambda_g, \rho_g$ such that $\lambda_g g = g = g \rho_g$.

An orbit of the groupoid $G$ over $A$ is an equivalence class for the relation $a_j \sim G a_k$ if and only if there is a groupoid element $g$ with $\alpha(g) = a_j$ and $\beta(g) = a_k$. Following Cannas Da Silva and Weinstein (1999), a groupoid is called transitive if it has just one orbit. The transitive groupoids are the building blocks of groupoids in that there is a natural decomposition of the base space of a general groupoid into orbits. Over each orbit there is a transitive groupoid, and the disjoint union of these transitive groupoids is the original groupoid. Conversely, the disjoint union of groupoids is itself a groupoid.

The isotropy group of $a \in X$ consists of those $g$ in $G$ with $\alpha(g) = a = \beta(g)$. These groups prove fundamental to classifying groupoids.

If $G$ is any groupoid over $A$, the map $(\alpha, \beta) : G \to A \times A$ is a morphism from $G$ to the pair groupoid of $A$. The image of $(\alpha, \beta)$ is the orbit equivalence relation $\sim G$, and the functional kernel is the union of the isotropy groups. If $f : X \to Y$ is a function, then the kernel of $f$, $ker(f) = [(x_1, x_2) \in X \times X : f(x_1) = f(x_2)]$ defines an equivalence relation.

Groupoids may have additional structure. As Weinstein (1996) explains, a groupoid $G$ is a topological groupoid over a base space $X$ if $G$ and $X$ are topological spaces and $\alpha, \beta$ and multiplication are continuous maps. A criticism sometimes applied to groupoid theory is that their classification up to isomorphism is nothing other than the classification of equivalence relations via the orbit equivalence relation and groups via the isotropy groups. The imposition of a compatible topological structure produces a nontrivial interaction between the two structures. Below we will introduce a metric structure on manifolds of related information sources, producing such interaction.

In essence a groupoid is a category in which all morphisms have an inverse, here defined in terms of connection by a meaningful path of an information source dual to a cognitive process.

As Weinstein (1996) points out, the morphism $(\alpha, \beta)$ suggests another way of looking at groupoids. A groupoid over $A$ identifies not only which elements of $A$ are equivalent to one another (isomorphic), but *it also parameterizes the different ways (isomorphisms) in which two elements can be equivalent*, i.e., all possible information sources dual to some cognitive process. Given the information theoretic characterization of cognition presented above, this produces a full modular cognitive network in a highly natural manner.

Brown (1987) describes the basic structure as follows:

> A groupoid should be thought of as a group with many objects, or with many identities... A groupoid with one object is essentially just a group. So the notion of groupoid is an extension of that of groups. It gives an additional convenience, flexibility and range of applications...
>
> EXAMPLE 1.      A   disjoint   union   [of groups] $G = \cup_\lambda G_\lambda, \lambda \in \Lambda$, is a groupoid: the product $ab$ is defined if and only if $a, b$ belong to the same $G_\lambda$, and $ab$ is then just the product in the group $G_\lambda$. There is an identity $1_\lambda$ for each $\lambda \in \Lambda$. The maps $\alpha, \beta$ coincide and map $G_\lambda$ to $\lambda$, $\lambda \in \Lambda$.
>
> EXAMPLE 2. An equivalence relation $R$ on [a set] $X$ becomes a groupoid with $\alpha, \beta : R \to X$ the two projections, and product $(x, y)(y, z) = (x, z)$ whenever $(x, y), (y, z) \in R$. There is an identity, namely $(x, x)$, for each $x \in X$...

Weinstein (1996) makes the following fundamental point:

Almost every interesting equivalence relation on a space $B$ arises in a natural way as the orbit equivalence relation of some groupoid $G$ over $B$. Instead of dealing directly with the orbit space $B/G$ as an object in the category $S_{map}$ of sets and mappings, one should consider instead the groupoid $G$ itself as an object in the category $G_{htp}$ of groupoids and homotopy classes of morphisms.

It is possible to explore homotopy in paths generated by information sources.

### Global and local groupoids

The argument next follows Weinstein (1996) fairly closely, using his example of a finite tiling.

Consider a tiling of the euclidean plane $R^2$ by identical 2 by 1 rectangles, specified by the set $X$ (one dimensional) where the grout between tiles is $X = H \cup V$, having $H = R \times Z$ and $V = 2Z \times R$, where $R$ is the set of real numbers and $Z$ the integers. Call each connected component of $R^2 \backslash X$, i.e. the complement of the two dimensional real plane intersecting $X$, a tile.

Let $\Gamma$ be the group of those rigid motions of $R^2$ which leave $X$ invariant, i.e., the normal subgroup of translations by elements of the lattice $\Lambda = H \cap V = 2Z \times Z$ (corresponding to corner points of the tiles), together with reflections through each of the points $1/2\Lambda = Z \times 1/2Z$, and across the horizontal and vertical lines through those points. As noted in Weinstein (1996), much is lost in this coarse-graining, in particular the same symmetry group would arise if we replaced $X$ entirely by the lattice $\Lambda$ of corner points. $\Gamma$ retains no information about the local structure of the tiled plane. In the case of a real tiling, restricted to the finite set $B = [0, 2m] \times [0, n]$ the symmetry group shrinks drastically: The subgroup leaving $X \cap B$ invariant contains just four elements even though a repetitive pattern is clearly visible. A two-stage groupoid approach recovers the lost structure.

We define the transformation groupoid of the action of $\Gamma$ on $R^2$ to be the set

$$G(\Gamma, R^2) = \{(x, \gamma, y | x \in R^2, y \in R^2, \gamma \in \Gamma, x = \gamma y\}$$

with the partially defined binary operation

$$(x, \gamma, y)(y, \nu, z) = (x, \gamma \nu, z).$$

Here $\alpha(x, \gamma, y) = x$, and $\beta(x, \gamma, y) = y$, and the inverses are natural.

We can form the restriction of $G$ to $B$ (or any other subset of $R^2$) by defining

$$G(\Gamma, R^2)|_B = \{g \in G(\Gamma, R^2) | \alpha(g), \beta(g) \in B\}.$$

1. An orbit of the groupoid $G$ over $B$ is an equivalence class for the relation $x \sim_G y$ if and only if there is a groupoid element $g$ with $\alpha(g) = x$ and $\beta(g) = y$.

Two points are in the same orbit if they are similarly placed within their tiles or within the grout pattern.

2. The isotropy group of $x \in B$ consists of those $g$ in $G$ with $\alpha(g) = x = \beta(g)$. It is trivial for every point except those in $1/2\Lambda \cap B$, for which it is $Z_2 \times Z_2$, i.e. the direct product of integers modulo two with itself.

By contrast, embedding the tiled structure within a larger context permits definition of a much richer structure, i.e. the identification of local symmetries.

We construct a second groupoid as follows: Consider the plane $R^2$ as being decomposed as the disjoint union of $P_1 = B \cap X$ (the grout), $P_2 = B \backslash P_1$ (the complement of $P_1$ in $B$, i.e. the tiles), and $P_3 = R^2 \backslash B$ (the exterior of the tiled room). Let $E$ be the group of all euclidean motions of the plane, and define the local symmetry groupoid $G_{loc}$ as the set of triples $(x, \gamma, y)$ in $B \times E \times B$ for which $x = \gamma y$, and for which $y$ has a neighborhood $\mathcal{U}$ in $R^2$ such that $\gamma(\mathcal{U} \cap P_i) \subseteq P_i$ for $i = 1, 2, 3$. The composition is given by the same formula as for $G(\Gamma, R^2)$.

For this groupoid-in-context there are only a finite number of orbits:

$\mathcal{O}_1$ = interior points of the tiles.

$\mathcal{O}_2$ = interior edges of the tiles.

$\mathcal{O}_3$ = interior crossing points of the grout.

$\mathcal{O}_4$ = exterior boundary edge points of the tile grout.

$\mathcal{O}_5$ = boundary 'T' points.

$\mathcal{O}_6$ = boundary corner points.

The isotropy group structure is, however, now very rich indeed:

The isotropy group of a point in $\mathcal{O}_1$ is now isomorphic to the entire rotation group $O_2$.

It is $Z_2 \times Z_2$ for $\mathcal{O}_2$.

For $\mathcal{O}_3$ it is the eight-element dihedral group $D_4$.

For $\mathcal{O}_4, \mathcal{O}_5$ and $\mathcal{O}_6$ it is simply $Z_2$.

These are the 'local symmetries' of the tile-in-context.

## 12.2	Stochastic Differential Equations

### Martingales

Suppose a player of a game of chance begins with an initial fortune of some given amount, and bets $n = 1, 2, \dots$ times according to a stochastic process in which a stochastic variable $\mathbf{X}_n$, which represents the size of the player's fortune at play $n$, takes values $\mathbf{X}_n = x_{n,i}$ with probabilities $P_{n,i}$ such that $\sum_i P_{n,i} = 1$, where $i$ represents a particular outcome at step $n$.

Assume for all $n$ there exists a value $0 < C < \infty$ such that the expectation of $\mathbf{X}_n$,

$$E(\mathbf{X}_n) \equiv \sum_i x_{n,i} P_{n,i} < C \qquad (12.1)$$

for all $n$. That is, no infinite or endlessly increasing fortunes are permitted.

We note that the state $\mathbf{X}_n = 0$, having probability $P_n^0$, i.e., the loss of all a player's funds, terminates the game.

We suppose it possible to define conditional probabilities at step $n + 1$ which depend on the way in which the value of $\mathbf{X}_n$ was reached, so that we can define the conditional expectation of $\mathbf{X}_{n+1}$:

$$E(\mathbf{X}_{n+1}|\mathbf{X}_1, \mathbf{X}_2, ...\mathbf{X}_n) \equiv E(\mathbf{X}_{n+1}|n).$$

The 'sample space' for the probabilities defining this conditional expectation is the set of different possible sequences of the $x_{m,i} > 0$: $x_{1,i}, x_{2,j}, x_{3,k}...x_{n,q}$

We call the sequence of stochastic variables $\mathbf{X}_n$ defining the game a *Submartingale* if, at each step $n$,

$$E(\mathbf{X}_{n+1}|n) \geq \mathbf{X}_n,$$

a *Martingale* if

$$E(\mathbf{X}_{n+1}|n) = \mathbf{X}_n$$

and a *Supermartingale* if

$$E(\mathbf{X}_{n+1}|n) \leq \mathbf{X}_n.$$

$\mathbf{X}_n$ is, remember, the player's fortune at step $n$.

Clearly a submartingale is favorable to the player, a martingale is an absolutely fair game, and a supermartingale is favorable to the house.

Regardless of the complexity of the game, the details of the playing instruments, the ways of determining gains or loss or their amounts, or any other structural factors of the underlying stochastic process, the essential content of the Martingale Limit Theorem is that in all three cases the sequence of stochastic variables $\mathbf{X}_n$ converges in probability 'almost everywhere' to a well-defined stochastic variable $\mathbf{X}$ as $n \to \infty$. That is, for each kind of martingale, no matter the actual sequence of winnings $x_{1,i}, x_{2,j}, ...x_{n,k}, x_{n+1,m}, ...$, you get to the same limiting stochastic variable $\mathbf{X}$. Sequences for which this does not happen have zero probability.

A simple proof of this result runs to several pages of dense mathematics using modern theories of abstract integration on sets. Indeed, all the asymptotic theorems we have cited require more or less arduous application of measure theory and Lebesgue integration, topics which are themselves relatively straightforward, elegant and worth study. Proofs using more elementary approaches run to full chapters.

**Nested Martingales**

Consider a compound stochastic process in which the 'winnings' at the 'smaller' scale, played by one set of rules, contribute to a quite different game having completely different rules on a 'larger' scale. These games are bounded by the condition $E(\mathbf{X}_n) < C$, for some finite positive $C$.

The simplest version of this extension assumes that the compound game is, in some sense, a subset of the original:

$$\mathbf{X}_{n+1} = \mathbf{X}_n + \mathbf{A}_n(\mathbf{Y}_{n+1} - \mathbf{Y}_n). \qquad (12.2)$$

Assume the filter, $\mathbf{A}_n \geq 0$, is a non-negative stochastic variable, that can take the value 0. This may, for example, be greater than zero only one time in ten or a hundred, on average. Taking the conditional expectation gives

$$E(\mathbf{X}_{n+1}|n) = \mathbf{X}_n + \mathbf{A}_n(E(\mathbf{Y}_{n+1}|n) - \mathbf{Y}_n) \qquad (12.3)$$

where the conditional expectation of any variate $\mathbf{Z}_n$ at step $n$ is just its value.

Since $\mathbf{A}_n \geq 0$, *the game described by the attenuated sequence* $\mathbf{X}_n$ *has the same martingale classification as does the nested central city game described by* $\mathbf{Y}_n$.

**The Martingale Transform**

The X-processes in equation (12.2) is the *Martingale transform* of $\mathbf{Y}_n$, and the result is classic, representing the impossibility of a successful betting system.

Note that the basic Martingale transform can be rewritten as

$$\frac{\mathbf{X}_{n+1} - \mathbf{X}_n}{\mathbf{Y}_{n+1} - \mathbf{Y}_n} \equiv \frac{\Delta\mathbf{X}_n}{\Delta\mathbf{Y}_n} = \mathbf{A}_n \qquad (12.4)$$

or

$$\Delta\mathbf{X}_n = \mathbf{A}_n\Delta\mathbf{Y}_n. \qquad (12.5)$$

Induction gives

$$\mathbf{X}_{n+1} = \mathbf{X}_0 + \sum_{j=1}^{n} \mathbf{A}_j \Delta \mathbf{Y}_j. \tag{12.6}$$

This notation is suggestive: In fact the Martingale transform is the discrete analog of Ito's stochastic integral relative to a sequence of stopping times, (Protter 1990, p. 44). In the stochastic integral context the Y-process is called the 'integrator' and the A-process the 'integrand.' Further development leads toward generalizations of Brownian motion, the Poisson process, and so on (Protter 1990).

The basic picture is of the transmission of a signal, $\mathbf{Y}_n$, in the presence of noise, $\mathbf{A}_n$.

**Stochastic Differential Equations**

A more realistic extension of the elementary denumerable Martingale transform for our purposes is

$$\mathbf{X}_{n+1} = \mathbf{X}_n + (\mathbf{B}_{n+1} - \mathbf{B}_n)\mathbf{X}_n + \mathbf{A}_n(\mathbf{Y}_{n+1} - \mathbf{Y}_n) \tag{12.7}$$

where $\mathbf{B}_n$ is another stochastic variable.

Using the more suggestive notation of equations (12.4) and (12.5) this becomes the fundamental stochastic differential equation

$$\Delta \mathbf{X}_n = \mathbf{X}_n \Delta \mathbf{B}_n + \mathbf{A}_n \Delta \mathbf{Y}_n. \tag{12.8}$$

Taking conditional expectations gives

$$E(\mathbf{X}_{n+1}|n) - \mathbf{X}_n =$$
$$\mathbf{X}_n(E(\mathbf{B}_{n+1}|n) - \mathbf{B}_n) + \mathbf{A}_n(E(\mathbf{Y}_{n+1}|n) - \mathbf{Y}_n). \tag{12.9}$$

If $\mathbf{X}_n, \mathbf{A}_n \geq 0$, the martingale classification of $\mathbf{X}$ depends on those of $\mathbf{B}$ and $\mathbf{Y}$.

Extending the argument to a hierarchically-linked network is straightforward, leading to the Ito stochastic integral

$$\mathbf{X}_{n+1} \approx \mathbf{X}_0 + \sum_{k=1}^{n} \mathbf{A}_k \Delta \mathbf{Y}_k. \tag{12.10}$$

The complete hierarchical system, then undergoes an iterative Z-process defined by the integrator $\mathbf{X}_j$:

$$\mathbf{Z}_{m+1} \approx \mathbf{Z}_0 + \sum_{j=1}^{m} \mathbf{C}_j \Delta \mathbf{X}_j. \tag{12.11}$$

Extension of this development to intermediate times is complicated and involves taking the continuous limit of the Riemann-type sums of the previous equations. This produces the stochastic differential equation

$$dX_t = X_t dB_t + A_t dY_t \qquad (12.12)$$

whose solution depends critically on the behavior of the second-order step-by-step 'quadratic variation,' a variance-like limit of the stochastic processes. Letting $U_n, V_n$ be two arbitrary processes with $U_0 = V_0 = 0$, their quadratic variation is

$$[U_n, V_n] \equiv \sum_{j=1}^{n-1} (U_{j+1} - U_j)(V_{j+1} - V_j). \qquad (12.13)$$

Taking the 'infinitesimal limit' of continuous time, a term-by-term expansion of this sum can be shown to give (Protter 1990)

$$[U_t, V_t] = U_t V_t - \int_0^t U_s dV_s - \int_0^t V_r dU_r. \qquad (12.14)$$

To put this in some perspective, classical Brownian motion has the 'structure equation' $[X_t, X_t] \propto t$.

That is, for Brownian motion the jump-by-jump quadratic variation increases linearly with time. While much of the contemporary theory of financial markets is based on Brownian analogs, real processes are likely to be more complex, subject to sudden, massive, discontinuous 'phase changes' which cannot be simply characterized as diffusional.

The quadratic variation is critical to the Ito chain rule for stochastic integrals. If $X$ is a continuous semimartingale and $f$ a twice-differentiable function, then Ito's clever but surprisingly direct calculation shows, in terms of stochastic integrals (Protter 1990)

$$f(X_t) - f(X_0) = \int_0^t f'(X_s) dX_s + \frac{1}{2} \int_0^t f''(X_s) d[X, X]_s. \qquad (12.15)$$

The SDE version of this becomes

$$df_t = f' dX_t + \frac{1}{2} f'' d[X, X]_t \qquad (12.16)$$

although, strictly speaking, only the integral relation is actually defined.

Applying the Ito chain rule to equation (12.12) gives a classic result (Protter 1990). We assume for simplicity no discontinuous jumps, and first study the 'exponential' equation

$$dX_t = X_t dB_t \rightarrow$$

$$X_t = X_0 + \int_0^t X_s dB_s. \qquad (12.17)$$

Following Protter (1990 p. 78), this has the solution

$$\mathbf{X}_t = \epsilon(\mathbf{B})_t = \mathbf{X}_0 \exp(\mathbf{B}_t - 1/2[\mathbf{B}_t, \mathbf{B}_t]). \qquad (12.18)$$

Next we define

$$\mathbf{H}_t \equiv \int_0^t \mathbf{A}_s d\mathbf{Y}_s. \qquad (12.19)$$

This can be restated as

$$\mathbf{X}_t = \mathbf{H}_t + \mathbf{X}_0 + \int_0^t \mathbf{X}_s d\mathbf{B}_s. \qquad (12.20)$$

For the continuous case, this has the formal solution (Protter 1990, p.266)

$$\epsilon_\mathbf{H}(\mathbf{B})_t =$$

$$\epsilon(\mathbf{B})_t [\mathbf{H}_0 + \int_0^t 1/\epsilon(\mathbf{B})_s d(\mathbf{H}_s - [\mathbf{H}, \mathbf{B}]_s)] \qquad (12.21)$$

with

$$1/\epsilon(\mathbf{B}) = \epsilon(-\mathbf{B} + [\mathbf{B}, \mathbf{B}]). \qquad (12.22)$$

The structure equations defining $[\mathbf{B}, \mathbf{B}]$ and $[\mathbf{H}, \mathbf{B}]$ are critical in determining transient behavior, but not likely to have simple Brownian form.

## 12.3 Morse Theory

Morse theory examines relations between analytic behavior of a function – the location and character of its critical points – and the underlying topology of the manifold on which the function is defined. We are interested in a number of such functions, for example information source uncertainty on a parameter space and 'second order' iterations involving parameter manifolds determining critical behavior, for example sudden onset of a giant component in the mean number model of Chapter 3, and universality class tuning in the mean field model described above. These can be reformulated from a Morse theory perspective. Here we follow closely Kastner (2006), and Pettini (2007).

The essential idea of Morse theory is to examine an $n$-dimensional manifold $M$ as decomposed into level sets of some function $f : M \to \mathbf{R}$ where $\mathbf{R}$ is the set of real numbers. The $a$-level set of $f$ is defined as

$$f^{-1}(a) = \{x \in M : f(x) = a\},$$

the set of all points in $M$ with $f(x) = a$. If $M$ is compact, then the whole manifold can be decomposed into such slices in a canonical fashion between two limits, defined by the minimum and maximum of $f$ on $M$. Let the part of $M$ below $a$ be defined as

$$M_a = f^{-1}(-\infty, a] = \{x \in M : f(x) \leq a\}.$$

These sets describe the whole manifold as $a$ varies between the minimum and maximum of $f$.

Morse functions are defined as a particular set of smooth functions $f : M \to \mathbf{R}$ as follows. Suppose a function $f$ has a critical point $x_c$, so that the derivative $df(x_c) = 0$, with critical value $f(x_c)$. Then $f$ is a Morse function if its critical points are nondegenerate in the sense that the Hessian matrix $\mathcal{J}$ of second derivatives at $x_c$, whose elements, in terms of local coordinates are

$$\mathcal{J}_{i,j} = \partial^2 f / \partial x^i \partial x^j,$$

has rank $n$, which means that it has only nonzero eigenvalues, so that there are no lines or surfaces of critical points and, ultimately, critical points are isolated.

The index of the critical point is the number of negative eigenvalues of $\mathcal{J}$ at $x_c$.

A level set $f^{-1}(a)$ of $f$ is called a critical level if $a$ is a critical value of $f$, that is, if there is at least one critical point $x_c \in f^{-1}(a)$.

Again following Pettini (2007), the essential results of Morse theory are:

1. If an interval $[a, b]$ contains no critical values of $f$, then the topology of $f^{-1}[a, v]$ does not change for any $v \in (a, b]$. Importantly, the result is valid even if $f$ is not a Morse function, but only a smooth function.

2. If the interval $[a, b]$ contains critical values, the topology of $f^{-1}[a, v]$ changes in a manner determined by the properties of the matrix $\mathcal{J}$ at the critical points.

3. If $f : M \to \mathbf{R}$ is a Morse function, the set of all the critical points of $f$ is a discrete subset of $M$, i.e., critical points are isolated. This is Sard's Theorem.

4. If $f : M \to \mathbf{R}$ is a Morse function, with $M$ compact, then on a finite interval $[a, b] \subset \mathbf{R}$, there is only a finite number of critical points $p$ of $f$ such that $f(p) \in [a, b]$. The set of critical values of $f$ is a discrete set of $\mathbf{R}$.

5. For any differentiable manifold $M$, the set of Morse functions on $M$ is an open dense set in the set of real functions of $M$ of differentiability class $r$ for $0 \leq r \leq \infty$.

6. Some topological invariants of $M$, that is, quantities that are the same for all the manifolds that have the same topology as $M$, can be estimated and sometimes computed exactly once all the critical points of $f$ are known: let the Morse numbers $\mu_i (i = 0, ..., m)$ of a function $f$ on $M$ be the number of critical points of $f$ of index $i$, (the number of negative eigenvalues of $H$). The Euler characteristic of the complicated manifold $M$ can be expressed as the alternating sum of the Morse numbers of any Morse function on $M$,

$$\chi = \sum_{i=1}^{m} (-1)^i \mu_i.$$

The Euler characteristic reduces, in the case of a simple polyhedron, to

$$\chi = V - E + F$$

where $V, E$, and $F$ are the numbers of vertices, edges, and faces in the polyhedron.

7. Another important theorem states that, if the interval $[a, b]$ contains a critical value of $f$ with a single critical point $x_c$, then the topology of the set $M_b$ defined above differs from that of $M_a$ in a way which is determined by the index, $i$, of the critical point. Then $M_b$ is homeomorphic to the manifold obtained from attaching to $M_a$ an $i$-handle, i.e., the direct product of an $i$-disk and an $(m - i)$-disk.

Again, Matsumoto (2002) and Pettini (2007) contain mathematical details and further references.


## 12.4   The Groupoid Atlas

The probability argument leading to equation (6.7) inherently defines a groupoid atlas in the sense of Bak et al. (2006). Following closely Glazebrook and Wallace (2009a, b), the set of groupoids $G_\alpha$ comprise a groupoid atlas $\mathcal{A}$ as follows.

A family of local groupoids $(G_\mathcal{A})$ is defined with respective object sets $(X_\mathcal{A})_\alpha$, and a *coordinate system* $\Phi_\mathcal{A}$ of $\mathcal{A}$ equipped with a reflexive relation $\leq$. These satisfy the following conditions:

1. If $\alpha \leq \beta$ in $\Phi_\mathcal{A}$ then $(X_\mathcal{A})_\alpha \cap (X_\mathcal{A})_\beta$ is a union of components of $(G_\mathcal{A})$, that is, if $x \in (X_\mathcal{A})_\alpha \cap (X_\mathcal{A})_\beta$ and $g \in (G_\mathcal{A})_\alpha$ acts as $G : x \to y$, then $y \in (X_\mathcal{A})_\alpha \cap (X_\mathcal{A})_\beta$.

2. If $\alpha \leq \beta$ in $\Phi_\mathcal{A}$, then there is a groupoid morphism defined between the restrictions of the local groupoids to intersections

$$(G_\mathcal{A})_\alpha|(X_\mathcal{A})_\alpha \cap (X_\mathcal{A})_\beta \to (G_\mathcal{A})_\beta|(X_\mathcal{A})_\alpha \cap (X_\mathcal{A})_\beta,$$

and which is the identity morphism on objects.

Thus each of the $G_\alpha$ with its associated dual information source $H_{G_\alpha}$ constitutes a component of an atlas that incorporates the dynamics of an interactive system by means of the intrinsic groupoid actions.

These are matters currently under active study.

# Bibliography

Ackoff, R., 1979, The future of operational research is past, *Journal of the Operational Research Society*, 30:93-97.

Adami, C., C. Ofria, and T. Collier, 2000, Evolution of biological complexity, *Proceedings of the National Academy of Sciences*, 97:4463-4468.

Adelman, L., 1994, Molecular computation of solutions to combinatorial problems, *Science*, 266:1021-1024.

Aiello W., F. Chung, L. Lu, 2000, A random graph model for massive graphs, in *Proceedings of the 32nd Annual ACM Symposium on the Theory of Computing*.

Albert R., A. Barabasi, 2002, Statistical mechanics of complex networks, *Reviews of Modern Physics*, 74:47-97.

Asanovic, K., R. Bokik, B. Catanzaro, J. Gebis, et al., 2006, The landscape of parallel computing research: a view from Berkeley. www.eecs.berkeley.edu/Pubs/TechRpts/2006/EECS-2006-183.pdf.

Ash R., 1990, *Information Theory*, Dover Publications, New York.

Atkinson, D., 2015, Emerging cyber-security issues of autonomy and the psychopathology of intelligent machines. In *Foundations of Autonomy and Its (Cyber) Threats: Papers from the 2015 AAAI Spring Symposium*, Technical Report No. SS-15-01, AAAI Press, Menlo Park, CA.

Atlan H., I. Cohen, 1998, Immune information, self-organization and meaning, *International Immunology*, 10:711-717.

Atmanspacher, H., 2006, Toward an information theoretical implementation of contextual conditions for consciousness, *Acta Biotheoretica*, 54:157-160.

Baars B., 1988, *A Cognitive Theory of Consciousness*, Cambridge University Press, New York.

Baars B., and S. Franklin, 2003, How conscious experience and working memory interact, *Trends in Cognitive Science*, 17:166-172.

Baars, B., 2005, Global workspace theory of consciousness: toward a cognitive neuroscience of human experience, *Progress in Brain Research*, 150:45-53.

Bak, A., R. Brown, G. Minian, T. Porter, T., 2006, Global actions, groupoid atlases and related topics, *Journal of Homotopy and Related Structures*, 1:1-54. Available from ArXiv depository.

Balasubramanian, K., 1980, The symmetry groups of nonrigid molecules as generalized wreath products and their representations, *Journal of Chemical Physics*, 72:665-677.

Balasubramanian, K., 2004, Relativistic double group spinor representations of nonrigid molecules, *Journal of Chemical Physics*, 120:5524-5535.

Balkwill, F., A. Mantovani, 2001, Inflammation and cancer: back to Virchow?, *Lancet*, 357:539-545.

Baron-Cohen, S. (ed), 1997, *The Maladapted Mind : Classic Readings in Evolutionary Psychopathology*, Psychology Press, Hove, East Sussex, UK.

Baverstock K., 2000, Radiation-induced genomic instability: a paradigm-breaking phenomenon and its relevance to environmentally induced cancer, *Mutation Research*, 454:89-109.

Belletti, F., M. Huo, X. Litrico, A. Bayen, 2015, Prediction of traffic convective instability with spectral analysis of the Aw-Rascle-Zhang model, *Physics Letters A*, 379:2319-2330.

Bennett, C., 1988, Logical depth and physical complexity. In *The Universal Turing Machine: A Half-Century Survey*, R. Herkin (ed.), pp. 227-257, Oxford University Press.

Bennett M., and P. Hacker, 2003 *Philosophical Foundations of Neuroscience*, Blackwell Publishing, London.

Binney J., N. Dowrick, A. Fisher, M. Newman, 1986, *The Theory of Critical Phenomena*, Clarendon Press, Oxford.

Birkoff, G., 1960, *Hydrodynamics: A study in logic, fact, and similitude*, Second Edition, Princeton University Press, Princeton, NJ.

Black, F., M. Scholes, 1973, The pricing of options and corporate liabilities, *Journal of Political Economy*, 81:637-654.

Blandin S., et al., 2011, A general phase transition model for vehicular traffic, *SIAM Journal of Applied Mathematics* 71:107-127.

Bohannon, J., 2015, Fears of an AI pioneer, *Science*, 349:252.

Bos, R., 2007, Continuous representations of groupoids, arXiv:math/0612639.

Bossdorf, O., C. Richards, M. Pigliucci, 2008, Epigenetics for ecologists, *Ecology Letters*, 11:106-115.

Brown, R., 1987, From groups to groupoids: a brief survey, *Bulletin of the London Mathematical Society*, 19:113-134.

Buneci, M., 2003, *Representare de Groupoizi*, Editura Mirton, Timisoara.

Burago, D., Y. Burago, S. Ivanov, 2001, *A Course in Metric Geometry*, American Mathematical Society, Providence, RI.

Burgin, M., B. Gupta, 2012, Second-Level Algorithms, Superrecursivity, and Recovery Problem in Distributed Systems, Theory of Computing Systems, 50:694-705.

Burgin, M., N. C. Debnath, 2010, Reusability as Design of Second-Level Algorithms. CATA 2010:147-152.

Burgin, M., 1992, Reflexive Calculi and Logic of Expert Systems, in Creative processes modeling by means of knowledge bases, Sofia, pp. 139-160.

Burgin, M., 1993, Reflexive Turing Machines and Calculi, Vychislitelnyye Sistemy (Logical Methods in Computer Science), 148:94-116, 175-176 (in Russian).

Bureau of Investigative Journalism, 2013, www.thebureauinvestigates.com/category/projects/drones

Burns J., D. Job, M. Bastin, H. Whalley, T. Macgillivray, E. Johnstone, and S. Lawrie, 2003, Structural disconnectivity in schizophrenia: a diffusion tensor magnetic resonance imaging study, *British Journal of Psychiatry*, 182:439-443.

Butler, D., 2007, The petaflop challenge, *Nature*, 5 July, 448:6-7.

Byrk, A., S. Raudenbusch, 2001, *Hierarchical Linear Models: Applications and Data Analysis Methods*, Sage Publications, New York.

Cannas Da Silva, A., A. Weinstein, 1999, *Geometric Models for Noncommutative Algebras*, American Mathematical Society, Providence, RI.

Cartmill M., 2000, Animal consciousness: some philosophical, methodological, and evolutionary problems, *American Zoologist*, 40:835-846.

Cassidy, M., K. Jang, C. Daganzo, 2011, Macroscopic fundamental diagrams for freeway networks, *Transportation Researcj Record*, 2260:8-15.

Champagnat, N., R. Ferriere, and S. Meleard, 2006, Unifying evolutionary dynamics: from individual stochastic processes to macroscopic models, *Theoretical Population Biology*, 69:297-321.

Chung, K., R. Williams, 1990, *Introduction to Stochastic Integration*, Second edition, Birkhauser, Boston, MA.

Ciliberti, S., O. Martin, A. Wagner, 2007a, Robustness can evolve gradually in complex regulatory networks with varying topology, *PLOS Computational Biology*, 3(2):e15.

Ciliberti, S., O. Martin, A. Wagner, 2007b, Innovation and robustness in complex regulatory gene networks, *Proceedings of the National Academy of Sciences*, 104:13591-13596.

Cohen, I., 2000, *Tending Adam's Garden: Evolving the Cognitive Immune Self*, Academic Press, New York.

Cohen, I., 2006, Immune system computation and the immunological homunculus. In Nierstrasz, O., J. Whittle, D. Harel, and G. Reggio (eds.), *MoDELS 2006*, LNCS, 4199:499-512.

Cohen, I., D. Harel, 2007, Explaining a complex living system: dynamics, multi-scaling, and emergence, *Journal of the Royal Society: Interface*, 4:175-182.

Cohen, M., A. Varki, 2010, The sialome - far more than the sum of its parts, *OMICS*, 14:455-464.

Cohen, T., B. Blatter, C. Almeida, E. Shortliffe, V. Patel, V., 2006, A cognitive blueprint of collaboration in context: Distributed cognition in the psychiatric emergency department, *Artificial Intelligence in Medicine*, 37:73-83.

Columbia University Law School Human Rights Clinic, 2012, Counting Drone Strike Deaths, http://web.law.columbia.edu/human-rights-institute

Connes, A., 1994, *Noncommutative Geometry*, Academic Press, San Diego.

Coplan, J., 2005, personal communication.

Coplan, J., M. Altemus, S. Matthew, E. Smith, B. Scharf, P. Coplan, J. Kral, J. Gorman, M. Owens, C. Nemeroff, and L. Rosenblum, 2005, Synchronized maternal-infant elevations of primate CSF CRF concentrations in response to variable foraging demand, *CNS Spectrums*, 10:530-536.

Corless, R., G. Gonnet, D. Hare, D. Jeffrey, and D. Knuth, 1996, On the Lambert W function, *Advances in Computational Mathematics*, 4:329-359.

Courchesne, E., K. Pierce, 2005, Why frontal cortex in autism might be talking only to itself: local over-connectivity but long-distance disconnection, *Current Opinion in Neurobiology*, 15:225-230.

Coussens, L. Z. Werb, 2002, Inflammation and Cancer, *Nature*, 420:860-867.

Cover T., J. Thomas, 2006, *Elements of Information Theory* Second Edition, John Wiley and Sons, New York.

Cummings, R., 2009, The repertoire of glycan determinants in the human glycome, *Molecular BioSystems*, 5:1087-1104.

Dalgleish A., 1999, The relevance of non-linear mathematics (chaos theory) to the treatment of cancer, the role of the immune response and the potential for vaccines, *Quarterly Journal of Medicine*, 92:347-359.

Dalgleish, A., K. O'Byrne, 2002, Chronic immune activation and inflammation in the pathogenesis of AIDS and cancer, *Advances in Cancer Research*, 84:231-276.

Dam, T. T. Gerken, B. Cavada, K. Nascimento, T. Moura, C.F. Brewer, 2007, Binding studies of the $\alpha$-GalNAc-specific lectins to the $\alpha$-GalNAc(Tn-antigen) form porcine submaxilary mucin and its smaller fragments, *Journal of Biological Chemistry*, 38:28256-28263.

Damaso, A., 1989, Time-locked multiregional retroactivation: a systems-level proposal for the neural substrates of recall and recognition, *Cognition*, 33:25-62.

Daqing, L., J. Yinan, K. Rui, S. Havlin, 2014, Spatial correlation analysis of cascading failures: congestions and blackouts, *Scientific Reports* 4:5381.

Darwin C., 1889, *The Descent of Man, and Selection in Relation to Sex*, 2nd ed., Appleton, New York.

de Groot, S., R. Mazur, 1984, *Non-Equilibrium Thermodynamics*, Dover, New York.

Dehaene, S., L. Naccache, 2001, Towards a cognitive neuroscience of consciousness: basic evidence and a workspace framework, *Cognition*, 79:1-37.

Dehaene, S., J. Changeux, 2005, Ongoing spontaneous activity controls access to consciousness: a neuronal model for inattentional blindness, *PLOS Biology*, 3:e141.

del Hoyo, M., E. Minian, 2008, Classical invariants for global actions and groupoid atlases, *Applied Catagorial Structures*, 18:689-721.

Dembo, A., O. Zeitouni, 1998, *Large Deviations: Techniques and Applications*, 2nd Ed., Springer-Verlag, New York.

Derman, E., N. Taleb, 2005, The illusions of dynamic replication, *Quantitative Finance*, 5:323-326.

Diekmann, U., R. Law, 1996, The dynamical theory of coevolution: a derivation from stochastic ecological processes, *Journal of Mathematical Biology*, 34:579-612.

Dobson, I., 2007, Where is the edge for cascading failure?: challenges and opportunities for quantifying blackout risk. IEEE Power Engineering Society General Meeting. Tampa, Fl., USA, June, 2007. Available from dobson@engr.wisc.edu.

Dretske F., 1981, *Knowledge and the Flow of Information*, MIT Press, Cambridge, MA.

Dretske F., 1988, *Explaining Behavior*, MIT Press, Cambridge, MA.

Dretske, F., 1993, Mental events as structuring causes of behavior, in *Mental Causation* (ed. by A. Mele and J. Heil), pp. 121-136, Oxford University Press.

Dretske F., 1994, The explanatory role of information, *Philosophical Transactions of the Royal Society A*, 349:59-70.

DSM-IV, 1994, *Diagnostic and Statistical Manual, fourth edition*, American Psychiatric Association.

Duryea, P., 1978, Press release dated Friday, 27 January, Office of the New York State Assembly Republican Leader, Albany, NY. Copy available from R. Wallace.

Dzganzo, C., V. Gayah, E. Gonzales, 2010, Macroscopic relations of urban traffic variables: an analysis of instability, *Working Paper UCB-ITS-VWP-2010-4*, UC Berkeley Center for Future Urban Transit.

Dzhaparidze, K., P. Spreij, 1994, Spectral characteristics of the optional quadratic variation process, *Stochastic Processes and their Applications*, 54:165-174.

Edelman D., B. Baars, and A. Seth, 2005, Identifying hallmarks of consciousness in non-mammalian species, *Consciousness and Cognition*, 14:169-187.

Ellis, R., 1985, *Entropy, Large Deviations, and Statistical Mechanics*, Springer, New York.

Emery, M., 1989, *Stochastic calculus in manifolds*, Universitext series, Springer-Verlag, New York.

English, T., 1996, Evaluation of evolutionary and genetic optimizers: no free lunch, in *Evolutionary Programming V: Proceedings of the Fifth Annual Conference on Evolutionary Programming*, L. Fogel, P. Angeline, and T. Back eds., pp. 163-169. MIT Press, Cambridge, MA.

Erdos, P., A. Renyi, 1960, On the evolution of random graphs, reprinted in *The Art of Counting*, 1973, 574-618 and in *Selected Papers of Alfred Renyi*, 1976, 482-525.

Evan, G., T. Littlewood, 1998, A matter of life and cell death, *Science*, 281:1317-1322.

Fanon, F., 1966, *The Wretched of the Earth*, Grove Press, New York.

Farmer, P., 2003, *Pathologies of Power*, University of California Press.

Feynman, R., 1996, *Feynman Lectures on Computation*, Addison-Wesley, Reading, MA.

Ficici, S., O. Milnik, and J. Pollack, 2005, A game-theoretic and dynamical systems analysis of selection methods in coevolution, *IEEE Transactions on Evolutionary Computation*, 9:580-602.

Forlenza M. A. Baum, 2000, Psychosocial influences on cancer progression: alternative cellular and molecular mechanisms, *Current Opinion in Psychiatry*, 13:639-645.

Frankel, T., 2006, *The Geometry of Physics: An Introduction, Second Edition*, Cambridge University Press.

Freeman, W., 2003, The wave packet: an action potential of the 21st Century, *Journal of Integrative Neurosciences*, **2**, 3-30.

Fullilove, M., 2004, *Root Shock*, Ballantine, New York.

Gandy, M., A. Zumla, 2003, *The Return of the White Plague*, Verso, New York.

Geroliminis, N., J. Sun, 2011, Properties of a well-defined macroscopic fundamental diagram for urban traffic, *Transportation Research B*, 45:605-617.

Gilbert, P., 2001, Evolutionary approaches to psychopathology: the role of natural defenses, *Austrailian and New Zealand Journal of Psychiatry*, 35:17-27.

Gilbert, S., 2001, Mechanisms for the environmental regulation of gene expression: ecological aspects of animal development, *Journal of Biosciences*, 30:65-74.

Glazebrook, J., R. Wallace, 2009a, Rate distortion manifolds as model spaces for cognitive information, *Informatica*, 33:309-346.

Glazebrook, J.F., R. Wallace, 2009b, Small worlds and red queens in the global workspace: an information-theoretic approach, *Cognitive Systems Research*, 10:333-365.

Golubitsky, M., I. Stewart, 2006, Nonlinear dynamics and networks: the groupoid formalism, *Bulletin of the American Mathematical Society*, 43:305-364.

Goubault, E., M. Raussen, 2002, Dihomotopty as a tool in state space analysis, *Lecture Notes in Computer Science*, Vol. 2286, April, 2002, pp. 16-37, New York, Springer, New York.

Goubault, E., 2003, Some geometric perspectives in concurrency theory, *Homology, Homotopy, and Applications*, 5:95-136.

Gould, P., R. Wallace, 1994, Spatial structures and scientific paradoxex in the AIDS pandemic, *Geografiska Annaler*, 76B:105-116.

Gould S., 1991, Exaptation: a crucial tool for evolutionary psychology, *Journal of Social Issues*, 47:43-65.

Gould S., 2002, *The Structure of Evolutionary Theory*, Harvard University Press, Cambridge, MA.

Granovetter M., 1973, The strength of weak ties, *American Journal of Sociology*, 78:1360-1380.

Green, R., 1979, *Sampling Design and Statistical Methods for Experimental Scientists*, John Wiley, New York.

Griffin D., 1976, *The Question of Animal Awareness*, The Rockefeller University Press, New York.

Griffin D., 1992, *Animal Minds*, University of Chicago Press, Chicago.

Griffin D., 2000, Scientific approaches in animal consciousness, *American Zoologist*, 40:889-892.

Griffin D., and G. Speck, 2004, New evidence of animal consciousness, *Animal Cognition*, 7:5-18.

Grimmett, G., A. Stacey, 1998, Critical probabilities for site and bond percolation models, *The Annals of Probability*, 4:1788-1812.

Gunderson, L., 2000, Ecological resilience - in theory and application, *Annual Reviews of Ecological Systematics*, 31:425-439.

Gupta, G., A. Surolia, S. Sampath Kumar, 2010, Lectin microarrays for glycomic analysis, *OMICS*, 14:419-436.

Haug, E., N. Taleb, 2011, Option traders use (very) sophisticated heuristics, never the Black-Scholes-Merton formula, *Journal of Economic Behavior and Organization*, 77:97-106.

Hawley, J., 2006, Patriot Fratricides: The human dimension lessions of Operation Iraqui Freedom, *Field Artillery*, January-February.

Hawley, J., 2008, The Patriot Vigilance Project: A case study of Patriot fratricide mitigations after the Second Gulf War, *Third System of Systems Conference*, December 10.

Hayes C., 2003, Four routes of cognitive evolution, *Psychological Review1*, 110:713-727.

Hazewinkel, M., 2002, *Encylopedia of Mathematics*, 'Index Formulas', Springer, New York.

Heine S., 2001, Self as a cultural product: an examination of East Asian and North Amereican selves, *Journal of Personality*, 69:881-906.

Helbing, D., 2001, Traffic and related self-driven many-particle systems, *Reviews of Modern Physics*, 73:1067-1141.

Helgason, S., 1962, *Differential Geometry and Symmetric Spaces*, Academic Press, New York.

Herberman R., 1995, Principles of tumor immunology in Murphy G., Lawrence W. and Lenhard R. (eds.), *American Cancer Society Textbook of Clinical Oncology*, ACS, Second Edition, pp. 1-9.

Hollan, J., J. Hutchins, D. Kirsch, D., 2000, Distributed cognition: toward a new foundation for human-computer interaction research, *ACM Transactions on Computer-Human Interaction*, 7:174-196.

Holling, C., 1973, Resilience and stability of ecological systems, *Annual Reviews of Ecological Systematics*, 4:1-23.

Holloway R., 1996, Evolution of the human brain, in A. Lock and C. R. Peters (eds.), *Handbook of Human Symbolic Evolution*, pp. 74-125, Clarendon Press, Oxford.

Houghton, C., 1975, Wreath products of groupoids, *Journal of the London Mathematical Society*, 10:179-188.

Hu, J., M. Prandini, K. Johnasson, S. Sastry, 2001, Hybrid geodesics as optimal solutions to the collision-free motion planning problem. In M. Di Benedetto, A. Sangiovanni-Vincentelli (Eds.) *HSCC 2001*, LNCS 2034:305-318.

Hutchins, E., 1994, *Cognition in the Wild*, MIT Press, Cambridge, MA.

Ignall, E., 1972, What is a minute of response time worth? New York City Rand Institute Memo. Copy available from R. Wallace.

Jablonka, E., M. Lamb, 1998, Epigenetic inheritance in evolution, *Journal of Evolutionary Biology*, 11:159-183.

Jabolnka, E., M. Lamb, 2006, *Evolution in Four Dimensions*, MIT Press, Cambridge, MA.

Jin C., et al., 2013, Spontaneous phase transition from free flow to synchronized flow in traffic on a single-lane highway, *Physical Review E*, 87:012815.

Johnson-Laird, P., F. Mancini, A. Gangemi, 2006, A hyper-emotion theory of psychological illness, *Psychological Review*, 113:822-841.

Kahraman, A., 2009, The geometry and physicochemistry of protein binding sites and ligands and their detection in electron density maps, PhD Dissertation, Cambridge University.

Kastner, M., 2006, Phase transitions and configuration space topology, ArXiv cond-mat/0703401.

Kerner, B., S. Klenov, 2009, Phase transitions in traffic flow on multilane roads, *Physical Review E*, 80:056101.

Kerner, B., M. Koller, S. Klenov, H. Rehborn, M. Leibel, 2015, Empirical features of spontaneous and induced traffic breakdowns in free flow at highway bottlenecks, ArXiv:1502.02862v2 [physics.soc-ph].

Khasminskii, R., 2012, *Stochastic Stability of Differential Equations*, 2nd Edition, Spriner, New York.

Khinchin A., 1957, *The Mathematical Foundations of Information Theory*, Dover Publications, New York.

Kiecolt-Glaser, J., McGuier L., Robles T., and Glaser R., 2002, Emotions, morbidity, and mortality: new perspectives from psychoneuroimmunology, *Annual Review of Psychology*, 53:83-107.

Kinney, R., P. Crucitti, R. Albert, V. Latora, 2005, Modeling cascading failures in the North American power grid, *European Physics Journal, B*, 46:101-107.

Kleinman, A., and B. Good, 1985, *Culture and Depression: Studies in the Anthropology and Cross-Cultural Psychiatry of Affect and Depression*, University of California Press, Berkeley.

Kleinman, A., 1988, *Rethinking Psychiatry: From Cultural Category to Personal Experience*, Free Press, New York.

Kleinman, A., and A. Cohen, 1997, Psychiatry's Global Challenge, *Scientific American*, March, 86-89.

Knoll A, and S. Carroll, 1999, Early animal evolution: emerging views from comparative biology and geology, *Science*, 284:2129-2137.

Kozma, R., M. Puljic, P. Balister, B. Bollobas, W. Freeman, 2004, Neuropercolation: a random cellular automata approach to spatio-temporal neurodynamics, *Lecture Notes in Computer Science*, 3305:435-443.

Kozma, R., M. Puljic, P. Balister, B Bollobas, 2005, Phase transitions in the neuropercolation model of neural populations with mixed local and nonlocal interactions, *Biological Cybernetics*, **92**, 367-379.

Krebs, P., 2005, Models of cognition: neurological possibility does not indicate neurological plausibility, in Bara, B., L. Barsalou, and M. Bucciarelli (eds.), *Proceedings of CogSci 2005*, pp. 1184-1189, Stresa, Italy. Available at http://cogprints.org/4498/.

Landau L., E. Lifshitz, 2007, *Statistical Physics*, Third Edition, Part 1, Elsevier, New York.

Laxmisan, A., F. Hakimzada, O. Sayan, R. Green, J. Zhang, V. Patel, 2007, The multitasking clinician; Decision-making and cognitive demand during and after team handoffs in emergency care. *International Journal of Medical Informatics*, 76:801-811.

Lee, J., 2000, *Introduction to Topological Manifolds*, Springer, New York.

Lee, V., D. Singleton, 1990, 29th was Red Friday, New York Daily News, January 1, p. 21.

Li, D., B. Fu, Y. Wang, G. Lu, Y. Berezin, H.E. Stanley, 2015, Percolation transition in dynamical traffic network with evolving critical bottlenecks, *Proceedings of the National Academy of Sciences USA*, 112:669-672.

Longuett-Higgins, H., 1963, The symmetry groups of non-rigid molecules, *Molecular Physics*, 6:445-460.

Luchinsky, D., 1997, On the nature of large fluctuations in equilibrium systems: observations of an optimal force, *Journal of Physics, A*, 30:L577-L583.

Luczak T., 1990, *Random Structures and Algorithms*, 1:287.

Maass W., T. Natschlager, H. Markram, 2002, Real-time computing without stable states: A new framework for neural computation based on perturbations, *Neural Computation*, 14:2531-2560.

Mack A., 1998, *Inattentional Blindness*, MIT Press, Cambridge, MA.

Macdonald, J., L. Yang, M. Sutovic, H. Lederman, K. Pendri, W. Lu, B. Andrews, D. Stefanovic, M. Stojanovic, 2006, Medium scale integration of molecular logic gates in an automaton, *Nano Letters*, 6:2598-2603.

Massimini, M., F. Ferrarelli, R. Huber, S. Esser, H. Singh and G. Tononi, 2005, Neural activity spreads to distant areas of the brain in humans when awake but not when sleeping, *Science*, 309:2228-2232.

Masuda, T., R. Nisbett, 2006, Culture and change blindness, *Cognitive Science*, 30:381-399.

Matsumoto, Y., 2002, *An Introduction to Morse Theory*, American Mathematical Society, Providence, RI.

Maturana H., F. Varela, 1980, *Autopoiesis and Cognition*, Reidel Publishing Company, Dordrecht, Holland.

Maturana, H., F. Varela, 1992, *The Tree of Knowledge*, Shambhala Publications, Boston, MA.

McCauly, L., 1993, *Chaos, Dynamics, and Fractals: An Algorithmic Approach to Deterministic Chaos*, Cambridge University Press.

McGuire M.T., and A. Troisi, 1998, *Darwininan Psychiatry*, Oxford University Press, Oxforf, UK.

Mega, C., 1978, Report of the New York State Assembly Republican Task Force on Urban Fire Protection, Office of the Assembly Minority Leader. Available from R. Wallace.

Memmi, A., 1965, *The Colonizer and the Colonized*, Beacon Press, Boston.

Memmi, A., 1969, *Dominated Man*, Beacon Press, Boston.

Mezey, P., 1997, Fuzzy measures of molecular shape and size, Chapter 5 in *Fuzzy Logic in Chemistry*, Rouvray, D. (ed.), Academic Press, New York, pp.139-224.

Mnif, M., C. Muller-Schloer, 2006, Quantitative Emergence. In *Proceedings of the 2006 IEEE Mountain Workshop on Adaptive and Learning Systems*, IEEE SMCals2006, 78-84.

Molloy M., B. Reed, 1995, A critical point for random graphs with a given degree sequence, *Random Structures and Algorithms*, 6:161-179.

Molloy M., B. Reed, 1998, The size of the giant component of a random graph with a given degree sequence, *Combinatorics, Probability, and Computing*, 7:295-305.

Morris S., 2000, Perspectives: the Cambrian 'explosion': slow fuse or megatonnage? *Proceedings of the National Academy of Sciences*, 97:4426-4429.

Nair, G., et al., 2007, Feedback control under data rate constraints: an overview *Proceedings of the IEEE*, 95:108-137.

Nesse, R., 2000, Is depression an adaptation?, *Archives of General Psychiatry*, 57:14-20.

Newman, M., S. Strogatz, and D. Watts, 2001, Random graphs with arbitrary degree distributions and their applications, *Physical Review E*, 64:026118, 1-17.

Newman, M., 2003, Properties of highly clustered networks, arXiv:cond-mat/0303183v1.

NFPA, 1976, *Fire Protection Handbook*, National Fire Protection Association, Boston MA.

Nix A., M. Vose, 1992, Modeling genetic algorithms with markov chains, *Annals of Mathematics and Artificial Intelligence*, 5:79-88.

Nunney L., 1999, Lineage selection and the evolution of multistage carcinogenesis, *Proceedings of the London Royal Society, B*, 266:493-498.

O'Byrne, K., Dalgleish A., 2001, Chronic immune activation and inflammation as the cause of malignancy, *British Journal of Cancer*, 85:473-483.

Onsager, L., S. Machlup, 1953, Fluctuations and irreversible processes, *Physical Review*, 91:1505-1512.

O'Nuallain, S., 2008, Subjects and objects: metaphysics, biology, consciousness, and cognition, *Biosemiotics*, 1:239-251.

Orosz, G., R.E. Wilaon, G. Stepan, 2010, Traffic jams: dynamics and control, *Philosophical Transactions of the Royal Society A*, 368:4455-4479.

Park, H., S. Amari, K. Fukumizu, 2000, Adaptive natural gradient learning algorithms for various stochastic models, *Neural Networks*, 13:755-765.

Panskepp, J., 2003, At the interface of the affective, behavioral, and cognitive neurosciences: Decoding the emotional feelings of the brain, *Brain and Cognition*, 52:4-14.

Patel, V., 1998, Individual to collaborative cognition: a paradigm shift? *Artificial Intelligence in Medicine*, 12:93-96.

Pepperberg I., 2006, Cognitive and communicative abilities of Grey parrots, *Applied Animal Behavior Science*, 100:77-86.

Pettini M., 2007, *Geometry and Topology in Hamiltonian Dynamics and Statistical Mechanics*, Springer, New York.

Pielou, E., 1977, *Mathematical Ecology*, John Wiley and Sons, New York.

Pohl, W., 1962, Differential geometry of higher order, *Topology* 1:169-211.

Prandolini R., M. Moody, 1995, Brownian nature of Time-Base Error in tape recordings, *Journal of the Auditory Engineering Society*, 43:241-247.

Pratt, V., 1991, Modeling concurrency with geometry, *Proceedings of the 18th ACM SIGPLAN-SIGACT Symposium on Principles of Programming Languages*, 311-322.

Pretzel, O., 1996, *Error-Correcting Codes and Finite Fields*, Clarendon Press, Oxford.

Privman, V., M. Fisher, 1983, Finite-size effects at first-order transitions, *Journal of Statistical Physics*, 33:385-417.

Protter, P., 1990, *Stochastic Integration and Differential Equations*, Springer, New York.

Rabinovich, M., R. Huerta, G. Laurent, 2008, Transient dynamics for neural processing, *Science*, 321:48-50.

Ramaswamy, S., 2010, The mechanics and statistics of active matter, *Annual Reviews of Condensed Matter Physics*, 1:323-345.

Rand Fire Project, 1979, *Fire Deployment Analysis: A public policy analysis case study*, North Holland, New York.

Richerson P., and R. Boyd, 2006, *Not by Genes Alone: How Culture Transformed Human Evolution*, Chicago University Press.

Richter, U., M. Mnif, J. Branke, C. Muller-Scholer, H. Schmeck, 2006, Towards a generic observer/controller architecture for organic computing, p. 112 in *INFORMATIK 2006*, Lecture Notes in Informatics, Hochberger and Liskowsky (eds.), Gesellschaft fur Informatik, Bonn, Germany.

Ridley, M., 1996, *Evolution*, Second Edition, Blackwell Science, Oxford, UK, 1996.

Rockafellar, R., 1970, *Convex Analysis*, Princeton University Press, Princeton, NJ.

Roman, S., 1997, *Introduction to Coding and Information Theory*, Springer, New York.

Rosenfeld, A., 1971, Fuzzy groups, *Journal of Mathematical Analysis and Applications*, 35:512-517.

Ruelle, D., 1983,Turbulent dynamical systems, *Proceedings of the International Congress of Mathematicians*, Aug. 16-24, Warsaw, pp. 271-286.

Sarshar N., X. Wu, 2007, On Rate-Distortion models for natural images and wavelet coding performance, *IEEE Transactions on Image Processing*, 16:1383-1394.

Sasidharan, R., M. Gerstein, 2008, Protein fossils live on as RNA, *Nature*, 453:729-731.

Savante, J., Knuth, T. Luczak, and B. Pittel, 1993, The birth of the giant component, arXiv:math.PR/9310236v1.

Scharre, P., 2016, Autonomous weapons and operational risk, Center for a New American Security, Washington DC
http://www.cnas.org/autonomous-weapons-and-operational-risk.vtISHGO-RiY

Scherrer, K., J. Jost, 2007a, The gene and the genon concept: a functional and information-theoretic analysis, *Molecular Systems Biology*, 3:87-93.

Scherrer, K., J. Jost, 2007b, Gene and genon concept: coding versus regulation, *Theory in Bioscience*, 126:65-113.

Seth A., B. Baars, and D. Edelman, 2005, Criteria for consciousness in humans and other mammals, *Consciousness and Cognition*, 14:119-139.

Shannon, C., 1959, Coding theorems for a discrete source with a fidelity criterion, *Institute of Radio Engineers International Convention Record*, 7:142-163.

Shirkov, D. V. Kovalev, 2001, The Bogoliubov renormalization group and solution symmetry in mathematical physics, *Physics Reports*, 352:219-249.

Silani, G., U. Frith, J. Demonet, F. Fazio, D. Perani, C. Price, C. Frith, and E. Paulesu, 2005, Brain abnormalities underlying altered activation in dyslexia: a voxel based morphometry study, *Brain*, 128(Pt 10):2453-2461.

Simmonds M., 2006, Into the brains of whales, *Applied Animal Behavior Science*, 100:103-116.

Simons, D., C. Chabris, 1999, Gorillas in our midst: sustained inattentional blindness for dynamic events, *Perception*, 28:1059-1074.

Simons, D., 2000, Attentional capture and inattentional blindness, *Trends in Cognitive Sciences*, 4:147-155.

Skierski, M., A. Grundland, J. Tuszynski, 1989, Analysis of the three-dimensional time-dependent Landau-Ginzburg equation and its solutions, *Journal of Physics A*, 22:3789-3808.

Skoyles, J., 1999, Neural plasticity and exaptation, *American Psychologist*, 54:438-439.

Snow, E., 1997, The role of DNA repair in development, *Reproductive Toxicology*, 11:353-365.

Somers, S. P. Guillou, 1994, Tumor strategies for escaping immune control: implications for psychoimmunotherapy", in Lewis C., O'Sullivan C. and Barraclough J. (eds.), *The Psychoimmunology of Cancer: Mind and body in the fight for survival*, Oxford Medical Publishing, pp. 385-416.

Stanford/NYU 2012, Living under drones: death, injury, and trauma to civilians from US drone practices in pakistan, http://livingunderdrones.org/.

Starr, R., 1978, Making New York Smaller, *New York Times Magazine*, 14 November, p. 32.

Stewart, I., M. Golubitsky, M. Pivato, 2003, Symmetry groupoids and patterns of synchrony in coupled cell networks, *SIAM Journal of Applied Dynamical Systems*, 2:609-646.

Stewart I., 2004, Networking opportunity, *Nature*, 427:601-604.

Stojanovic, M., T. Mitchell, D. Stefanovic, 2002, Deoxyribozyme-based logic gates, *Journal of the American Chemical Society*, 124:3555-3561.

Stone, M., 1977, Let big cities die?, *US News and World Report*, 8 August, p. 80.

Striedter, G. F., 2004, *Principles of Brain Evolution*, Sinauer Associates, Sunderland, MA.

A. Tauber, 1997, Historical and philosophical perspectives concerning immune cognition, *Journal of the History of Biology*, 30:419-440.

Tenaillon, O., Taddei F., Radman M. and Matic I., 2001, Second-order selection in bacterial evolution: selection acting on mutation and recombination rates in the course of adaptation, *Research in Microbiology*, 152:11-16.

Thaler, D. 1999 Hereditary stability and variation in evolution and development, *Evolution and Development*, 1:113-122.

Thayer J., and R. Lane, 2000, A model of neurovisceral integration in emotional regulation and dysregulation, *Journal of Affective Disorders*, 61:201-216.

Thayer J., and B. Friedman, 2002, Stop that! Inhibition, sensitization, and their neurovisceral concomitants, *Scandinavian Journal of Psychology*, 43:123-130.

Timberlake, W., 1994, Behavior systems, associationationism and Pavlovian conditioning, *Psychonmic Bulletin*, Rev. 1, 405-420.

Tishby, N., F. Pereira, W. Bialek, 1999, The information bottleneck method, *37th Annual Conference on Communication, Control, and Computing*, pp. 368-377.

Tompa, P., C. Szasz L. Buday, 2005, Structural disorder throws new light on moonlighting, *Trends in Biochemical Sciences*, 30:484-489.

Toulouse, G., S. Dehaene, J. Changeux, 1986, Spin glass model of learning by selection, *Proceedings of the National Academy of Sciences*, 83:1695-1698.

van Lint, J., 1999, *Introduction to coding Theory*, Springer, New York.

Van Valen, L., 1973, A new evolutionary law, *Evolutionary Theory*, 1:1-30.

Villalobos, M., A. Mizuno, B. Dahl ,N. Kemmotsu, and R. Muller, 2005, Reduced functional connectivity between V1 and inferior frontal cortex associated with visumotor performance in autism, *Neuromage*, 25:916-925.

Volz, E., 2004, Random networks with tunable degree distribution and clustering, *Physical Review E*, 70:056115.

Vose, M., 1999, *The Simple Genetic Algorithm: Foundations and Theory*, MIT Press, Cambridge, MA.

Waddington, C., 1957, *The Strategy of the Genes*, Macmillan, New York.

Wallace, D., R. Wallace, 1998, *A Plague on Your Houses*, Verso, New York.

Wallace, D., R. Wallace, 2011, Consequences of massive housing destruction: the New York City fire epidemic, *Building Research and Information*, 39:395-411.

Wallace, R., 1988, A synergism of plagues: 'planned shrinkage', contagiouis housing destruction and AIDS in the Bronx, *Environmental Research* 47:1-33.

Wallace, R., 1990, Urban desertification, public health and public order: 'planned shrinkage', violent death, substance abuse, and AIDS in the Bronx, *Social Science and Medicine* 31:801-813.

Wallace, R., 1993, Recurrent collapse of the fire service in New York City: the failure of paramilitary systems as a phase change, *Environment and Planning A*, 25:233-244.

Wallace, R., 2000, Language and coherent neural amplification in hierarchical systems: renormalization and the dual information source of a generalized spatiotemporal stochastic resonance, *International Journal of Bifurcation and Chaos*, 10:493-502.

Wallace, R., 2002, Adaptation, punctuation and information: a rate-distortion approach to non-cognitive 'learning plateaus' in evolutionary process, *Acta Biotheoretica*, 50:101-116.

Wallace R., 2004, Comorbidity and anticomorbidity: autocognitive developmental disorders of structured psychosocial stress, *Acta Biotheoretica*, 52:71-93.

Wallace R., 2005a, *Consciousness: A Mathematical Treatment of the Global Neuronal Workspace Model*, Springer, New York.

Wallace R., 2005b, A global workspace perspective on mental disorders, *Theoretical Biology and Medical Modelling*, 2:49, http://www.tbiomed.com/content/2/1/49.

Wallace R., 2006, Pitfalls in biological computing: canonical and idiosyncratic dysfunction of conscious machines, *Mind and Matter*, 4:91-113.

Wallace R., 2007, Culture and inattentional blindness, *Journal of Theoretical Biology*, 245:378-390.

Wallace, R., 2008a, Toward formal models of biologically inspired, highly parallel machine cognition, *International Journal of Parallel, Emergent, and Distributed Systems*, 23:367-408.

Wallace, R., 2008b, Developmental disorders as pathological resilience domains, *Ecology and Society*, 13:29 (online).

Wallace, R., 2009, Programming coevolutionary machines: the emerging conundrum, *International Journal of Parallel, Emergent, and Distributed Systems*, 24:443-453.

Wallace, R., 2010a, Tunable epigenetic catalysis: programming real-time cognitive machines, *International Journal of Parallel, Emergent, and Distributed Systems*, 25:209-222.

Wallace, R., 2010b, Expanding the modern synthesis, *Comptes Rendus Biologie*, 333:701-709.

Wallace, R., 2011a, Multifunction moonlighting and intrinsically disordered proteins: information catalysis, non-rigid molecule symmetries and the 'logic gate' spectrum, *Comptes Rendus Chimie*, 14:1117-1121.

Wallace, R., 2011b, On the evolution of homochirality, *Comptes Rendus Biologies*, 334:263-268.

Wallace, R., 2012, Spontaneous symmetry breaking in a non-rigid molecule approach to intrinsically disordered proteins, *Molecular BioSystems*, 8:374-377.

Wallace, R., 2012b, Consciousness, crosstalk, and the mereological fallacy: an evolutionary perspective, *Physics of Life Reviews*, 9:426-453.

Wallace, R., 2014, A formal approach to the molecular fuzzy lock-and-key, *International Journal of Unconventional Computing*, 10:93-110.

Wallace, R., 2014b, Extending Swerdlow's hypothesis: statistical models of mitochondrial deterioration and aging, *Journal of Mathematical Chemistry*, 52:2663-2679.

Wallace, R., 2015a, *An Ecosystem Approach to Economic Stabilization: Escaping the neoliberal wilderness*, Routledge, New York.

Wallace, R., 2015b, *An Information Approach to Mitochondrial Dysfunction: Extending Swerdlow's Hypothesis*, World Scientific, Singapore.

R. Wallace, R., 2015c, Closed-system 'economic' models for psychiatric disorders: Western atomism and its culture-bound syndromes, *Cognitive Processing*, 16:279-290.

Wallace, R., 2016, Subtle noise structures as control signals in high-order biocognition, *Physics Letters A*, 380:726-729.

Wallace, R., D. Wallace, 1977, *Studies on the Collapse of Fire Service in New York City 1972-1976: The impact of pseudoscience in public policy*, University Press of America, Washington DC.

Wallace, R., D. Wallace, 1990, Origins of public health collapse in New York City: the dynamics of planned shrinkage, contagious urban decay, and social disintegration, *Bulletin of the New York Academy of Medicine*, 66:391-434.

Wallace R., R.G. Wallace, 1998, Information theory, scaling laws, and the thermodynamics of evolution, *Journal of Theoretical Biology*, 192:545-559.

Wallace R., and R.G. Wallace, 1999, Organisms, organizations, and interactions: an information theory approach to biocultural evolution, *BioSystems*, 51:101-119.

Wallace, R., D. Wallace, R.G. Wallace, 2003, Toward cultural oncology: the evolutionary information dynamics of cancer, *Open Systems and Information Dynamics*, 10:159-181.

Wallace R., D. Wallace, 2004, Structured psychosocial stress and therapeutic failure, *Journal of Biological Systems*, 12:335-369.

Wallace, R., M. Fullilove, 2008, *Collective Consciousness and its Discontents: Institutional Distributed Cognition, Racial Policy, and Public Health in the United States*, Springer, New York.

Wallace R., D. Wallace, 2008, Punctuated equilibrium in statistical models of generalized ceovolutionary resilience: How sudden ecosystem transitions can entrain both phenotype expression and Darwinian selection, *Transactions on Computational Systems Biology IX* LNBI 5121:23-85.

Wallace, R., D. Wallace, 2009, Code, Context, and epigenetic catalysis in gene expression, *Transactions on Computational Systems Biology XI*, LNBI 5750:283-334.

Wallace, R.G., R. Wallace, 2009, Evolutionary radiation and the spectrum of consciousness, *Consciousness and Cognition* 18:160-167.

Wallace, R., D. Wallace, 2010, *Gene Expression and its Discontents: The social production of chronic disease*, Springer, New York.

Wallace, R., D. Wallace, 2013, *A Mathematical Approach to Multilevel, Multiscale Health Interventions: Pharmaceutical industry decline and policy response*, Imperial College Press, London.

Waliszewski, P., Molski M., and Konarski J. (1998) On the holistic approach in cellular and cancer biology: nonlinearity, complexity, and quasi-determinism of the dynamic cellular network, *Journal of Surgical Oncology*, 68:70-78.

Wang, M., G. Uhlenbeck, 1945, On the theory of the Brownian Motion II, *Reviews of Modern Physics*, 17:323-342.

Wayand J., D. Levin, A. Varakin, 2005, Inattentional blindness for a noxious multimodal stimulus, *American Journal of Psychology*, 118:339-352.

Weinstein A., 1996, Groupoids: unifying internal and external symmetry, *Notices of the American Mathematical Association*, 43:744-752.

West-Eberhard, M., 2005, Developmental plasticity and the origin of species differences, *Proceedings of the National Academy of Sciences*, 102:6543-6549.

Wiegand, R., 2003, *An analysis of cooperative coevolutionary algorithms*, PhD Thesis, George Mason University.

Wilson, K., 1971, Renormalization group and critical phenomena. I. Renormalization group and the Kadanoff scaling picture, *Physical Review B*, 4:3174-3183.

Wolpert, D., W. MacReady, 1995, No free lunch theorems for search, Santa Fe Institute, SFI-TR-02-010.

Wolpert, D., W. MacReady, 1997, No free lunch theorems for optimization, *IEEE Transactions on Evolutionary Computation*, 1:67-82.

Wolpert, D., W. MacReady, 2005, Coevolutionary free lunches, *IEEE Transactions on Evolutionary Computation*, 9:731-735.

Wymer, C., 1997, Structural nonlinear continuous-time models in econometrics, *Macroeconomic Dynamics*, 1:518-548.

Yeung, R., 2008, *Information Theory and Network Coding*, Springer, New York.

Zhang, L., 2015, *Realistic, efficient and secure geographic routing in vehicular networks*, PhD Thesis in the Department of Computer Science, University of Victoria, Canada.

Zhu R., A. Riberio, D. Salahub, and S. Kauffman, 2007, Studying genetic regulatory networks at the molecular level: Delayed reaction stochastic models, *Journal of Theoretical Biology*, 246:725-745.

# Index

Printed in the United States
By Bookmasters